Maintaining a Minority Language

MULTILINGUAL MATTERS SERIES
Series Editor: Professor John Edwards,
St. Francis Xavier University, Antigonish, Nova Scotia, Canada

Other Books in the Series
Beyond Bilingualism: Multilingualism and Multilingual Education
Jasone Cenoz and Fred Genesee (eds)
Beyond Boundaries: Language and Identity in Contemporary Europe
Paul Gubbins and Mike Holt (eds)
Bilingualism: Beyond Basic Principles
Jean-Marc Dewaele, Alex Housen and Li Wei (eds)
Can Threatened Languages be Saved?
Joshua Fishman (ed.)
A Dynamic Model of Multilingualism
Philip Herdina and Ulrike Jessner
English in Africa: After the Cold War
Alamin M. Mazrui
Identity, Insecurity and Image: France and Language
Dennis Ager
Ideology and Image: Britain and Language
Dennis Ager
Language and Society in a Changing Italy
Arturo Tosi
Language Attitudes in Sub-Saharan Africa
Efurosibina Adegbija
Language, Ethnicity and Education
Peter Broeder and Guus Extra
Language in Jewish Society
John Myhill
Language Planning in Malawi, Mozambique and the Philippines
Robert B. Kaplan and Richard B. Baldauf, Jr. (eds)
Language Planning in Nepal, Taiwan and Sweden
Richard B. Baldauf, Jr. and Robert B. Kaplan (eds)
Linguistic Minorities in Central and Eastern Europe
Christina Bratt Paulston and Donald Peckham (eds)
Motivation in Language Planning and Language Policy
Dennis Ager
Multilingualism in Spain
M. Teresa Turell (ed.)
Politeness in Europe
Leo Hickey and Miranda Stewart (eds)
The Other Languages of Europe
Guus Extra and Durk Gorter (eds)
Where East Looks West: Success in English in Goa and on the Konkan Coast
Dennis Kurzon

Please contact us for the latest book information:
**Multilingual Matters, Frankfurt Lodge, Clevedon Hall,
Victoria Road, Clevedon, BS21 7HH, England
http://www.multilingual-matters.com**

MULTILINGUAL MATTERS 129
Series Editor: John Edwards

Maintaining a Minority Language
A Case Study of Hispanic Teenagers

John Gibbons and Elizabeth Ramirez

MULTILINGUAL MATTERS LTD
Clevedon • Buffalo • Toronto

Library of Congress Cataloging in Publication Data
Gibbons, John
Maintaining a Minority Language: A Case Study of Hispanic Teenagers
John Gibbons and Elizabeth Ramirez.
Includes bibliographical references and index.
1. Language Maintenance–Australia–Sydney. 2. Bilingualism–Australia–Sydney.
3. Literacy–Australia–Sydney. 4. Spaniards–Australia–Sydney–Languages.
5. Teenagers–Australia–Sydney–Language. 6. Spanish language–Social aspects–
Australia–Sydney. I. Ramirez, Elizabeth. II. Title.
P40.5.L322A844 2004
404'.2'0994–dc22   2004002824

British Library Cataloguing in Publication Data
A catalogue entry for this book is available from the British Library.

ISBN 1-85359-741-4 (hbk)
ISBN 1-85359-740-6 (pbk)

Multilingual Matters Ltd
UK: Frankfurt Lodge, Clevedon Hall, Victoria Road, Clevedon BS21 7HH.
USA: UTP, 2250 Military Road, Tonawanda, NY 14150, USA.
Canada: UTP, 5201 Dufferin Street, North York, Ontario M3H 5T8, Canada.

Typeset by Wordworks Ltd.
Printed and bound in Great Britain by the Cromwell Press Ltd.

Contents

Acknowledgements

Earlier versions of some of the material in this book were published in the following papers:

Gibbons, J. and Lascar, E. (1998) Operationalising academic language proficiency in bilingualism research. *Journal of Multilingual and Multicultural Development* 19 *(1), 40–50.*

Gibbons, J. (1999) Register aspects of literacy in Spanish. *Written Language and Literacy* 2(1), 63–88.

Gibbons, J., Lascar, E. and Mizón Morales, M.I. (1999) The role of social class and home literacy practices in literacy proficiency in a group of Chilean adolescents. In T. O'Brien (ed.) *Language and Literacies* (pp. 26–42). Clevedon: Multilingual Matters.

Gibbons, J. and Ramirez, E. (2003) The role of attitudes in the development of a full literate proficiency in Spanish. In P. Ryan and R. Terborg (eds) *Language: Issues of Inequality* (pp. 187–213). Mexico: CELE, Universidad Nacional Autónoma de México.

The Sydney research reported in this book was funded by two ARC small grants to the Spanish English Biliteracy Project:

- in 1996, A$7000 through the University of Western Sydney;
- in 1998, A$10,000 through the University of Sydney.

Conventions

The following conventions are used in this book.

Tables

In the statistical tables, correlations that are significant at 0.05 are shown in **bold,** and findings that are near this level are shown in *italics*.

Questionnaires

In reporting the results of the questionnaire/test instruments used, each questionnaire/test is indicated by a hash symbol (#), and the question number (**Q**). So questionnaire 4, question 75 is referred to as **#4 Q75.**

Network conventions

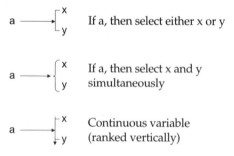

a ⟶ ⌐x ⌐y   If a, then select either x or y

a ⟶ ⌠x ⌡y   If a, then select x and y simultaneously

a ⟶ ⌐x ⌐y   Continuous variable (ranked vertically)

Chapter 1

Introduction

Objectives

This book has two overarching objectives. The first is to present an understanding of the factors that lead to the development of biliteracy and bilingualism in the individual and the maintenance of these in communities, particularly minority communities. Second, it attempts to explore and test out these understandings in a particular community – the Spanish-speaking community in Sydney, Australia. In particular it looks at the bilingualism and biliteracy of 106 Hispanic teenagers.

A major challenge for linguistic minorities, whether indigenous, refugee or migrant, is the maintenance of their language and culture. In almost all societies around the world, the nationalist myths that societies are (or can be) homogenous culturally, linguistically and ethnically, have led to the overt or covert suppression of cultural and linguistic difference, and sometimes the 'cleansing' of ethnic difference (including genocide). Hornberger (1997) refers to English as one of the main 'predator' languages that is endangering languages around the world, particularly in Australia where it has overwhelming cultural and economic dominance.

However, the issue of maintenance of minority languages is not a simple yes–no polar issue. The extent and degree of maintenance are also major concerns. A more nuanced understanding of minority language maintenance and shift requires the examination of the degree of acquisition of various elements of proficiency, including spoken language, basic literacy skills, grammar and high register.

There is an extensive literature that reports the success of bilingual education in producing high levels of bilingualism and biliteracy – for general surveys see Cummins (1996, 2000), Baker (2001) and, for a recent example, Lindhold-Leary (2001). However, the unfortunate reality is that bilingual education is not accessible to most language minorities. Transitional bilingual education, tapering out after the early years of primary school, is more widely available, but full bilingual education throughout schooling is rare. In New South Wales, Australia, where the research reported in this book was carried out, full bilingual education, in which subjects other than language are taught in two languages, hardly exists

(Gibbons, 1997). The same is true in many other countries. The reasons for this include practical problems (for instance it can be difficult and expensive to organise bilingual education for students that comprise a small language minority in a school), resources and mistaken beliefs (see Cummins, 2000).

If mainstream education does not provide an appropriate education for all children, it is left to the individual, the family, the minority community and non-mainstream institutions to support bilingualism in children, including second and subsequent generations from a migrant background. In this case, we must ask what are the arguments for and against maintaining a minority language.

The arguments against maintenance include the psychological risk, and the investment of time, energy and money that may be involved. The psychological risk is one of identity conflict and discomfort, and sometimes this is found among people who do not gain a good mastery of both languages (people with high proficiency in both languages are usually comfortable in both language contexts, and therefore tend not to suffer from this conflict). The other possible disadvantage is that minorities may have to invest time, money and effort in seeking out and utilising situations that favour the development of a minority language. In concrete terms, minority language children in New South Wales may need to attend minority language classes (mostly at the weekend) in addition to regular schooling.

Some of the possible benefits of minority language maintenance are:

for the individual:
- higher majority language proficiency and literacy (see Cummins, 1996, and the interdependence hypothesis);
- more positive self concept/self esteem;
- travel and employment opportunitie;
- cognitive flexibility (Hamers & Blanc, 2000: 88–92);

for the family:
- it strengthens contact within the family and maintains contact with relatives, especially overseas;

for the community:
- it contributes to community maintenance and pride;

for the nation:
- it meets the need for culturally-aware fluent bilinguals within the nation and for contacts with other nations.

Edwards (1994: 136) writes 'Questions of language ... of the protection of threatened collectivities are ... especially significant for minority groups. Unlike powerful mainstream societies, they do not have the luxury of ignoring these matters.'

Given the above, and using a financial metaphor, it is for the individual, the family and the community to decide whether the returns on bilingual proficiency are worth the investment and the risks. Many bilingual communities, particularly minority-language communities, are profoundly concerned about creating and sustaining high levels of proficiency in *both* the languages that are used in the community. The majority language will often be needed for interaction with friends, family and colleagues from outside the minority community, for participation in the mainstream society, and for access to the mainstream economy, institutions and services. As noted above, the minority language is often viewed as essential to cultural continuity and identity and to maintaining contact with people in the minority community (and often the region of origin). Furthermore, all else being equal, it is a bonus to know two languages rather than one, and there are few advantages to being monolingual. One of our teenage interviewees wrote 'I think to have the chance to be able to communicate in more than one language is a marvellous gift that opens doors to another world (cultures, customs, traditions)'.

For those who have made a decision in favour of high level bilingualism in the absence of bilingual education, we hope to provide information that may assist in this endeavour. In particular we wish to thank and to assist the Spanish-speaking community in Sydney.

Factors in the Development of Bilingualism and Biliteracy

Bilingualism has many aspects: one is the nature of the bilingual mind, whether bilinguals have a single fused representation of their languages, or separate representations; another is the patterning of bilingual code choice; and a third is the development and maintenance of proficiency in two languages. This book deals with the last of these three, examining two interlinked issues. First, what are the factors that lead to the development of two languages in an individual, and thereby the maintenance of two languages in a community? The second issue is the level and nature of the *proficiency* in the two languages. Are they both equally developed? Is there some type of functional specialisation such that certain domains of life are best handled in one language, while other domains are handled in the other language? And finally, what is the *linkage* between our issues – do certain factors lead to certain types and levels of proficiency? Haugen (1972) refers to this area as 'language ecology'.

Proficiency

Minority-language maintenance is, in effect, an attempt to resist the cultural power of languages that are spoken by a majority of the population, and/or languages that are, for some reason, socially dominant. Most minority languages lack both an official status and a role within national life – they tend to be used only in the home, and to some degree in the minority-language community (see the classic Fishman *et al.*, 1971). These facts mean that, for second generations and beyond, it is difficult to achieve a full and literate proficiency in both languages. While home use often means that children develop a domestic variety of the minority language, the lack of a place for it outside the home and community may mean that the children have little opportunity to develop aspects of the language that relate to more complex and more public uses. On the other hand, their experience of the second language may lack an intimate or domestic register. Early bilingualism studies tended to focus on whether or not a conversational command is developed in two languages. More recently, we have seen a shift in emphasis, and bilingualism researchers such as Cummins (1996), Verhoeven (1991a; 1991b) and Hamers (1994) are examining the extent to which minority-language speakers develop fuller and more literate proficiency in both languages.

Looking at the process of development, the first language experienced by minority-language children will be the home language, mostly the minority language. However, they will meet the majority language in the environment – increasingly so as they have contact with the wider community and its media. If education is available only in the majority language, then once a child starts school, the second language will begin to play a major role. In time it will overtake the home language, and the child may well develop a stronger command of the second language than the mother tongue. On the other hand, Cummins (1984) claims that children who begin school with little command of the school language can remain behind mother-tongue students in their command of the school language for up to seven years. There is a risk that these children will have an age-appropriate control of neither the mother tongue nor the school language (see Slade & Gibbons, 1987, for evidence of this in Australia). Biliterate language proficiency is therefore an issue of concern for the parents/caregivers, and for the students themselves.

We have looked at the advantages of bilingualism in general, and it may be good to consider the advantages of biliteracy. In general biliteracy enhances all the advantages discussed for bilingualism, in particular:

- *access* to written and specialist registers of language, and consequently;
- *access* across time, space and culture, to material that even in a post-literate age is still less available in the spoken language. In particular it gives access to the minority world view;
- *employment and travel* – the spoken language is useful, but literacy increases possibilities;
- *literacy in one language supports literacy in the other.*

These themes will be developed further in this book.

In this book we will attempt to examine the development of a fuller bilingual proficiency in both languages but, since it is more likely to be underdeveloped, we will examine proficiency in the minority language in more detail, and we will attempt to establish linkages with the following factors.

Factors

The factors that create and sustain bilingualism are often grouped into three main categories, that we shall refer to as societal, contact, and attitudinal. This type of categorisation (not always with the same titles) is used by, amongst others, Hamers and Blanc (2000) and Allard and Landry (1994). The *societal* layer is a broad socio-structural area, and is manifested concretely in the existence of social institutions and media. *Contact* concerns the individual's experience of the social world, particularly social interaction – what language does an individual use with neighbours, in shops and cafés, and with the doctor? *Attitudes* and beliefs exist within the mind of the individual, although they are mostly socially constructed, and are to some degree shared with others as part of culture.

It is important to note, however, that these categories interact in complex ways. For instance publishing a newspaper in a minority language (a *societal* phenomenon) enables *contact* with a more formal style of the language, and enhances the prestige of the language, affecting *attitudes*. However, the decision to publish a newspaper is itself likely to be influenced by attitudes and beliefs about the minority language. This type of circularity bedevils much of the discussion about bilingualism. It is perhaps best to see these categories as the layers through which various factors and variables are projected. These themes will all be expanded upon considerably in later chapters. The categories and their interaction are summarised in Figure 1.1.

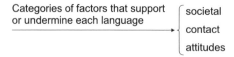

Figure 1.1 Categories of factors

(for the meaning of the conventions used, see p. *x*)

The Organisation of the Book

The organisation of this book follows roughly the structure of the preceding section. Chapter 2 examines in greater depth the issue of language proficiency. This is followed by a discussion of the measurement of bilingual proficiency in Chapter 3. Chapter 4 looks at the influence on bilingualism of broad socio-structural and demographic factors. Chapter 5 examines the role of interpersonal interaction in the development and maintenance of bilingualism. Chapter 6 concentrates more on biliteracy, particularly the influence of media use, literacy practices and education. Chapter 7 discusses the role of attitudes and beliefs in the creation of bilingual proficiency, including attitudes to languages and their speakers, to bilingualism itself, and to the vitality of languages and communities. Chapter 8 attempts to weave together all these factors and their proficiency outcomes, and to make suggestions for language maintenance in minority communities.

Chapters 5 to 7 share a similar structure: the first part of each chapter is a general discussion of the issues, including some reporting of findings from elsewhere. The second part then shows how we investigated the issues in the Sydney Hispanic community, and what we discovered.

The Context of the Studies

The studies reported in this book are set in the national context of Australia, a country of recent immigration that still receives a *per capita* migration that is among the world's highest. With the exception of the treatment of its Aboriginal minority, Australia is comparatively tolerant of ethnic, linguistic and cultural differences. Nevertheless, the dominance of English in Australia is absolute. While one can survive in Australia without English, this is only possible on the margin of society. Mainstream employment, education and access to services (for instance department stores) is feasible only if one speaks English. As in many migrant societies, it is expected that the second generation of refugee or migrant minorities will become 'Australian', in effect that they will act in accordance with Anglo-Australian behavioural norms, and that they will be native speakers of Australian English. The overwhelming hegemony of English, and its sheer cultural 'weight' makes the maintenance of minority languages a daunting challenge for minority communities in Australia. In practice, ghettoisation is unusual in second and subsequent generations, who generally use English to participate fully in the mainstream economy and culture, while maintaining alongside this varying levels of the minority language and culture. As Tuominen (1999: 57) remarks 'We have evidence that language use among immigrant groups often shifts towards a society's majority language'.

More specifically, the context of the study is Sydney, by far the largest city in Australia, with a population of over 4 million. It is also Australia's most multicultural city, and more than half the population is not of Anglo-Celtic heritage. The multilingualism of the school population can be seen in the fact that around a third of children present at primary school speaking little or no English (Abdoolcader, 1989). More than 90% of the schoolchildren in some areas speak English as a second language (Gibbons *et al.*, 1994).

The community within which the studies took place is that of Spanish speakers. The Spanish-speaking community is an interesting candidate for study, because it is a middle-sized community, that is neither notably disadvantaged (unlike in some parts of the USA) nor advantaged. To look at the community in general, we used census data to examine the role of societal factors, since such broad social factors need broad social data. However, if we take, for example, media, education and socio-economic status (SES), we can also look at their impact in a particular smaller population. Most of our data comes from such a smaller population.

We focused on teenagers, because it is in the teens that higher levels of language proficiency are acquired, so this is a crucial time for the development of full bilingualism and biliteracy. We interviewed 106 Hispanic teenagers in their homes, each interview taking around two hours. The interviews were conducted in 1997–1998.

The interviews

The interviews had two main elements: an 'open' element, where interviewees were asked in very broad terms to discuss their ideas about language in their lives and their identity as Hispanics; they were also asked more specific open questions, such as 'where do you use Spanish?' Interviewees entered their responses into a laptop computer.

There was also a 'closed' element in which the interviewees were asked to complete questionnaires with a fixed choice of responses. More detail is given in the relevant chapters. With regard to proficiency, there was also an 'open' element, since there were free-conversation parts of the interviews that were assessed for oral proficiency, and we also used self evaluation. In addition there were the language tests described in detail in Chapter 3. Home literacy resources were also examined, and the caregiver was interviewed.

The interviewees

Our intention was to examine students attending secondary school, to examine their level of bilingualism in Spanish, and to see what factors in their life and environment affected it.

Sampling procedure

We found no neutral way of locating Spanish-speaking families – for example, using Hispanic surnames would have excluded the many Argentinian Australian families who have Italian or German surnames. Even if we had been able to locate interviewees at random, we doubted that we could obtain a truly random sample, since our participants would of necessity be people willing to surrender their time and privacy. Instead, to find such people we used a mixture of advertising for volunteers in the local Spanish newspapers, and – following Milroy (1980) – the network contacts of Elizabeth Ramirez and our main research assistants César Luzardo and Vicky Rovira. At the end of each interview, the interviewee and caregiver were asked for contact details of other Hispanic teenagers that they felt might be willing to participate in the research, and thus one interview often led to another. This non-random sampling may have been biased towards the recruitment of interviewees who were willing to acknowledge their Spanishness, and with some level of confidence in the Spanish ability, but it became apparent that this was not universally the case.

Basic demographics

There were 106 interviewees, and all future figures are given in relation to this number. There were 63 females and 43 males. The ages of the interviewees at the time of the interview are given in Table 1.1 (5 interviewees did not provide their birth date). The great majority of the interviewees were in the 12–16 year range.

Language of education

Our intention was to focus on Australian-educated interviewees.

Table 1.1 Ages of the interviewees ($n = 106$)

Age in years	Number of interviewees of that age
18	2
17	6
16	9
15	28
14	18
13	16
12	17
11	5
Missing	5

However, it was often the case that, if there was more than one possible interviewee in the family, the older sibling/s had been educated in the country of origin before migration. We therefore included such interviewees in the data collection, since we were unwilling to forego potentially useful interviews. However there is a possibility that education in a Spanish-speaking country could mask the effects of various Australian factors. Where preliminary analysis revealed a possible difference of this kind, only the results for the Australian-educated group (defined as interviewees born in Australia, or who immigrated before the age of 6 years) will be given; 84 interviewees fell into this category, 59 interviewees were Australian born, and 47 were born overseas.

Substantially more information about the sample, and the relationship between demographic variables and bilingual proficiencies, is given in Chapter 4.

The Chilean sample

In the past, the standards for bilinguals have sometimes been set at unrealistic ideal levels, particularly for language proficiency. To avoid this issue, and to obtain relevant yardstick data, we used some of our proficiency measures and other research instruments on Chilean adolescents with the help of two schools in Santiago de Chile (Chile is the largest source of Spanish-speaking migrants to Australia). This sample comprised 96 girls aged around 13–14 years. One of the schools was a prestigious private school, and the other was a systemic school. The students from the private school were mainly from upper-middle-class homes, while those from the systemic school were mainly from lower-middle-class homes, with a proportion from working-class homes.

Chapter 2

Language Proficiency

Introduction

A (not always fruitful) distinction may be made between those who study the development of the mother tongue (particularly the development of literacy and school language), and those who study the development of the second language. Generalising is dangerous, but one can observe a difference in emphasis, with researchers into second-language development tending to focus more on grammar and vocabulary, while those who are concerned with mother tongue issues tend to concentrate on less linguistic aspects such as literacy practices. This book is about a group of people who do not fit comfortably into either of these categories – people born into a minority-language community.

Both approaches are relevant to such people. We need to know first whether a more basic command of language, particularly grammar and vocabulary, develops to age norms in both languages. Silva-Corvalán (1991) showed that some more complex aspects of Spanish morphology were not fully developed in the second-generation Hispanic American community she investigated. She presents her data in the form of implicational scales, which seem to reveal progressive simplification and reduction in grammar according to the generation of immigration. Zentella (1997: 180–212) also documents attrition in the complex Spanish tense and voice system. Dorian (1981) documents similar phenomena as part of the process of language shift in a community of Scottish Gaelic speakers. In Australia Yagmur *et al.* (1999) present findings from vocabulary and grammar tests showing clearly that there is language attrition in both middle- and working-class first-generation Turkish migrants. Other studies reveal language attrition of other languages in Australia, including Italian (Bettoni, 1985) and Dutch (Ammerlaan, 1995). Among minority language speakers, it is therefore important to assess grammatical morphology and vocabulary to see whether mastery of the majority language is to some degree at the expense of the minority language – Lambert's (1977) 'subtractive bilingualism' – perhaps indicating incipient language shift.

Other indicators of loss of proficiency may include accent with extensive transfer from the other language, and code mixing in more formal contexts

11

where it is inappropriate. Both phenomena are documented by Bettoni (1981) in the Italian community in North Queensland, where the progressive invasion of the Italian language by English over three generations represents a form of creeping language shift. Language shift is sometimes mistakenly discussed as a black-and-white issue rather than as a process of gradual shading over, involving language mixing and language attrition.

Examination of the language proficiency of second and subsequent generations of bilinguals will need to elicit oral language (both monitored and free) to check accent and mixing, and also to assess some of the more elusive aspects of oral proficiency, such as fluency and idiomaticity (the ability to generate language that is not only grammatically accurate, but also uses forms of expression that are common or natural in the language).

The mother-tongue orientation involves the notions of literacy and biliteracy, which are examined in Chapter 6. Proficiency includes low-level aspects of literacy, such as basic command of the writing system – including the ability to both read and write the written symbols, spelling and punctuation . In Spanish there is the additional complication of the diacritics – the accent (´) and tilde (~). These cause problems for both native-speaker children and second-language learners, and require checking. Other aspects of basic literacy can be assessed by more global measures such as cloze tests.

While regular home use has the potential to develop most basic grammatical systems, it is much less certain that more formal, academic and literate aspects of the language will develop without help from the education system. This is another typical concern of mother tongue-studies, and involves the language features of academic and formal registers that develop through literacy practices.

These complex interplays of different elements and types of language proficiency that emerge from different sociolinguistic contexts make one issue clear. It is important to take seriously the issue of language proficiency among bilinguals, and examine it using adequate measures. While there are richer models and more varied evaluation techniques in both second-language and mother-tongue assessment, these are less commonly deployed among bilinguals, where in many cases only self assessment or grammar measures are used (see for instance Zentella, 1997). We argue here for a more complex and fuller vision of language proficiency, and therefore for more varied measures.

Traditional models of second-language competence such as those found in Canale and Swain (1980) and Bachman (1990) have used a division into four main types of language proficiency (under slightly differing names): grammatical, discoursal, sociolinguistic and strategic (the ability to actually deploy the other three types). However, the careful large-scale testing of these in Harley, Allen *et al.* (1990) challenged this model. A factor analysis revealed instead a two-factor structure that divided language competence into a general language proficiency, linked particularly to lexico-grammatical ability (which is well documented and does not need further description here), and a written–spoken dimension that corresponds to the literacy arena discussed below.

Biliterate proficiency

In a range of publications, Cummins (1979, 1984, 1996) has divided the bilingual proficiency of minority language children into two elements, everyday conversational language, and cognitive academic language. Cummins relates the latter to education and literacy, and observes that it is mostly acquired in educational contexts. A cogent attack was mounted on Cummins by Martin-Jones and Romaine (1986), who based their critique partly on the inadequate linguistic modelling of the distinction. More recently, Cummins (1996: 67–68) has stated that everyday language is more context embedded, while academic language tends to context reduced. Cummins is not a linguist, and counters the criticism of his linguistic modelling by calling on the work of Biber (1988, 1995) for adequate description and evidence that the distinction has linguistic reality.

Context embeddedness and the reference to Biber's work give two strong indicators of the nature of this phenomenon. Biber describes his work as register analysis, and context embeddedness is a defining feature of the Hallidayan register parameter 'mode', which examines the linguistic effects produced by the distance (in terms of time, space and abstractness) between a text and the context to which it refers, and also the distance between listener/reader and speaker/writer. In the bilingualism literature, this type of register variation is often associated with literacy, for instance Hamers and Blanc (1989: 68) refer to 'the "literacy" use of language which requires a decontextualised use of language'. In referring to this register as literate register, we are not claiming that this register equates with literacy, but there a strong case that it constitutes an important element of literacy – see for example Baynham (1995) and Christie (1990). Despite the knowledge of register that has been emerging over the last decade or more, and the importance of the concept for understanding higher-level bilingualism, there have been few attempts to incorporate it into bilingualism studies or to attempt to operationalise it for bilingualism studies involving languages other than English.

We should at this juncture state that we recognise, value and indeed speak varieties of language other than the standard, decontextualised and written. However, the social status and communicative utility of the latter suggest that it is desirable for a full bilingual proficiency to encompass such registers within its repertoire.

Register is a product of the relationship between the linguistic systems, and the contexts of their use. So academic register is the type of language that is used in the process of education, while everyday register is the language used for social interaction in home and community. In most countries, apart from the small numbers of children who receive bilingual education, bilingual children experience only one language as the medium of education. While there may be some opportunity for study *of* the other language, there is usually little or no opportunity to learn *through* the other language, which severely limits opportunities to acquire the academic register of that language. In Australia, as in most nations where there is a dominant language, apart from the minute proportion of children who receive bilingual education, minority-language children experience only the majority language (English) as a medium of instruction. This may explain the unease of many second- and third-generations speakers of minority languages concerning their own minority-language proficiency; as one of our interviewees wrote (# 4 Q75; capitals in the original): I SPEAK INFORMAL WITH THEM AND FIND IT HARD TO SPEAK FORMALLY

While they often have a well-developed domestic register of their first language, they have not had the chance to acquire many other registers, particularly the academic register. Yet some minority-language children manage to acquire a good level of biliteracy and some command of academic register in both languages. A major concern of the parents of our interviewees, although not always articulated in these terms, is that their children might not fully acquire formal and written registers of Spanish. It therefore seems important to discover what levels are attained, and how.

This book attempts to do so. This involves three tasks. The first task is to uncover and understand academic register, which is poorly described for most languages other than English (including Spanish): this is done in the remainder of this chapter. The second task to examine and measure the development of both everyday and academic registers, a core issue in the study of full bilingual development: this is discussed in Chapter 3. A third task is to examine the various factors that might contribute to this development, the topic of subsequent chapters.

The concept 'cognitive academic language' or academic register is widely used in the literature on bilingualism, but has been subjected to a limited amount of research. Indeed, the great majority of work in bilingualism has concentrated on the spoken rather than the written language.

Academic Register in English

In the history of the study of language in education debates, there have been many attempts to show, firstly, that the language of education, or 'academic register', is different from and more complex than everyday language and, secondly, that certain types of home language experience provide a closer match to the language of the school, and therefore provide a better preparation for school. Brice Heath's (1983) important study illuminates cultural differences between school and home, and gives limited information on language differences. There is, however, an emerging literature on the first need mentioned above, the description of academic register, although it is mostly concerned with English. The differences seem to emerge mostly from the fact that schooling concerns itself to a significant extent with written texts; in other words, there is a central concern with literacy (and here with the linguistic variation that distinguishes written from spoken language).

Biber (1988) undertook a study of a very large corpus of texts, both oral and written. He performed a factor analysis of the linguistic correlates of text types, and arrived at seven factors, all of which are highly significantly correlated with variation in text type, although no single dimension can be associated with any single text type. Three of these, dimensions 1, 3 and 5, Biber (1988: 162) says could be considered 'oral/literate dimensions'.

- *Dimension 1* seems to be based on whether the writer/speaker's purpose is 'informational' or 'interactive, affective and involved', and on the circumstances in which the text is produced: '... careful editing possibilities ... versus circumstances dictated by real-time constraints'(Biber, 1988: 107).
- *Dimension 3* 'seems to distinguish between highly explicit context-independent reference and nonspecific, situation-dependent reference' (Biber, 1988: 110).
- *Dimension 5* has to do with the distinction between abstract and non-abstract information.

Biber (1988) provides examples of text types at the extremes of these dimensions, and discusses the formal linguistics features that distinguish them. Table 2.1 below summarises these findings.

These three dimensions conform to the type of differences we mentioned above as likely to distinguish academic register from everyday language. They also share properties with the Hallidayan register categories of Tenor, Mode and Field. These categories, while not making absolute

Table 2.1 Biber's three oral/literate dimensions

Dimension	Examples of text types at the extremes of the dimensions	Linguistic realisations
1 Informational versus involved production (Biber, 1988: 107)	official documents, telephone conversations	high proportion of nouns and prepositional phrases, longer words and varied vocabulary
3 Explicit versus situation-dependent reference (Biber, 1988: 110)	official documents, broadcasts	relative clauses
5 Abstract versus non-abstract information (Biber, 1988 : 112)	academic prose, telephone conversations	passives

predictions about the language forms used in any given context, posit a probabilistic relationship between context and form.

In relation to academic text, Hallidayan linguists, particularly Halliday and Hasan (1985) and Halliday and Martin (1993) have found the following linguistic correlates of academic register.

Mode

Written texts, because of their composing processes and storage possibilities, tend to be better planned and less dependent on context (see for example Chafe, 1985; Chafe & Tannen, 1987). These distinctions between the spoken and written language – context embedding and planning – are not absolute, however. A note to oneself, despite being written, can be unplanned and spontaneous, and deeply context embedded and therefore highly inexplicit, if the writer assumes that s/he will remember the context of writing. On the other hand, we have free-standing and well-planned oral literature. Further confusing the issue are the facts that television news is a scripted oral performance, while dialogue in a novel is a written representation of oral language – in Crystal and Davy's (1969) terms, spoken as written, and written as spoken respectively.

Linguists, particularly Halliday (1985) have resolved this issue by noting that there is a continuum, running from least planned and highly contextualised to most planned and context reduced. He refers to this as the 'mode continuum', and explores the linguistic consequences of decontextualisation and planning. One important linguistic outcome when con-

Table 2.2 Noun phrases in the development of ideas

The text (elements that provide the language context are in brackets)	Notes
(The mechanism by which) glass cracks	*glass*, a thing, appears in its congruent form – a noun *crack*, a process, appears in its congruent form – a verb
(The stress needed) to crack glass	glass cracking becomes a unit dependent on 'need'
(as) a crack grows	*crack* has now become a noun – i.e. it is now grammatically metaphorical *grow*, a process, is introduced congruently as a verb *glass* is assumed
(will make) slow cracks grow	the rate of cracking, which is an attribute, is introduced congruently as an adjective *slow*
(speed up) the rate at which cracks grow	*rate* now becomes a noun – it is structurally separated from *crack* and *grow*
The rate of crack growth (depends not only on ...)	grow now becomes a noun *growth* *rate* is now more closely linked with *crack* and *grow*
(we can decrease) the crack growth rate (1000 times)	all the concepts developed over the preceding text are now packaged as a single dense noun phrase *crack growth rate*

structing long connected texts is that, as an understanding or issue grows steadily through a text, that growing understanding may be summarised in a noun phrase, as the starting point for the next development of the ideas. The examples in Table 2.2, taken from Halliday (1988), show this in action. They are taken from an article 'The fracturing of glass' in *Scientific American* (1987) and are presented in the order in which they occur in this text.

This cumulation within the noun phrase explains much about the nature of academic register. As Halliday shows, when ideas are first introduced they generally appear in a simple 'congruent' form – things appear as nouns, processes as verbs, attributes as adjectives, logical connections as conjunctions such as 'therefore', and so on. However, as the last example shows, the accumulation of concepts skews these relationships between form and semantics. Halliday calls this 'grammatical metaphor'.

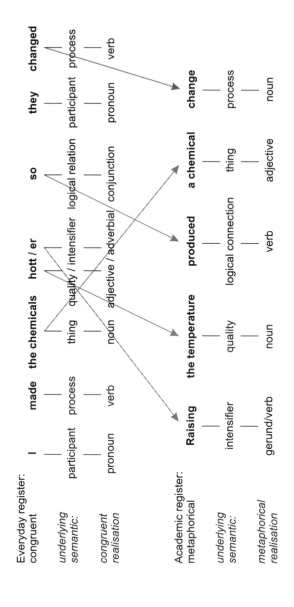

Figure 2.1 An example of grammatical metaphor in English

Figure 2.1 gives another illustration of how in English the change to academic register leads to a skewing of the relationship between the underlying semantic concepts – in this case extending beyond nominalisations. So 'things' *chemicals* are realised congruently as a noun in the first sentence, but metaphorically in the second sentence as an adjective; the 'logical connection' appears congruently as a conjunction *so* in the first sentence, but metaphorically as a verb *produced* in the second, and a 'process' *change* appears as a verb in the first sentence, but metaphorically as a noun in the second. The notion of grammatical metaphor includes, but is much more powerful than, 'nominalisation'.

In English, grammatical metaphor permits the dense packaging of information, particularly in the noun phrase, or nominal group. Its importance in functional literacy is discussed by Baynham (1995: 234) and others. Halliday (1975) also shows that the congruent form is learned first among children. Campbell (1994) demonstrates that mastery of grammatically metaphorical form, in particular, good and appropriate control of nominalisation, is highly variable among minority-language speakers, and is learned late. Indeed higher levels of language acquisition appear in part to consist of the development of register, of learning how grammatical resources can be redeployed once they have been mastered.

Halliday and Martin (1993) also show that, in scientific language (although probably not in legal language, see Gibbons, 1994b: 7, or in history texts, like the ones discussed later in this chapter) this increased complexity at the level of the phrase, or 'group' in Hallidayan terms, is offset by less complexity in the sentence structure or syntax. Indeed many sentences in scientific language seems to consist of complex noun phrases with the verb 'to be' or an equivalent joining them, a simple syntactic structure. In Figure 2.1, we see exactly this, with a two-clause dependent syntactic structure in the first sentence reduced to a simple single clause, but with increased complexity in the noun phrases.

Other possible consequences of a text becoming more written are:

- *increased lexical density,* i.e. there are more content words and fewer structure words – in part a consequence of grammatical metaphor (see also Biber, 1988);
- *exophoric reference becomes endophoric,* i.e. reference is made to things within the text rather than to the surrounding context. An extreme cases of context embeddedness and linguistic inexplicitness is 'pass me that one', where only the verb is explicit because the referents of 'me' and 'that one' are made obvious by the context. Another extreme example is the operating surgeon's 'scalpel!' where only the

particular object needs to be made explicit – what needs to be done (i.e. handing it over), who is to do so and to whom are again assumed from the context. In a text not embedded in the same context, the participants and processes need to be made more explicit e.g. 'the surgeon had the nurse pass him the scalpel';

• *increased explicitness in the logical structure* – as a consequence of planning, and because links are made to other parts of the text rather than the outside world, the logical structure or argument is made more explicit, less of 'and' but more of 'therefore', less of 'next' but more of 'first, second, third' (see Biber, 1988)

• *more passives* (see Biber, 1988), these enable us to reorganise the information flow in a text, and often work hand in hand with grammatical metaphor. One role of passives is to facilitate the placing of old information at the beginning of the sentence, even if the old information is the logical recipient of the verb's action. An example is 'When the Prime Minister arrived at Parliament, he was jeered by striking public servants', where, in the second half, the Prime Minister is old information, so he can be placed first by means of a passive, and the remainder of the clause adds information.

These phenomena have been noted by a number of scholars working in a range of linguistic schools, see Biber, 1988, and Danet and Bogoch (1994: especially 119–123).

Field

Field has to do with the specialisation of knowledge being realised through the specialised use of language – mostly vocabulary. Specialists organise their understanding of the world in ways that differ from common everyday understandings. Sometimes this leads to new words for new concepts – for instance 'precipitation' is not an everyday word, but it enables a weather expert or geographer to package together the related phenomena of rain, snow and hail. In scientific texts there are frequent uses of such words ('hyponyms') to group related phenomena. Sometimes, perhaps confusingly, everyday words are used in a specialised sense. For example in a courtroom the following everyday words are used with specialised reference: 'offence', 'costs', 'order'. Martin (1990: 86) writes 'scientists simply cannot do their jobs without technical discourse. Not only is it compact and therefore efficient, but, most importantly it codes an alternative perspective on reality to common sense ... It constructs the world in a different way.'

Tenor

This element of register relates to the social relationship between writer and reader, or between speakers. This is the element that is most commonly handled in standard sociolinguistic accounts. Important to this is the relative *status* of these people, is one talking 'down', 'up' or to a peer? What roles are the people playing? Another variable that may affect language is *affect*, both feelings at the moment of communication and long-term attitudes. A final factor is *contact*, how well the people involved know each other. All three of these aspects of tenor form part of politeness, and the process of negotiating social relationships.

The *status* element affects illocutionary acts – for instance when getting someone else to do something, whether one begs, requests or orders is a result of the status relationship. Status differences also tend to produce more 'hedges', including less direct commitment to the truth of a statement. From the lower status party, they can be realised through modal verbs such as 'might' and adjuncts such as 'perhaps'. The language written for young children is often affected by status, using exclamations, and perhaps also diminutives – sometimes to the point of seeming patronising. Status also contributes to selecting forms of address.

Affect often affects modality – a strong emotional charge is reflected in emotional language, including augmentative expression such as 'utterly' in 'utterly stupid'. Written academic language is usually emotionally neutral and shuns such expressions, even the relatively mild 'very'.

Contact, which leads to familiarity, also affects language. If one is writing for an unknown audience, one must take care not to appear familiar. This can lead to some outcomes that appear bizarre – for instance writers of factual texts may avoid referring to the reader at all, and if they do so may use the third person ('the reader may wish to consider the alternatives') rather than the second person ('you may wish to consider the alternatives'), even though they are addressing the reader directly. Overall, texts used in schooling tend to be more impersonal than conversation.

These phenomena are comparatively well described for English – see Chafe (1985), Chafe & Tannen (1987), Halliday (1985), Halliday & Martin (1993) and Biber (1988) – but we have been able to find almost nothing on this topic for Spanish, nor indeed have Lavandera and a range of other eminent Spanish language experts whom we have consulted. Yet, in the context of the role of Spanish as a major world language, and as an important minority language in the USA and Australia, this type of information could be of great importance in the education of Spanish speakers. This study does not represent a long term and detailed analysis of Spanish academic register, but rather an initial effort to initiate such an analysis, and operationalise the concept.

Academic Register in Spanish

In order to break into this topic, we gathered school textbooks that are used in Argentina and Uruguay for teaching natural science and social science, in years 2 and 3 in primary schools, and in years 7 and 8 in secondary schools. We did this on the basis that early primary texts are likely to be close to the students' everyday language, since at this stage students would have had little chance to acquire academic register. By the middle years of high school, however, students would be expected (rightly or wrongly) to have acquired some aspects of academic register, and would be expected to need exposure to other aspects. Therefore we looked for texts that covered closely-related topics in the earlier and later years. This produced a total of eight texts: four primary texts matched with four secondary texts, evenly divided between social science and natural science. Extracts from seven of those texts are used in following discussion.

In other words, we chose texts that covered similar content, but were written for different ages, in order to see whether there were substantial differences in the language used. Any such differences would indicate the higher levels of academic register that students are expected to handle in the upper years, and would provide evidence of the way register operates in Spanish. Rather than handling field, mode and tenor separately, since all three are manifested in the texts, extracts from the texts are presented in columns, with the primary level texts on the left, and equivalents from the secondary level texts on the right. In this way the contrasts between the language resources used can be clearly viewed.

First, however, we need to note something of the formal differences between English and Spanish that might affect the realisation of register. In the area of mode, we earlier noted the particular importance of grammatical metaphor in English, particularly in the construction of complex noun phrases. Spanish does not permit the direct modification of one noun by another with the same ease that English does. Spanish has a form that corresponds to the English 'of' construction, but one noun cannot be simply placed before another in a manner similar to adjectives, as in English. So, while Spanish has a translation equivalent of 'the fracture of glass' and 'the power of the wind', it does not have a word-for-word translation equivalent of 'glass fracture' or 'wind power'. We can therefore predict that grammatical metaphor in Spanish will not exactly parallel that of English.

With regard to 'planning', as noted earlier, an important resource in

English is the use of passives to organise the information flow in texts. While passives exist in Spanish, they are less favoured stylistically – indeed they are mostly avoided in speech, being replaced with reflexive or impersonal constructions. Reflexive constructions permit the omission of the agent and the fronting of the recipient of the action in a similar manner to passives. Furthermore, word order in Spanish is freer than in English, and phrases may well appear at various points in the structure, even though SVO (subject/verb/object) is generally regarded as the unmarked structure. Once more, given these differing resources, we would expect that information flow through text might be managed somewhat differently in Spanish, in part by using reflexives or marked orderings of elements within active sentences to play the role of less frequent passives.

Let us now look at examples from the primary and secondary parallel texts: the primary level text is in the left column, and equivalents from the secondary level texts are on the right, so that the contrasts in the use of the language resources can be clearly viewed. Word-for-word glosses into English are provided in italics.

Primary (Text A)	*Secondary (Text B)*
El ciclo del agua	**¿Cómo se forman las nubes?**
The Water Cycle	*How are clouds formed?*
Al enfriarse las nubes,	Las precipitaciones tienen lugar cuando
When the clouds cool,	
las gotitas de agua se juntan	*Precipitation takes place when*
the little drops of water join	aumenta el tamaño de las partículas de agua o hielo
y forman gotas más grandes.	*the size of the particles of water or ice increases*
and form bigger drops.	
Estas gotas, como pesan más,	y ellas caen por acción de la gravedad.
These drops, since they weigh more,	
caen a la tierra en forma de lluvia, nieve y granizo.	*and they fall by the action of gravity.*
fall to the ground in the form of rain, snow and hail.	

These particular extracts happen to describe exactly the same phenomenon, but are written for different age levels – the text on the right is for secondary schools, while the text to the left is for primary schools. W will now compare elements of the two texts which have parallel content, but different wording.

a nieve y granizo	Las precipitaciones
rain snow and hail	*Precipitation*

This is a very clear example of the use of technical vocabulary (field), with the lower-level text using everyday words, while the higher-level text uses a specialist hyponym 'precipitation'.

más grandes	aumenta el tamaño de
bigger (lit. more big)	*increases the size of*

This example illustrates grammatical metaphor in action. 'Size' is an attribute, so in congruent language it would appear as an adjective, and 'moreness' an intensifier, would be realised as a type of adverb, as indeed happens in the primary text. In the secondary text however moreness is realised as a verb 'aumenta' *increase*, (not, it should be noted, a nominalisation) and size as a noun 'tamaño'.

gotitas de agua	las partículas de agua
little drops of water	*particles of water*

This example is an interesting combination of specialised language from the scientific field and characteristics of child/adult relations. The use of *particles* rather than 'drops' is clearly a (possibly unnecessary) use of a technical versus an everyday term (i.e. in Hallidayan terms a field difference). However, 'gotitas' has a diminutive ending, of a type that would not normally appear in a scientific text, since '-ito' has an emotive loading similar to 'little' (in contrast to 'small') in English. Gooch (1967: 2) writes that 'the so-called diminutive suffixes are often not used primarily to convey an idea of smallness, but to express affection or to produce a favourable reaction in the person addressed'. The '-ito' diminutive is typical of language used by adults to younger children, and therefore may be a manifestation of the social relationship (i.e. tenor).

caen a la tierra	ellas caen
they fall to the ground	*they fall*

Since it is easy to over-interpret textual differences, the following is tentative only, but why did the writers include *to the ground* for the younger children? It is clearly over-specific and redundant, but there is little doubt that skilled communicators with younger children use redundancy and highly explicit language, perhaps because they feel that nothing should be taken for granted among younger children. This may then be another tenor marker.

como	por acción de
since	*by the action of*

This is another clear case of grammatical metaphor. The linkage between gravity/mass and falling is causal. In the primary text this is congruently expressed by a causative conjunction. In the secondary text, however, this relationship is expressed by a prepositional phrase centred on *action*, which is multilayered in its incongruence, being derived from the verb 'act', which here means 'cause'.

pesan más   la gravedad
they weigh more   *gravity*

The difference here is in part one of knowledge – younger children may not have mastered the explicit concept *gravity*. This knowledge difference is manifested in field-specific scientific language. Since mass is an attribute, the congruent form would be an adjective, 'heavy'. As an aside, it is interesting to note that in neither English nor Spanish can we say the more scientifically accurate 'mass more' instead of *weigh more*, and 'more massive' does not have this exact meaning – a case where our concepts have outpaced our language.

It is difficult to find texts whose content is matched with this degree of exactness, but these short examples provide evidence of academic register differences in Spanish that is convincing linguistically, as well as intuitively when the whole texts are examined.

It is not only scientific texts that display such characteristics. Texts C and D below both deal with heroes of independence struggles, San Martín in Argentina, and Lavalleja in Uruguay. Because the texts deal with different men, their content is not exactly equivalent. However, there are sufficient parallels to provide interesting comparisons.

Primary (Text C)	*Secondary (Text D)*
San Martín, un gran hombre	**(Lavalleja)**
En un pueblito llamado Yayepú nació José Francisco de San Martín.	Juan Antonio Lavalleja nació el 24 de Junio de 1784 en los alrededores
In a little village called Yayepú was born José Francisco de San Martín.	*Juan Antonio Lavalleja was born on 24th of June 1784 near*
Era el menor de los cinco hijos de Juan de San Martín (militar español)	de la Villa de Concepción de Minas, siendo sus padres Manuel Pérez de La Valleja y
He was the youngest of the five children of Juan de San Martín (a Spanish soldier)	*Villa de Concepción de Minas, his parents being Manuel Pérez de La Valleja and*
y doña Gregoria Matorras.	Ramona Justina de La Torre.
and Doña Gregoria Matorras.	*Ramona Justina de La Torre.*

De pequeño prefería el juego de los soldaditos. ¡Cómo los hacía marchar!
As a child he liked playing with toy soldiers. How he made them march!

Cuando tenía seis años sus padres decidieron volver a España.
When he was six yeasr old his parent decided to go back to Spain.

Allí estudió la carrera militar y siendo muy joven participó en batallas.
There he took military studies and while still very young participated in battles.

¡Era un soldado muy valiente!
He was a very brave soldier!

Regresó a Buenos Aires para ayudar en la lucha contra el enemigo.
He returned to Buenos Aires to help in the fight against the enemy.

Creó el Regimento de Granaderos a Caballo
He created the Horse Grenadiers

Regimentel que venció a los españoles en la batalla de San Lorenzo.
which defeated the Spanish in the battle of San Lorenzo.

En Mendoza preparó el Ejercito de los Andíes. Las damas mendocinas bordaron la bandera.
In Mendoza he trained the Army of the Andes. The Mendoza women embroidered the flag.

San Martín cruzó la cordillera de los Andíes para libertar Chile y Perú.
San Martín crossed the Andes chain to liberate Chile and Peru.

Murió en Francia. Sus restos descansan en la Catedral de Buenos Aires.
He died in France. His remains lie in the Cathedral of Buenos Aires.

Durante su adolescencia ayudó a su padre, que era estanciero, en las tareas rurales.
During his adolescence he helped his father, who was a gentleman farmer, with farm work

En 1811 se incorporó desde sus comienzos a la Revolución Oriental
In 1811 he became part from its very beginning of the Uruguayan Revolution

y participó en la batalla de Las Piedras, en el Éxodo y en la marcha de retorno
and took part in the battle of Las Piedras, in the Exodus and in the return march

que culminó con el segundo sitio...
which finished with the second siege ...

En 1825 participó activamente en el movimiento revolucionario
In 1825 he took an active part in the revolutionary movement

cuya jefatura le fue confiada
whose leadership was entrusted to him

y vivió hasta 1828 sus años más gloriosos como principal protagonista de la gesta emancipadora.
and lived until 1828 his most glorious years as the main protagonist of our heroic emancipation.

... En 1853, cuando ya había retirado a la vida privada fue designado como miembro ...
In 1853, when he had already retired to private life he was appointed a member

del Triunvirato que sucedió al presidente Giró.
of the triumvirate which succeeded President Giró.

En el ejercicio de su alto cargo falleció el 22 de octubre de ese mismo año
In the exercise of his high office he expired on the 22nd of October of that same year.

We will now compare elements of the two texts.

Era el menor de los cinco hijos de
He was the youngest of the five children of
Juan de San Martín (militar español)
Juan de San Martín (a Spanish soldier)
y doña Gregoria Matorras.
and Doña Gregoria Matorras.

siendo sus padres Manuel Pérez de La
Valleja y
*his parents being Manuel Pérez de La
Valleja and*
Ramona Justina de La Torre.
Ramona Justina de La Torre

Here, unlike the scientific texts discussed by Halliday, we can see that the secondary level text is more syntactically complex than the primary text, using a dependent construction. Overall, there are many more examples of greater syntactic complexity in the secondary-level history text.

Siendo muy joven
Being very young
De pequeño
As a child

Durante su adolescencia
During his adolescence

'Age' is an attribute, and is therefore congruently expressed as an adjective, as in text C, as 'joven' *young* and 'pequeño' *small*. In text D, however, a nominalisation *adolescence* is used – an example of grammatical metaphor.

Era un soldado
He was a soldier

(ayudó a su padre ...) en las tareas rurales
(helped his father ...) with farm work

'Work' is an action, and therefore congruently expressed as a verb. In text D it appears as a noun – grammatical metaphor again. The adjective 'rurales' is translated into English by a noun *farm*, showing a tendency for Spanish to qualify nouns by adjectives, where English might use another noun.

regresó (a Buenos Aires)
(He) returned (to Buenos Aires)

la marcha de retorno
the return march

Both marching and returning are actions, and would therefore be congruently expressed as verbs. In text D, however, both appear as nouns, using grammatical metaphor, while text C uses the congruent form.

creó el Regimento de Granaderos
created the Grenadier Regiment

cuya jefatura le fué confiada
whose leadership was entrusted to him

The extract from text D is extremely complex in its grammar, with a passive within a possessive relative clause (both are rarely used in Spanish conversation). Furthermore 'to lead' is an action, and would therefore be congruently realised as a verb, but it appears as the noun *leadership*, which has an extra layer of complexity added by the suffix '-tura' *-ship*, which creates an abstract noun from a concrete one 'jefe' *leader.*

¡Era un soldado muy valiente!	sus años más gloriosos como principal
He was a very brave soldier!	protagonista
	his most glorious years as the main hero

Bravery is an attribute, and it appears congruently in the form of a adjective 'valiente' *brave* in text C. In text D it appears as a noun in 'protagonista' *hero* (brave person) and his glory is also projected on to 'his years' (at a deeper level it was Lavalleja who was glorious, not his years). We also have a field phenomenon in the use of the elevated 'protagonist' rather than 'hero', although this difference is less marked in Spanish than in English since this is a common word for 'hero' in Spanish. The entire extract from text D is also in the form of a very complex noun phrase, in comparison with the simple sentence from text C.

para libertar Chile y Perú	la gesta emancipadora
to liberate Chile and Peru	*our heroic emancipation*(lit. *the*
	emancipatory geste/saga)

Two of the three bilingual dictionaries we consulted did not contain the word 'gesta' – an indication of its degree of specialisation. The adjective 'emancipatory' probably does not exist in English. This is a reflection of the fact that Spanish is very rich in adjectives, because nouns are less easy to use as modifiers. In general the secondary version is in a more elevated style.

Murió en Francia. Sus restos descansan	En el ejercicio de su alto cargo falleció
en la Catedral de Buenos Aires.	el 22 de octubre de ese mismo año.
He died in France. His remains lie in the	*In the exercise of his high office he expired*
Cathedral of Buenos Aires.	*on the 22nd of October of that same year.*

The two words for dying, 'murió' *died* and 'falleció' *expired* provide a classic register example, where a more elevated lexical item is used in text D, compared to the everyday one in text C. Notice, too, the two simple sentences in the primary text, compared with the nominalisation 'En el ejercicio', which uses grammatical metaphor to combine two elements, by replacing a clause with a prepositional phrase.

Turning now to scientific texts, E and F, we can see more instances of register phenomena.

Primary (Text F)	Secondary (Text E)

El Ecosistema
The Ecosystem

Integrantes de un ecosistema
The constituents of an ecosystem

En un ecosistema, cada ser vivo encuentra todo lo que necesita ...
In an ecosystem, every living being finds all it needs ...

... dependen unos de otros. Cada uno tiene un lugar y una función
... they depend on each other. Each one has its place and its function

que cumplir en el medio en que vive, porque en la naturaleza todo está en equilibrio.
to perform in the medium in which it lives, because in nature everything is in equilibrium.

La comunidad biótica o biocenosis es el conjunto de vegetales y animales
The biotic community or biocenosis is the group of flora and fauna

que habitan en un medio (acuático o terrestre), y mantienen entre ellos relaciones
that inhabit a medium (aquatic or terrestrial), and maintain among themselves relationships

de alimentación, sostén, refugio, etc. Una comunidad y el medio en que ella vive,
of alimentation, support, shelter, etc. A community and the medium in which it lives,

interrelacionados, constituyen un ecosistema.
interrelated, constitute an ecosystem.

... (1) La comunidad biótica o biocenosis, integrada por todos los seres vivos que habitan un ecosistema ...
The biotic community or biocenosis, constituted by all the living beings that inhabit an ecosystem.

Cada comunidad biótica o biocenosis (del griego *bios*: vida; *oinos*: en comun)
Each biotic community or biocenosis (from the Greek 'bios' life; 'oinos' in common)

incluye, por tanto, el conjunto de seres vivos que viven en un determinado ambiente físico (...).
includes, therefore, the group of living beings that live in a particular physical environment.

Esta comunidad normalmente presenta interdependencia entre los seres vivos
This community normally displays interdependence among the living beings

que la integran, fundamentalmente de naturaleza nutritiva, pues unos se alimentan de los otros.
which constitute it, fundamentally of a nutritive nature, since some feed upon others.

Pero también hay dependencia de los factores físicos ambientales, es decir, del biotopa.
But there is also dependence on physical environmental factors, that is, on the biotope.

La biocenosis constituye, pues, una asociación en equilibrio relativamente estable en el tiempo.
The biocenosis constitutes, then, an association in relatively stable equilibrium through time.

It may be worth mentioning that the English translations in this example represent the Spanish poorly in register terms. For example,

vegetales y animales ... medio acuático   seres vivos ... ambiente físico
o terrestre   *living beings ... physical environment*
flora and fauna ... aquatic or terrestrial
medium

In a similar English language school text, 'seres vivos' would probably be *life forms*. 'Vegetales y animales' does not translate well in English, because while we use *animals*, we do not use the corresponding *vegetals*. Finally 'environment', 'aquatic' and 'terrestrial' are all more elevated in style than their Spanish equivalents. Overall the English translation is more inflated than the Spanish.

However, comparing the Spanish texts, in the higher-level text we find clear use of the field phenomenon of overarching hyponyms, in this case more abstract terms, for the more specific terms in the lower-level text: 'seres vivos' for 'vegetales y animales', and 'físico' for 'acuático o terrestre'.

los seres vivos dependen unos de otros   ... presenta interdependencia entre los
the living beings depend on each other   seres vivos
                                                              displays interdependence among the living
                                                              beings

en la naturaleza todo está en equilibrio   constituye ... una asociación en
in nature everything is in equilibrium   equilibrio relativamente estable en el
                                                              tiempo
                                                              constitutes an association in relatively
                                                              stable equilibrium through time

The extracts from text E in these two examples show complexity at phrase level, following a verb similar to the verb *to be* 'presenta' and 'constituye'. In the first example, note particularly the nominalisation 'interdependencia' (*interdependence*) which corresponds to the verb 'depende' (*depend*) in the primary text. The long noun phrase beginning 'una asociación' in the second example has two qualifying prepositional phrases, which seems unnecessarily complex. Indeed, when it is compared with the lower-level text, the 'en el tiempo' (*through time*) element seems an example of the wordiness condemned in Labov (1969).

There was one further example of a text fragment that provided a particularly clear example of the manner in which Spanish uses specialist adjectives to handle cases where in English a noun would be used as a qualifier.

la fuerza del aire para mover   energía eólica
the strength of wind to move (things)   *wind power*
                                                              (lit. *aeolian energy*)

The first thing to note is that the primary text (on the left) is clumsy in its need to avoid specialist terms. The second is the use in the secondary text of the adjective 'eólica'. *Aeolian* in English is a word we have encountered only in association with *harp*. It is rare and literary. In Spanish, however, it has become a technical terms as the adjective relating to wind. Similar examples that were noted earlier are 'rurales' and 'emancipadora'. We remarked previously that Spanish has fewer linguistic resources for combining nouns into complex noun phrases. It seems that this is to some degree compensated for in Spanish (and other Romance languages) by a richness in technical and elaborate adjectives, which are both more common and more varied than in English. This can also be found in quite everyday expressions such as 'exposición felina' – literally 'feline exhibition', meaning 'cat show' – note that in the English the structure is noun–noun, while Spanish uses a noun–adjective construction.

Complexity

One question that arises from the above is whether the language of Spanish secondary school texts is more complex than that of primary school texts. Over recent years systemic linguists have developed a number of measures of text complexity that relate to register phenomena. The first developed was *lexical density* (Halliday, 1985). This is a measure of the ratio of content words – the more content or lexical words, the more dense and difficult the text. The measure is arrived at by dividing the number of clauses by the number of content words. Another type of complexity is *phrasal intricacy*, the amount of information in the noun phrase, which systemic linguists sometimes refer to as 'nominal structure'. A complex nominal group or noun phrase is defined as one that contains more elements than one determiner and/or one adjective and one noun. A complexity measure is obtained by dividing the number of complex noun phrases by the number of clauses. A third type of complexity is in the syntactic structure, referred to here as *syntactic intricacy* – Halliday (1985) calls this 'grammatical intricacy'. It is measured by counting the number of clauses and the 'depth' of the syntactic structure in terms of the number of layers of structural dependency, and dividing this by the number of sentences. The final measure is one of the extent of use of *grammatical metaphor*. This is measured by counting the number of cases and dividing by the number of sentences. These measures were used on several texts, including those from which these examples and the cloze tests in Chapter 3 are derived. The measures are given in Table 2.2.

It can be seen from these data that, apart from the one result in bold, on all measures the secondary texts are more complex than the primary texts

Table 2.2 Complexity measures for eight texts

		Phrasal intricacy	*Syntactic intricacy*	*Lexical density*	*Grammatical metaphor*	*Total*
History texts						
Liberators	primary	0.50	3.10	4.06	0.00	7.66
	secondary	0.64	4.30	5.00	1.50	11.44
Aztecs	primary	0.40	**3.50**	3.38	0.25	7.53
	secondary	0.57	**3.38**	3.67	0.88	8.50
Science texts						
Water	primary	0.53	3.78	3.47	0.33	8.11
	secondary	0.82	4.43	3.88	1.00	10.13
Ecosystems	primary	0.45	3.30	4.00	2.33	10.08
	secondary	1.00	4.20	4.45	4.00	13.65

(the difference in the result in bold is probably not significant). It is inter-esting to note that this holds true for syntactic intricacy as well as phrasal intricacy, despite Halliday's predictions. Much more grammatical meta-phor is used is the secondary texts. These results show that there is a need to process more complex language later in schooling, and these complexities provide some targets for higher levels of Spanish acquisition.

Conclusion

The conclusion that can be clearly drawn from these examples is that Spanish does indeed have register characteristics that resemble those of English, and the differences between the two languages have to do with the formal resources available in the two languages to perform the functions that higher-level literacy demands. The technique discussed here, of finding and analysing parallel texts written for different age groups, is one way to gain access to the characteristics of this register.

Since the textbook samples that we have examined show quite clearly that this type of register is associated with secondary education, a major issue for bilingual communities whose children are receiving a monolin-gual education is whether adolescents are or are not developing this literate register in both languages. For minority-language communities, given the majority-language education of their younger members, it is the minority language that is less likely to have achieved this, and therefore the minority language is the main source of concern. So far as we are aware, these higher levels of bilingual proficiency have not been examined using adequate models of register. We also saw in the first part of this chapter a number of other areas where minority-language proficiency may be endangered, such as grammar (particularly morphology) and various aspects of oracy, indicating a range of proficiency issues that may challenge minority-language communities, and underlining the need to take bilingual proficiency seriously. Means of assessing various elements of proficiency are discussed in the next chapter.

Chapter 3
Measuring Proficiency

Introduction

This book is not a text on language testing, which has a rich literature (see, for example, Alderson *et al.*, 1995; Bachman & Palmer, 1996). However the issue of academic register, particularly in Spanish, is not overtly addressed in most language-testing literature, although in general the literature supports the notion that testing should be tailored to its objectives. In this study, the objective is to establish a relationship between the factors discussed in subsequent chapters and different areas of language proficiency, including the development of academic register in Spanish.

For these purposes a balance had to be struck between the need for useful and convincing measures of language proficiency (for instance in much of the work done in the framework of a social psychology of language, only questionable self assessment of language proficiency is used), and the exigencies of examining various aspects of the interviewees' beliefs and lives. All this within a limited budget and without placing undue demands upon them (remembering that they were comparatively young, were volunteers, and in some cases were already under pressure from school work). Our assessments therefore needed to gather the maximum of information within the minimum time, and make limited demands upon the researchers for processing time. Our assessments were a compromise, but we believe a reasonable one, given that the results were not to be used for gate keeping, but as proficiency guides for research purposes.

Assessing Proficiency

Developing register sensitive multiple choice cloze measures

One primary purpose of our study, as described in the previous chapter, was to assess the development of literate academic proficiency in our bilingual interviewees. Initially we performed a pilot study on 24 Hispanic Australian university students, in which we used cloze measures based on some of the school texts we had identified as exemplifying academic register, including the secondary texts that were examined in Chapter 2.

We piloted eight clozes, and then selected the two that discriminated best. The cloze tests involved deletion of every sixth word, but with some shifts to the left or right to include a greater number of content words. Unfortunately, such tests proved to be difficult even for highly literate native Spanish speakers. When we looked at the responses on the cloze tests, it became clear, however, that, on a number of the deletions, the interviewees supplied words that were semantically accurate, but were wrong in terms of register. This gave us the idea of developing multiple-choice clozes, in almost all cases using as the four choices, *wording that our interviewees had supplied*. In this way, the use of multiple-choice cloze tests enabled us to include items in which candidates chose between register alternatives, creating register-sensitive items. While we are well aware of the criticisms directed at cloze testing, we needed a technique that was comparatively simple to use, and that enabled us to utilise the texts that we had found which clearly exemplified register differences. This form of test met these practical criteria.

Figure 3.1 is one of the multiple-choice cloze tests, based on text A discussed in Chapter 2. The instructions for this test illustrate an important characteristic of the instruments used in Sydney – all rubrics and questions were bilingual in Spanish and English.

Clearly, some of these choices can be eliminated because their meaning or their grammar is wrong in context. In more than half of them, however, register plays a role in selecting the original word. If we look, for example, at number 14, the sentence says (in Spanish) 'droplets increase in size and fall by ____ of gravity'. The choices roughly translate as 'fault', 'action', 'because', and 'effect'. While saying that it is 'gravity's fault' that the droplets fall is reasonably accurate in meaning, it is of course entirely inappropriate in an academic text. 'Because of gravity' is more acceptable, but still not adequate in register terms. The original term 'action of gravity' is what we would expect. So, as well as having right or wrong choices in our multiple-choice, we could also grade responses for their appropriateness, assigning numerical values to the possible choices – the original word 'acción' scored 4, 'efecto' scored 3, 'causa' 2, and 'culpa' 1. A team of three university-educated Spanish speakers had little problem in reaching a consensus on the values to be assigned to the choices. The main problem with this test is that it has relatively few items. This was a compromise, since the text could have included more text from the original school textbook, but we did not wish to overload our interviewees. As it was, completion of the measures and the rest of the interview took around two hours.

The other cloze we selected for the main study was developed in the

From the choices below the passage, select the BEST word to fill the gap. Several of the words are possible – your task is to find the best one and enter it on the computer. The word may be shorter or longer than the line. The numbered groups of words correspond to the numbers in the text. The first one is done for you. Read the whole passage before you start.

Del grupo de palabras que aparece debajo del texto, elige la palabra MÁS APROPIADA para reemplazar la línea _____ 0. Hay varias palabras posibles – tu tienes que elegir la más apropiada y marcarla en la computadora. La palabra puede ser más corta o más larga que la línea. Los números de cada grupo de palabras correponden a los números en el texto. La primera ya está hecha. Lee todo el pasaje antes de comenzar.

¿Cómo se forman las nubes?

Las nubes suelen formarse _____ (*ejemplo*) el encuentro de dos masas de aire a diferente temperatura. El vapor del aire caliente _____(01) nubes cuando se mezcla con el aire _____(02). La zona atmosférica en _____(03) se forman las nubes se _____(04) 'frente'. Las nubes a que da _____(05) un frente cálido son en _____(06) de láminas y capas llamadas 'estratos'. Si al formarse las nubes la _____(07) es muy baja, la condensación _____(08) produce en forma de cristales _____(09) hielo y las nubes se denominan 'cirros'. Cuando las nubes presentan un _____(10) grisáceo oscuro reciben el nombre _____(11) 'nimbos'. Las precipitaciones tienen lugar cuando _____(12) el tamaño de las _____(13) de agua o hielo y ellas caen por _____(14) de la gravedad.

*Select the best word to fill the numbered gaps in the passage. Enter it on the computer. Elige la palabra **más apropiada** para reemplezar la línea en el texto. Entrala en la computadora.*

(*Ejemplo/Example*)	(04)	(08)	(12)
a. de	a. denomina	a. alta	a. aumenta
b. por	b. llama	b. las	b. reducen
c. antes	c. hace	c les	c. tiene
d. después	d. vuelve	d. se	d. forman
(01)	**(05)**	**(09)**	**(13)**
a. hace	a. peso	a. llamado	a. cristales
b. produce	b. mucho	b. mucho	b. masas
c. forma	c. orígen	c. de	c. gotas
d. hay	d. lugar	d. el	d. partículas
(02)	**(06)**	**(10)**	**(14)**
a. helado	a. mayoría	a. aspecto	a. culpa
b. frígido	b. estado	b. tono	b. acción
c. frío	c. forma	c. color	c. causa
d. glacial	d. conformación	d. cubierto	d. efecto
(03)	**(07)**	**(11)**	
a. donde	a. temperatura	a. nubes	
b. que	b. presión	b. de	
c. cual	c. cual	c. tormenta	
d. cuanto	d. atmósfera	d. en	

Figure 3.1 The science multiple-choice cloze test

same way, but in order to maintain some content balance, this one was a history text about Lavalleja (text D in Chapter 2).

In order to check the reliability of the test, we used Guttman split-half estimates (but see Bachman, 1990, on the problems of using split-halves in this type of test) performing correlations of responses to the odd and even questions within each cloze. On the Sydney sample the results were for the science cloze a correlation of 0.50, $p =< 0.0001$, and for the history cloze 0.58, $p = < 0.0001$ ($n = 104$, 2 missing values). The Spearman Brown split half prophecy formula therefore gives a reliability of 0.667 and 0.734 respectively. These figures are below what is desirable, but when the science cloze was used with the 96 Chilean adolescents to establish mother tongue yardstick data, this resulted in a more robust split-half estimate of 0.88. Some of our Sydney interviewees were simply incapable of doing the test, so their guesses may have distorted the picture. The correlation between the two clozes was 0.63 ($p = < 0.0001$), demonstrating reasonable inter-test reliability; the difference between them can be explained by the fact that they do not examine the same register field.

The C-test

Apart from measures of literate register, we felt that it was important to use some other, more traditional, measures of language proficiency. We thought it was quite likely that some of our second-generation Hispanic teenagers would not have developed Spanish particularly well, so we needed to examine development of more basic proficiency. Silva-Corvalán (1991) who examined the Spanish of second-generation Hispanics in the USA, found significant underdevelopment of the rather complex morphology of Spanish. To examine this, we used a C-test (Klein-Braley & Raatz, 1984), a form of testing developed specifically to examine morphology in a language such as Spanish, where inflectional morphology is carried in the second half of the word, mainly in the form of suffixes. In a C-test every third or fourth word has its second half deleted. In our C-test, a passage about cholesterol, the interviewees were asked to supply the second half of the words and write out the complete word. This test also acts a test of vocabulary, since if the person does not know the word, supplying the second half, even if it contains a significant morphological component, and writing the whole word can be difficult or impossible.

Basic literacy

There is a common perception that Spanish is easy to spell because it is mostly phonic in its spelling, and accent marking is quite regular. Nevertheless, when we examined the completed C-tests, which required the interviewees to write the whole word, there were significant numbers of errors in spelling and accents. For example one interviewee wrote 'habeses' for *a veces*. This contains several of the spelling problems of Spanish: word division; silent *h*; *v* and *b* usually both pronounced [b]; and *c* before 'e' or 'i', *z*, and *s* all pronounced [s] in varieties of Spanish other than those of North and Central Spain. There were also frequent omissions of accents and tildes. These types of spelling and accent errors we called 'basic literacy' errors; our scoring controlled for the number of missing responses.

Oral assessment

We also assessed the spoken Spanish of the interviewees. The interviewer tape recorded the interview, which contains a segment dedicated to eliciting spoken Spanish, including the use of a picture story task (which the interviewees were given time to prepare), and an unprepared conversation about favourite school subjects and leisure activities. These were intended to elicit both more and less careful speech. Subsequently the tapes were listened to by three university-educated Spanish speakers, and scored for fluency, accent, code mixing, and idiomaticity – following in part Harley *et al.* (1990). The listeners soon became accustomed to listening for specific indicators of these various elements. The scoring chart is shown in Figure 3.2.

The accent was to some degree independent of the other variables. For the other elements, a lack of general proficiency manifested itself differently for different interviewees. Some were hesitant if they were uncertain how to express an idea (i.e. fluency), using many filled and unfilled pauses. Others drew on English, either shaping their Spanish according to English wordings (idiomaticity) or simply using English (mixing). Others used a simple Spanish, of a type more appropriate to much younger Spanish native speakers (idiomaticity). Some of the lower-proficiency interviewees sounded like English mother tongue, low-proficiency second-language speakers of Spanish, reflecting the relative dominance of their two languages. The best of the second-generation speakers sounded like native speakers of both languages.

Unfortunately one of the research assistants who performed the interviews did not follow the instructions for the oral assessment, and 18 of the tapes did not contain the data needed to score oral proficiency.

Self assessment

We gave interviewees some self-rating scales for language proficiency. These were not vague, open scales about writing and speaking, but rather

Fluency

(5) **Native** – no hesitations associated with the search for words or structures that might not be fully mastered.
(4) **Good** – fairly flowing, but with the occasional pause or search that might not be expected from a native speaker.
(3) **Reasonable** – noticeable competency-based hesitation, but easy to follow.
(2) **Poor** – many examples of hesitation, to the point where it is not always easy to follow an argument.
(1) **Very poor** – hesitation overwhelming normal speech patterns.

Accent

(5) **Native** – Indistinguishable from a native speaker on the basis of pronunciation.
(4) **Good** – Australian background detectable but not intrusive.
(3) **Reasonable** – clearly intelligible, but frequent English influence.
(2) **Poor** – sometimes hard to recognise words; extensive English interference.
(1) **Very poor** – sounds like a low-level second-language speaker.

Idiomaticity

(5) **Native** – expresses things in the same way that a native speaker would.
(4) **Good** – expresses things well, but occasionally uses a form of words that a native speaker is unlikely to use.
(3) **Reasonable** – some expressions are native-like, but some are clearly not – either they are very literal expressions of meaning, or there is some influence from the English form of expression.
(2) **Poor** – mostly very literal meaning making, and/or extensive influence from English form of expression.
(1) **Very poor** – apart from very common expressions, all sound like literal meaning making and/or the English form of expression

Code mixing

(5) **None** – pure Spanish.
(4) **Little English** – a few English words/expressions, mostly for Australian concepts.
(3) **Quite a lot of English words** – many words/expressions borrowed from English, but not sentence-fragment switching.
(2) **Lots of English** – words, expressions and switching in the middle of sentences.
(1) **Only low-level Spanish** – many whole sentences in English.

Figure 3.2 Assessment criteria for oral language

questions about specific uses of Spanish – we have to thank Josiane Hamers for this idea. The questions and the scoring used are shown in Figure 3.3.

It can be seen that some trouble was taken to examine a range of register variables, including written language versus spoken, formal and informal language, everyday and specialist language, and various specific fields, as well as both production and comprehension. The questions also examine tasks of varying level of difficulty, involving lower and higher levels of language proficiency.

The questions are constructed to elicit self-assessments that are as objective and targeted as possible, but such an instrument inevitably involves a subjective element. Interviewees who lack self-awareness of their language proficiency may make inaccurate ratings. Interviewees who lack confidence may underrate their language proficiency, while interviewees who are overconfident may overestimate their language proficiency. The issue

---

How easy or hard is it for you to do these things in Spanish?
¿Cuán fácil o dificil te resulta hacer lo siguiente en español?

Buy a loaf of bread in a baker's shop
Comprar pan en una panadería

Tell Spanish speakers the way to your school
Decirles a los hispanohablantes como llegar a tu escuela

Write a 'thank-you' letter to relatives
Escribir una carta de agradacimiento a tus familiares

Take notes at a meeting of Spanish speakers
Tomar apuntes en una reunión de hispanohablantes

Explain a Science lesson
Explicar una lección de ciencias

Read the Spanish language newspaper *The Spanish Herald*
Leer el periódico en lengua española *The Spanish Herald*

Write a book report
Escribir un somario de un libro

Read a social studies text book written in Spanish
Leer un libro de estudios sociales en español

The interviewees responded to each question by clicking on one of 5 boxes, which were scored as shown below:

(5)   very easy / muy fácil
(4)   fairly easy / bastante fácil
(3)   neither easy nor hard / ni fácil ni dificil
(2)   fairly hard / bastante dificil
(1)   very hard / muy dificil

Figure 3.3 Self ratings for Spanish proficiency

of confidence is part of what we refer to as 'attitudes' in Chapter 7. In the past, social psychologists have tended to correlate self assessments with attitude measures – the risk of contamination in so doing is obvious.

English measures

We felt it was important to include measures of our interviewees' English proficiency, even though this was not the main target of our investigation, in order to get a fuller picture of their bilingualism. The measures we used were cloze tests where each seventh word was deleted. They were not multiple-choice measures like the Spanish clozes, so they were more general measures of grammar and vocabulary as well as register. We tried to include register issues by taking our passages from school texts on hibernation and water. These cloze tests had been developed and evaluated by Nasrin Shokrpour (see Shokrpour & Gibbons, 1998).

Scores on the Measures

Table 3.1 gives information on the range of scores found on the C-test and cloze tests, and compares the Australian interviewees with the Chilean interviewees, giving some idea of how the Australians compared with the Chileans overall, and therefore how their Spanish proficiency compares with peers in a Spanish-speaking country.

Looking first at the scores on the register multiple-choice clozes, even in the Chilean sample (where the students were around 13 years of age) some students did not have a real command of academic register. Since the

Table 3.1 Basic statistics on multiple choice clozes and C-test

	Australian interviewees				Chilean interviewees			
	Science cloze	*History cloze*	*Sum of clozes*	*C-test*	*Science cloze*	*History cloze*	*Sum of clozes*	*C-test*
Mean	40.317	46.808	87.125	22.172	44.188	46.698	90.885	32.333
Std. Dev.	5.218	5.590	8.829	9.110	3.913	4.573	6.353	6.005
Min	15	34	51	4	32	33	74	13
Max	51	59	109	48	51	57	106	43
Number of respondents	104	104	104	99	96	96	96	96

Australian-educated interviewees in our sample had not been educated through the medium of Spanish, their opportunities to master the register were far fewer than those of the Chilean sample. A comparison of the two sets of figures reveals the effects of this, and a more accessible illustration is given in the graphs in Figure 3.4. While the better Australian students were comparable with the Chilean sample, the range of scores as shown by the standard deviation is higher for the Australian sample, and there are many

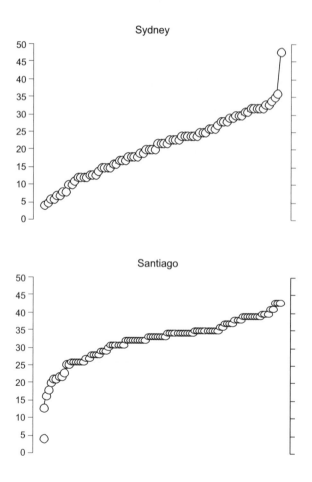

Figure 3.4 Sydney–Santiago comparative line charts: Summed scores of the clozes

more lower scores, giving a lower mean. In other words, a proportion of the Australian interviewees did not have an age-appropriate command of Spanish academic register, and they tended overall to have a lower command – an important if not surprising finding.

A similar picture emerges on the C-test (Figure 3.5), although the consistently lower scores in Sydney are more apparent.

What is particularly noticeable is that the mean of the Australian group

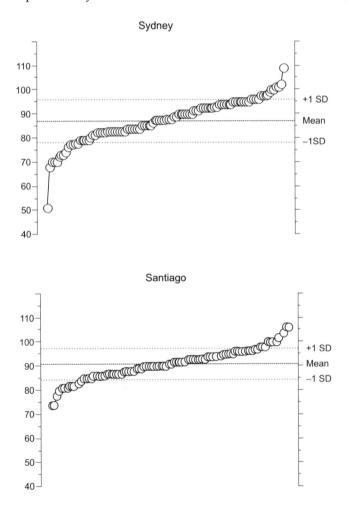

Figure 3.5 Sydney–Santiago comparative line: C-test

is well below (1.69 standard deviations) that of the Chilean interviewees. This is explained in part by the many scores in the lower range, as shown on the graph. When the Australian sample was limited to interviewees who were born in Australia or who migrated before the age of 5 years, the figure was not notably different from the score for all the Australians (the mean and standard deviation fell to 21.7556, and 8.950, but the minimum and maximum scores remained the same, indicating that the best grammatical performance came from one of the second-generation group). Like the cloze scores, the grammar scores indicate that a substantial number of Australian interviewees are well below their Chilean peers, suggesting English dominance. However nearly half of the Sydney sample have scores that place them in the same score range as the Santiago sample, indicating that others have a grammatical competence similar to their Santiago peers. Our concern is to discover how these different levels of achievement among the Sydney interviewees arise.

Relationships Between the Measures

Underlying proficiency structure

Following Harley *et al.* (1990), we performed a factor analysis to see whether there was an underlying structure of proficiency in our data. The basic finding however is contained in Table 3.2.

The factors are strong and distinct. Factor 1 is the oral assessment, Factor 2 the English measures, Factor 3 the Spanish multiple-choice clozes, Factor 4 the basic literacy (spelling and accents), and Factor 5 the C-test measure of grammar and vocabulary, and the self-proficiency rating. This suggests that the self rating of our interviewees is primarily self rating of grammar and vocabulary rather than other language elements. This analysis agrees with Harley *et al.*'s (1990) finding that there is a 'written' element in proficiency, which we would view as mainly constituted by written register. These factors also support our decision to evaluate separately these various aspects of language proficiency, since on the basis of these data they are to some degree discrete, although there may be a limited relationship between the C-test and the multiple-choice register clozes. These findings challenge notions of generalised proficiency, and are of interest for the models of communicative competence that are used in language testing.

Correlations between the measures

We followed up on this analysis by performing correlations between the various types of measure. We performed the analysis first without the oral

Table 3.2 Factor analysis of language measures: Oblique solution primary pattern matrix

	Factor 1	Factor 2	Factor 3	Factor 4	Factor 5
Spanish oral fluency	**0.906**	-3.295E-4	0.021	0.192	-0.051
Spanish oral accent	**0.852**	-0.035	-0.046	-0.119	1.758E-4
Spanish oral idiomaticity	**0.962**	-0.245	0.081	-0.044	-0.087
Spanish oral mixing	**0.864**	0.142	-0.127	-0.064	-0.139
Spanish C-test	0.126	0.292	0.018	-0.005	**0.720**
Spanish C-test (# of missing values)	-0.049	-0.252	0.015	-0.158	**-0.738**
Spanish self proficiency rating	0.019	-0.326	-0.046	-0.084	**0.922**
Spanish basic literacy	-0.022	-0.019	-0.048	**0.987**	-6.147E-5
Spanish history multiple-choice cloze	0.214	0.063	**0.910**	-0.060	-0.311
Spanish science multiple-choice cloze	-0.301	-0.125	**0.934**	2.561E-5	0.212
English cloze water	-0.204	**0.864**	-0.050	-0.072	0.099
English cloze hibernation	0.148	**0.861**	-0.005	0.035	-0.186

(< 0.5 in **bold**)

measures (Table 3.3), since there were many more missing values in the oral measures.

Basic literacy (the amount of non-standard spelling and accents) is not related to other aspects of written language proficiency, so is not further discussed here (however, there may be a message here for those involved in marking written work, and teaching literacy). There is some relationship between the C-test of grammar and vocabulary, and the multiple-choice cloze measures of register development. This is predictable, since register is a particular deployment of grammar and vocabulary resources: these elements of language are necessary, but not sufficient, for register development. The clozes are related to each other, but are not identical in their measurement, as one would expect from measures of development of different fields of register. The considerably stronger relationship between the science cloze and the C-test (compared with the correlation between the history cloze and the C-test) supports an impression gained from much analysis using the register measures, that the science cloze is a better measure of the more advanced register-based issues. The total of the cloze measures produces a slightly stronger correlation than the individual

Table 3.3 Correlation matrix: Spanish proficiency measures

	Basic literacy		C-test		History m/c cloze		Science m/c cloze		Multiple-choice cloze total	
	Corr.	p	Corr.	p	Corr.	p	Corr.	p	Corr.	p
C-test	0.049	0.6358								
History m/c cloze	-0.150	0.1419	0.212	**0.0371**						
Science m/c cloze	-0.038	0.7112	0.243	**0.0161**	0.630	**< 0.0001**				
M/c cloze total	-0.108	0.2921	0.253	**0.0121**						
Self assessment	0.043	0.6788	0.556	**< 0.0001**	0.110	0.2821	0.146	0.1546	0.142	0.1654

Observations = 97; missing values = 9

measures: this indicates that this joint measure is worth retaining in future analyses. Self assessment appears to be based on self assessment of grammar and vocabulary, confirming that interviewees do not appear to take into account their basic literacy and register development, and may be unaware of them. We should note that the significant correlations between the multiple choice clozes and the C-test indicate some level of inter-test reliability for the former, and the strong relationship of the C-test with a range of other measures (including the oral measures below) indicates inter-test reliability for that measure.

Turning now to the oral measures, it is apparent from Table 3.4 that the major relationship is with the C-test and self assessment measures. This adds pronunciation to the language abilities that are self assessed.

There is a significant relationship between the history multiple-choice cloze and oral idiomaticity. Oral idiomaticity is to some degree a measure of control of grammar and vocabulary, so it is understandable that it would correlate with the cloze measure that more strongly measures general proficiency. This relationship also appears in an attenuated form in the 'total' measures. Once more, basic literacy has no relationship with pronunciation, which provides evidence that pronunciation is little related to spelling, a finding that challenges, for Spanish at least, the view that regional or class accents affect such basic literacy.

Table 3.4 Correlations between written and spoken measures

Written measures	Oral fluency		Oral accent		Oral idiomaticity		Oral mixing		Oral total	
	Corr.	p	Corr.	p	Corr.	p	Corr.	p	Corr.	p
Basic literacy	0.11	0.3358	-0.10	0.3671	-0.09	0.4482	-0.06	0.5802	-0.04	0.7525
C-test	0.62	< 0.0001	0.58	< 0.0001	0.47	< 0.0001	0.52	< 0.0001	0.64	< 0.0001
Self proficiency rating	0.54	< 0.0001	0.49	< 0.0001	0.58	< 0.0001	0.43	< 0.0001	0.60	< 0.0001
History m/c cloze	0.21	0.0648	0.18	0.1168	0.28	**0.0102**	0.13	0.2359	0.24	**0.0323**
Science m/c cloze	0.11	0.3103	0.07	0.5185	0.07	0.5136	0.06	0.5673	0.10	0.3888
M/c cloze total	0.18	0.1031	0.14	0.2030	0.21	0.0620	0.11	0.3146	0.19	0.0844

Observations = 81, missing values = 25

Relationship between Spanish and English proficiency

In a variety of publications Cummins (1979, 1984, 1996), and various other scholars such as Francis (2000), have provided convincing evidence that there is a 'language interdependence' factor. This theory challenges the commonly-held view that, if minority-language students neglect their mother tongue and put all their efforts into mastering the socially dominant language, they will achieve higher standards in the dominant language. Instead there is convincing evidence from studies of 'language interdependence' that supporting the minority mother tongue leads to better standards in the dominant language, however counter-intuitive this may be.

To examine the possibility of 'language interdependence' we correlated scores on the Spanish proficiency measures with scores on the English proficiency measures. First we examined the whole sample (Table 3.5).

Alternative explanations for language interdependence have been proposed in terms of the contribution of general intelligence to the ability to take tests, and with our data it could also be claimed that differences in age might explain the result. Therefore we performed the same correlations

Table 3.5 Correlations of Spanish measures with English measures: All interviewees

Spanish measures	English cloze: water		English cloze: hibernation		Sum of the English clozes	
	Corr.	p	Corr.	p	Corr.	p
Spanish basic literacy	-0.04	0.6956	0.04	0.6999	0.00110	0.9915
Spanish C-test	0.31	**0.0020**	0.28	**0.0052**	0.34	**0.0006**
Spanish self assessment	-0.09	0.3945	-0.09	0.3915	-0.10	0.3239
Spanish history m/c cloze	0.11	0.2976	0.09	0.3599	0.12	0.2487
Spanish science m/c cloze	-0.02	0.8719	0.11	0.2828	0.06	0.5842
Spanish m/c cloze total	0.06	0.5841	0.11	0.2665	0.10	0.3332

inserting controls for non-verbal IQ, age, and both combined, but the correlations remained significant.

When we limited the sample to the interviewees wholly educated in

Table 3.6 Correlations of Spanish measures with English measures: Wholly Australian educated

Spanish measures	English cloze: water		English cloze: hibernation		Sum of the English clozes	
	Corr.	p	Corr.	p	Corr.	p
Basic literacy	-0.04	0.7546	0.15	0.1942	0.11	0.3591
C-test	0.34	**0.0025**	0.31	**0.0051**	0.37	**0.0007**
Self-assessment	0.08	0.4648	0.13	0.2586	0.12	0.2862
History cloze	-0.02	0.8398	0.07	0.5710	0.02	0.8378
Science cloze	0.04	0.7620	0.11	0.3445	0.08	0.4763
Spanish cloze total	-0.05	0.6579	-0.02	0.8327	-0.04	0.7065

Observations = 77; missing values = 7

Australia (Table 3.6), the C-test correlations were strengthened, although significances remained similar as a consequence of the smaller sample size.

These results provide yet more evidence that there is an underlying language interdependence. However, in line with research findings elsewhere, this factor can explain only part of language development. Later when we examine the effects of Spanish instruction, we will see that Spanish instruction is also correlated with the scores on *English* proficiency measures.

Conclusion

We have no illusions that the testing procedures we adopted as part of this research were ideal. However it should be remembered that, in much research of this type, only self-assessment measures are used. In subsequent chapters, it will emerge clearly that self assessment alone is inadequate as a means of assessing proficiency, and misses a range of interesting and important information since it seems that self assessment is limited mainly to grammar and vocabulary, as well as distorting the picture to the extent that such measures are measures of confidence as well as proficiency.

As with much language testing, there were competing criteria of reliability, validity and practicality. We needed to contain both the time and effort demanded of our young volunteer interviewees, in order to fit the research into the resources of time and energy available to both them and us. Nevertheless, we believe that the measures are sufficiently robust for them to serve the purposes for which they were intended – a guide to the level of development of various elements of language proficiency, so that this could be compared to a range of factors concerning the interviewees and their backgrounds.

There is evidence from these findings that different elements of language proficiency profile separately, raising doubts about excessive claims made for general proficiency. We also found support for Cummins' view that there is some degree of proficiency interdependence in bilinguals, although a general ability to do test tasks might also be involved in this finding.

Concerning the comparisons between our two samples, it is clear that only a proportion of the Sydney interviewees fall within the same proficiency range as the Santiago comparison group in both general lexico-grammatical competence and command of higher register. The remainder of this book will attempt to examine the complex range of variables that lead to these varying levels of proficiency

Chapter 4

The Societal

Introduction

This chapter deals with effect of various large-scale social structures and institutions upon the development and maintenance of bilingualism and biliteracy (these are summarised in Figure 4.1). The issues are discussed at the broadest level in this chapter – for instance the availability of media in various languages in the community. (Access to such media in particular homes, and whether individuals avail themselves of the opportunity, are discussed in subsequent chapters.) In this chapter, each issue will be raised then illustrated, rather than issues and investigation being separated as in subsequent chapters.

Large-scale surveys such as national censuses are a useful means of examining broad societal phenomena, and their relation to language proficiency. Another way of viewing this area is to see it as the impact of the wider societal and sociolinguistic context. This wider context frames, structures and contributes to the everyday existence and language behaviour of individuals, but these individuals still have scope to enact and assert their individual and small group beliefs and behavioural patterns.

The effects of social and structural variables on the development and maintenance of bilingualism in individuals and communities have long been the object of academic study. The model underlying this chapter has been influenced by Kloss (1966), Haugen (1972), Ferguson (1981), Clyne (1991), and Allard and Landry (1994). However, it largely follows that given by Giles *et al.* (1977). Baker (2001: 72) reports criticism of their model, because its dimensions and factors are not truly independent, because the model is not sufficiently contextualised in society and history (a criticism also made by Williams, 1992), and because it is difficult to measure the relative impact of the variables. The first of these issues, the difficulty of separating variables, was acknowledged earlier, but it does not mean that an analysis should not be attempted. All theories and models are abstractions from a complex and interwoven reality, and it is important to at least attempt this abstraction in order to enable language contexts to be compared, and generalisations to be made. The other two criticisms have been taken on board, and the issues they raise are addressed.

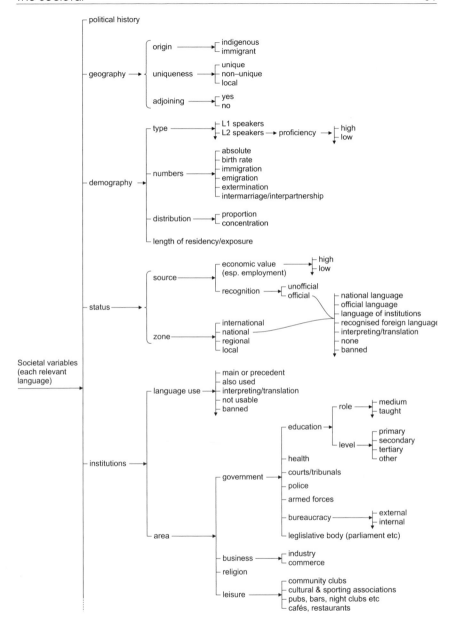

Figure 4.1 Societal/ecological variables that support or undermine languages
(continues overleaf)

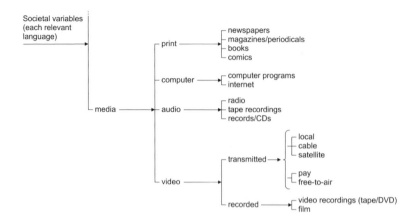

Figure 4.1 *Continued*

The particular factors outlined in Figure 4.1 have been suggested as likely factors in these studies, although there is probably no single decisive factor that leads to proficiency in one language or the other, producing bilingualism or monolingualism.

The model proposed in this chapter needs to be applied to all the relevant factors, in order to assess their likely influence on the maintenance of the languages. Allard and Landry (1994) speak of such variables as 'placing weights on a scale'. If sufficient weights go onto the plus side, there is an increased likelihood of a language being acquired by individuals, and maintained in a community. If sufficient of these variables are negative, then of course the reverse applies, and the language is endangered. Once the 'weights' of all the main languages used are assessed, the relative weights need to be considered. Even a healthy language can be overwhelmed by very powerful competitor.

Giles *et al.* (1977) do not limit their description, as I attempt to do here, to the wider societal and contextual arena, so the version in Figure 4.1 differs somewhat from theirs, although it does utilise their division into geographic, status, demographic and institutional variables. The discussion in this chapter uses this figure as a framework; each variable is examined in turn, with a general definition and an account of how it applies to the two candidate languages of the Hispanic community in Australia (particularly Sydney), namely Spanish and English.

Political History

The political history of a language and its community of speakers under-lies much of what is written in this book. What is now called Spanish is the standardised dialect of the region of Castile in Spain. As the Castilians gained power in Spain, their dialect became the national and standard language, although there has been long resistance, particularly from speakers of Catalan and Euskerra (Basque). In recent years other Spanish varieties have undergone a renaissance (see Turell, 2000).

By their conquest of South and Central America, the Spaniards estab-lished Spanish as the main language of their former territories, with some additional influences manifesting themselves in the local varieties. In Chile there is substantial influence from the Andalusian variety of Spanish, particularly in vocabulary. In Buenos Aires the largest ethnic group in the population were Italians, and there is therefore some influence from Italian on the local variety of Spanish, and the local argot *Lunfardo* has a substantial Italian component. There is also influence from the indigenous languages, particularly at the level of vocabulary, on all the Spanish varieties of Latin America.

English in Britain has a similar history, in that a variety of English spoken in the region of London became the national standard, and has now supplanted regional varieties, mostly leaving only accents. The Celtic languages Manx and Cornish have died, although their revival is in prog-ress. Welsh was suppressed and became mostly limited to North Wales, but is now being reasserted. Scottish Gaelic has been mostly lost on the main-land. The fate of these dialects and other languages in Britain was partly a consequence of power relations between speakers, but there was also delib-erate suppression, mainly through the education system, of languages other than standard English. The arrival and survival of other minority languages in Britain happened mostly after the settlement of Australia.

The establishment of Castilian in Spain and English in Britain illustrates the importance of political power and dominance in establishing one particular language variety rather than another as a standard language. In both societies, a combination of a nationalist ideology, and practical communication issues constituted the ideological basis for the suppression of other varieties. Political power can strongly support or profoundly undermine languages. We shall see many examples of how power is actual-ised through the factors examined in the rest of this book.

When European settlers arrived in Australia in 1787, there were around 240 Aboriginal languages. Most of these have disappeared, and only a few are expected to survive as mother tongues to the middle of this century.

Power relations, the establishment of European political, social and economic structures, new diseases and violent suppression explain most of these disappearances. There has been constant migration into Australia since this time, to the point where indigenous Australians are around 2% of the population. Until 1945, this migration was mainly from Britain and Ireland. British colonial government, and the preponderance of English speakers, meant that English became the *de facto* national language of Australia. There was a large migration mainly from continental Europe, including Spain, in the 1940s, 1950s and 1960s, followed by an opening up to the rest of the world. Asia is now a major source of immigrants, but there are significant numbers from Latin America.

From the late 1970s to the mid-1990s, the official policy of multiculturalism (in which Australia's ethnic and linguistic diversity was officially accepted) received majority support. In recent years attitudes towards multiculturalism have become more negative in parts of the population (interestingly, it appears to be the more recent immigrants that tend to be most strongly opposed to further immigration), and more culturally conservative politicians have taken power. This is reflected in changes in government policy in the late 1990s and early 2000s, including a reduction in the annual number of migrant places in Australia. Politics therefore affects both the numbers of speakers of various languages arriving in Australia, and the community's acceptance of minority-language institutions.

The reality is that immigrants into Australia have been absorbed, and the second generation has generally acculturated to Australian norms, becoming bicultural and bilingual, if not Australian monocultural and English monolingual. A major mechanism for this is the education system.

Given that migration is a difficult and disturbing experience for many immigrants, another socio-political question we may wish to ask is what are some of the causes of the migration of language communities? Two factors are often suggested: economic and political. Looking first at the 'pull' of Australia, since its independence from Britain in 1901 Australia has been a stable democracy, with a high level of individual freedom. Economically, although since the Second World War it has declined compared with other Western nations, Australia is still a prosperous first-world country with a high standard of living and reasonable wealth distribution. It therefore attracts immigrants from countries that have a much lower standard of living, and/or an oppressive government. Australia's migration policy has always had a component of political refugees, and for the last 30 years has had a preference for educated and skilled migrants, and for people who speak English. Often such people wish to leave their country only when conditions are particularly difficult.

Spain, in part as a consequence of the Civil War, had a considerably lower standard of living in the late 1940s and 1950s. At that time, the Franco regime was also at its most oppressive. This was the time when most migration from Spain took place. As economic development and political liberalisation took hold, migration from Spain to Australia almost ceased: the two countries now have a similar standard of living, and Spain is a lively democracy. Similarly in the 1970s oppressive military regimes took power in Chile, Argentina and Uruguay (the 'southern cone' countries), and at that time the economies of all three countries were quite depressed. It was at this time that migration to Australia from the southern cone was at its height. All three countries returned to democracy by the 1980s, and Chile's economy has experienced considerable success over the past 20 years. Migration from these countries has slowed markedly since these changes. It is possible that the economic and political problems of Argentina at the time of writing in 2002 will spark a new wave of migration. The pattern for Central American nations is similar. The mixture of political and economic factors in migration has meant that the Spanish-speaking migration to Australia, unlike the predominantly working-class economic immigration from some other countries, contained a mix of social classes (Valverde *et al.*, 1994: 27 mention 'the middle class background of a great proportion of the Spanish Speaking Background population').

This briefest of outlines shows how political and economic forces can lead to changes in the language composition of a nation such as Australia.

Geography

Origin

The distinction between migrant and indigenous languages can be made on the basis of where a language first developed. With Spanish, this was in Castile. However, there is also a case for saying that migrant languages over time become indigenised, particularly when distinct local varieties develop, such as Australian English or Chilean Spanish. Although English arrived in Australia only in the eighteenth century, it has become a distinct standard variety with its own dictionaries and grammars. Although the norm for Latin American varieties of Spanish is still mostly laid down by the *Real Academia de la Lengua* in Spain, that body recognises different varieties of Spanish in its publications.

The impact on language shift may be that people who speak an *indigenous* language may assign to that language a particular association with the

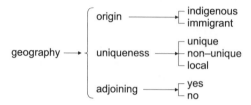

Figure 4.2 Geography

land, and this may lead to greater tenacity in maintaining it. On the other hand, *migrants* may decide to adjust to their new country by shifting languages, usually confident that their language is maintained in their country of origin.

English and Spanish in Australia are clearly immigrant languages, but English has also become indigenised. Bettoni (1981) makes a case for saying that Italian has developed a distinctive Australian variety, although it is not standardised. In a similar fashion, the Spanish of Australia shows certain local characteristics, in particular the impact of English can be observed in the use of *factoría* for 'factory', instead of *fábrica*, and the general use of *batería* for 'battery' rather than *pila*. There has also been some levelling of the differences between national varieties. Similar phenomena have also been observed in the Spanish of the United States.

In this case the indigenising and standardising of Australian English provide support for that language. The Spanish of Australia is less well supported since it is not a recognised standard variety.

Uniqueness

The essential question here is whether the language in question is found in only one place, or is widespread. For instance the local language, Taiap, discussed by Kulick (1992) is unique. It is spoken by only a few hundred people and, if the language shift described by Kulick continues, the language will disappear forever. However, if Spanish is lost in Australia, it will continue to be spoken in Spain and Latin America. This variable is important because, if a language is not unique, then there is the potential to bring in both speakers and language material from other places, and this supports the language. Where a language is unique, as is the case with many indigenous languages around the world, this is not possible. Yet, drawing on the ecological metaphor, the loss of a unique language is a loss of richness and diversity in human cultures and modes of thought. The awareness of uniqueness in a language community may spur the maintenance of their language. Even if a language is geographically unique, it may nevertheless be spread over a wide area, and thus may serve as a viable form of regional communication, supporting the language. This is the case with some Indian regional languages. Where a language is purely local, as with Taiap, this militates against its survival.

Looking at English and Spanish in Australia, neither language is unique, and for both there is a vast range of resources, and the potential for communication with other populations. This supports both languages.

Adjoining

If the communities that speak a language are geographically close, this facilitates sharing of resources, supporting the language. So German-speaking communities in Switzerland, Austria, Germany and other parts of central Europe can share resources, for instance by accessing each other's television and radio, or by examining each other's school books. A similar situation exists for speakers of varieties of Malay in Thailand, Malaysia, Indonesia, Brunei and the Philippines. By contrast, Dutch-speaking communities outside Europe lack such immediate contiguous support. The importance of this variable is lessened by modern means of communication and travel, but it plays a stronger role among poorer communities.

Australia is sufficiently remote from any other land mass to make the sharing of language resources problematic. Spanish in Australia is separated by the Pacific from the nearest Spanish-speaking country – Chile. English in Australia is widely geographically separated from the societies that have influenced it most –Britain and the USA. Even New Zealand is sufficiently distant to make sharing of language resources difficult. English is, however, emerging as the lingua franca of the Asia–Pacific region.

Status

Status has to do with the social place of a language within the broader society – whether it is recognised, and whether it grants access to social power, employment and prestige. Bourdieu and Passeron (1990: 73) refer to this as *linguistic capital*, defined as:

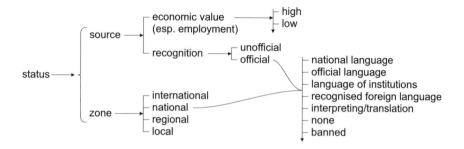

Figure 4.3 Status

... fluency in, and comfort with, a high-status, world-wide language which is used by groups who possess economic, social, cultural and political power and status in local and global society. The linguistic capital thesis, then, states that students who possess, have access to, or develop linguistic capital, thereby have access to better life chances. (Bourdieu & Passeron, 1990: 73)

As one of our teenage interviewees put it more starkly:

it helps to know a language if you want to get a job.

The reverse face of this can be seen in languages that lack some or all of these characteristics.

Unofficial recognition

Status may be acquired in a non-official way. The development of entertainment or practical uses for a language may raise the status of that language. In Indonesia, for example, English has quite a status in the general population because it is associated with fashion in clothes and, to a lesser degree, music. English is used extensively in advertising because of its prestige associations, and it is also the main language of the Internet and most overseas media. This drives language learning. The status of English may also help to explain the unusually high level of language maintenance in the long-established English-speaking minorities of Argentina and Chile.

In Australia, Spanish was accorded quite low status up to the mid-1990s (see Valverde *et al.*, 1994). However, with the advent of *salsa* and a range of high-profile Spanish-speaking singers and film stars, Spanish is now fashionable among younger Australians.

Official recognition

This is the language planning issue of the official status accorded to the language, and is decided by official bodies. It may be decided by legislative bodies; for example, in Australia there is a National Language Policy established by an Act of Parliament. In contrast, in Chile there is at the time of writing no official government policy on national language issues, although Spanish is the *de facto* national language, to some degree as a consequence of the official education policy, which establishes Castilian as the language of education.

International recognition

At the international level, official recognition is given by bodies such as the United Nations, which uses a limited number of languages in its sessions, and all debate is available in interpreted form in these languages. Both English and Spanish are accorded this status. Similarly, the European Union has official languages that consist of all the national languages including English and Spanish, but the three main working languages of the EU are English, German and French, but not Spanish. It should also be noted that the international language of shipping and aviation is English. There is an important sense in which English is the prime case of Bourdieu and Passeron's (1990) *global* reach.

It seems likely that the learning and maintenance of languages is influenced by international recognition. English is currently the dominant international language, and it is supplanting other languages around the world. Spanish, however, also has high international recognition. On this criterion English receives major support, and Spanish receives strong support.

An indication of how the international recognition of Spanish might affect language maintenance in Australia comes from a study made in a boys' school in Sydney (Gibbons, 1994a). Parents in this school were asked whether they spoke a language other than English in the home, and if so, whether they would like to see this language maintained in the school. The languages and the number of speakers are given in Table 4.1.

In the study, the question asked about maintenance was whether the parents would prefer their son to study the home language or a language other than English (LOTE) at school. When processing the results, languages were divided into 'international' languages (mainly those that are widely learned), and other languages.

The figures in Table 4.2 indicate that, among this groups of parents at least, international status affects choices about language maintenance – the parents are aware of the status and potential usefulness of their mother tongue, and this influences their decision about whether they wish to see

Table 4.1 Languages used at home ($n = 223$)

English only	161	Norwegian	1
Italian	6	Ukrainian	1
German	3	Hungarian	1
French	7	Assyrian	1
Malay/Indonesian	2	Sindhi	2
Japanese	2	Arabic	1
Mandarin Chinese	3	Farsi/Persian/Iranian	2
Other Chinese languages	12	Portuguese	1
Greek	11	Finnish	1
Spanish	1	Thai	1

the language maintained through mainstream education (the difference between 'international' and 'other' language speakers was significant on a t-test). This illustrates one of the mechanisms through which status may operate, since Frasure-Smith *et al.* (1975) also found a link between parental attitudes to language and educational choice. This type of decision is sometimes referred to as 'private language planning'.

Table 4.2 Cross-tabulation of language types by language study preference

	'International language'* speaker	*Other language speaker*	*All*
Support known LOTE at school	20 (90.91%)	9 (29.03%)	29
Learn another language	2 (9.09%)	22 (70.97%)	24
All	22 (100%)	31 (100%)	53

*(Spanish, French, Malay/Indonesian, Japanese, Mandarin Chinese, Arabic coded as 'international languages')
χ^2 19.884 with degrees of freedom = 1; $p<0.01$ (but notice one frequency less than 5)

This picture may be supported by Clyne and Kipp's (1997b: 22), comments (concerning 1996 national census data) that there is 'high intergenerational language shift among Polish, Hungarian and Maltese Australians' but 'relatively low inter-generational shifts among Spanish speakers and French Australians'.

National recognition

The list of possible types of national recognition in Figure 4.4 is not exhaustive, but it is important to note that they are ranked according to the level of status accorded to the language. Australia is unusual among predominantly English-speaking countries in having a National Language Policy. In 1987 this policy established English as the country's national and official language, which all citizens are expected to learn. The Policy also identified a number of other recognised languages that were intended to be taught in schools – initially their official status was 'Languages of Wider Teaching'. These languages have trading or regional importance, and/or a large resident community: Mandarin Chinese, Indonesian/Malay, Japanese, French, German, Italian, Modern Greek, Arabic and Spanish. Spanish was one of these officially-recognised languages because it meets the criterion of trading importance and, as we shall see in the section on demography, it has a significant community of speakers in Australia.

In the subsequent Australian Language and Literacy Policy of 1991, the list was extended to 14 'priority languages' (involving additions such as Korean, Russian, Aboriginal languages and Vietnamese) from which individual states should select eight for targeted Commonwealth support funding. The 'priority languages' for New South Wales (but not Victoria) included Spanish. Although the policy has varied slightly subsequently, Spanish maintains its status as a 'priority language' at both state and federal levels.

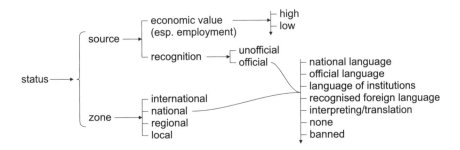

Figure 4.4 Levels of national recognition

In terms of national and state recognition, English is strongly supported, and Spanish is supported to some degree (to the maximum extent that any language other than English is supported in Australia). The recognition at state level is a form of *regional recognition*.

Recognition may need to be considered in relation to institutions – for instance in which institutions is interpreting and translation available, or a language actively prohibited. This will be considered when institutions are examined.

Regional and local recognition

Perhaps the best example of regional recognition can be found in the cantons of Switzerland, where the cantonal language (German, Italian, French or Romansh) is used for local institutional purposes, including education. A good example of official local recognition can be found in Toronto where certain suburbs have official signs in both English and the language of the local community (for instance Greek). In Sydney this is starting to happen in some areas, noticeably in Dixon Street, the traditional Chinatown, but there is at the time of writing no equivalent in Spanish-speaking areas.

Economic value

This must be recognised as an important variable in language maintenance and loss. It is common around the world for people to work on improving their language proficiency in order to get a better job, or earn more money (note the comment from Bourdieu & Passeron, 1990, quoted earlier).

Economic value may come from within the country, particularly if we are talking of proficiency in a dominant majority language, or it may come from the enhanced possibility of international communication. Within Australia, at the national level, Spanish has relatively little local economic value – unlike, for example, Japanese, which is useful for finding work in the tourism industry. There are relatively few newspaper advertisements mentioning Spanish as a requirement, but many for Japanese, despite the considerable economic potential of Spanish discussed in a 1992 Senate report (Senate Standing Committee on Foreign Affairs, Defence and Trade, 1992). In Fairfield in Sydney's West, the suburb that has the highest concentration of Spanish speakers, a range of businesses and services use both Spanish and English. These businesses may be favoured by Spanish speakers, and may prefer employees with Spanish proficiency, so Spanish can have limited economic value in this local context.

By contrast, English proficiency is strongly and directly related to employment and income in Australia. Table 4.3, taken from DIMA (2001) shows levels of employment and unemployment related to English proficiency in Australia. (In the 1996 census, people who reported using a language other than English in the home were asked 'How well does the person speak *English*' and the possible responses were 'Very well', 'Well', 'Not well', and 'Not at all'. The first two responses were then combined as 'good English' and the latter two as 'poor English'). In Table 4.3, both unem-

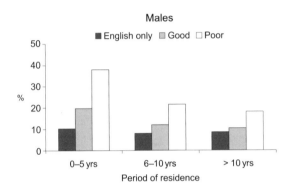

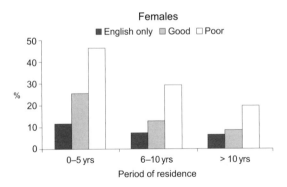

Figure 4.5 Unemployment rates by period of residence and English proficiency (overseas-born usual residents aged 15 years and over)

Source: 1996 Census Customised Matrix Table CS084 (DIMA, 2001)
    Usual residence basis – excludes overseas visitors

Table 4.3 Labour force status by proficiency in English (usual residents aged 15 years and over)

| | Other language spoken at home and English proficiency | | | | | | | | | |
| | English only | | Good | | Poor | | Total (a) | | Total (b) | |
	No.	%	No	%	No	%	No	%	No	%
Employed	6,579,578	58.2	916,667	52.1	102,103	23.6	1,033,101	46.5	7,636,536	54.9
Unemployed	607,364	5.4	121,814	6.9	36,900	8.5	161,276	7.3	772,301	5.6
In the Labour Force	7,186,942	63.6	1,038,481	59.1	139,003	32.1	1,194,377	53.7	8,408,837	60.4
Not in the Labour Force	4,043,089	35.8	695,478	39.6	285,832	66.1	995,021	44.8	5,173,952	37.2
Not Stated	73,702	0.7	24,274	1.4	7,684	1.8	33,574	1.5	332,497	2.4
Total:	11,303,733	100.0	1,758,233	100.0	432,519	100.0	2,222,972	100.0	13,915,286	100.0
Unemployment rate		8.5		11.7		26.5		13.5		9.2
Participation rate		64.0		59.9		32.7		54.6		61.9

(a) Includes proficiency not stated
(b) Includes language and proficiency not stated
Source: 1996 Census Customised Matrix Table CS084 (DIMA, 2001)
Usual residence basis – excludes overseas visitors

Table 4.4 Occupation by proficiency in English (Employed usual residents aged 15 years and over)

	English Only		Good		Poor		Total (a)		TOTAL (b)	
	\multicolumn{10}{l}{Other Language Spoken At Home and English Proficiency:}									
OCCUPATION	No.	%	No.	%	No.	%	No.	%	No.	%
Skilled Occupations										
Managers & Adminstrators	643,387	9.8	59,263	6.5	4,513	4.4	*64,736*	*6.3*	709,735	9.3
Professionals	1,151,418	17.5	151,353	16.5	2,766	2.7	*156,030*	*15.1*	1,309,461	17.1
Associate Professionals	750,546	11.4	100,256	11.0	7,134	7.0	*108,717*	*10.5*	861,151	11.3
Tradespersons & Related Workers	850,526	12.9	122,946	13.4	17,989	17.6	*143,040*	*13.9*	997,204	13.1
Total Skilled Occupations	*3,395,877*	*51.6*	*433,818*	*47.4*	*32,402*	*31.7*	*472,523*	*45.8*	*3,877,551*	*50.8*
Semi-skilled Occupations										
Advanced Clerical & Service Workers	294,510	4.5	33,301	3.6	817	0.8	*34,595*	*3.4*	329,849	4.3
Intermediate Clerical, Sales & Service Workers	1,077,381	16.4	135,313	14.8	5,009	4.9	*142,347*	*13.8*	1,223,013	16.0
Intermediate Production & Transport Workers	541,341	8.2	93,828	10.3	21,899	21.4	*117,350*	*11.4*	661,540	8.7
Total Semi-skilled Occupations	*1,913,232*	*29.1*	*262,442*	*28.7*	*27,725*	*27.1*	*294,292*	*28.5*	*2,214,402*	*29.0*
Unskilled Occupations										
Elementary Clerical, Sales & Service Workers	585,122	8.9	82,930	9.1	5,662	5.5	*89,818*	*8.7*	677,222	8.9
Labourers & Related Workers	527,749	8.0	104,181	11.4	30,195	29.5	*136,330*	*13.2*	667,351	8.7
Total Unskilled Occupations	*1,112,871*	*16.9*	*187,111*	*20.4*	*35,857*	*35.1*	*226,148*	*21.9*	*1,344,573*	*17.6*
Not Stated or Inadequate	158,363	2.4	31,986	3.5	6,247	6.1	*39,314*	*3.8*	200,221	2.6
TOTAL	6,580,343	100.0	915,357	100.0	102,231	100.0	*1,032,277*	*100.0*	7,636,747	100.0

(a) Includes proficiency not stated
(b) Includes language and proficiency not stated
Source: 1996 Census Customised Matrix Table CS085 (DIMA, 2001)
Note: Usual residence basis – excludes overseas visitors

ployment, and its opposite, participation in the workforce, are shown in relation to English proficiency.

It is clear from the information in Table 4.3 that employment and unemployment in Australia are linked to English proficiency. In addition Figure 4.5 shows that low proficiency in English is to some degree a factor independent of length of residence, in that even people with more than ten years' residence suffer higher rates of unemployment if their English proficiency is 'poor'.

It is not only unemployment that is affected by English proficiency in Australia, it is also the type of employment, and hence socio-economic status. Table 4.4 is taken from table B2 of DIMA (2001).

It is clear from Table 4.4 that there is a direct probabilistic relationship between level of English and status of employment. Perhaps the starkest

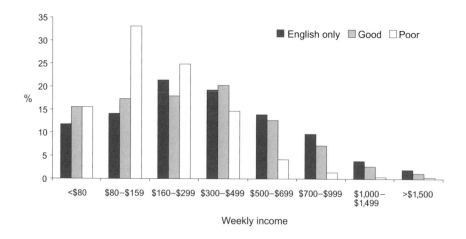

Figure 4.6 Weekly income distribution by proficiency in English

Source: 1996 Census Customised Matrix Table CS075A (DIMA, 2001)
　　　Usual residence basis – excludes overseas visitors

contrast is between 'Professionals' where there are very low numbers of 'poor' English speakers, and 'Labourers & related workers', where people with 'poor' English proficiency are greatly over represented. Findings such as these are predictable in a country like Australia where English is the public, official, and dominant working language. Skilled white collar workers who lack proficiency in English may be able to find work in one of the few environments where the working language is not English (the 'local' level), but they will be unlikely to achieve a senior position without the ability to interact effectively with the wider community.

One consequence of high rates of low-status employment or unemployment can be low income. Figure 4.6 shows once more a strong probabilistic relationship between income and English proficiency – those who have a 'poor' proficiency in English are strongly over-represented in the low income group, and are under-represented in the higher income group.

Demography

Number of speakers

If all else is equal, the greater the number of speakers of a language, the greater is the probability that this language will be maintained, transmitted and learned. As with all the factors, the numbers of speakers is only one weight in the scales: large communities have shifted to other languages, while some small communities have maintained theirs. For instance the Mennonites of Mexico, with their closed community, religiosity and low rates of intermarriage, have maintained their Germanic variety over more than a century. There are two issues concerning numbers of speakers: the absolute number of speakers, and factors that produce changes in these numbers, such as birth rate, immigration and emigration.

A useful source of information on numbers of speakers, including changes, are censuses, particularly those that ask questions about language and ethnic background. Australian census data provide a broad overview of language issues in the whole country. The last Australian census for which figures are available at the time of writing is the 1996 census. Since most of the data for our studies were gathered in 1997–1998, the census data compliments that gathered in our research.

Absolute numbers

If we begin at the international level, at the time of writing in the world at large the number of speakers of Spanish as a mother tongue is second only to Chinese and is greater than the number of native English speakers. However, if second-language speakers are included, the number of speakers of English far outnumbers speakers of any other language, including Spanish. These demographic characteristics mean that internationally both English and Spanish are highly favoured and supported by their number of speakers.

At the national level, turning to languages in Australia, the census of 1996 asked the following question: 'Does the person speak a language other than English at home?' If more than one language other than English was used at home, people were asked to record the one that was most commonly used. The responses were that 81.9% used only English at home, 15.4% used a language other than English, and 2.7% did not state their language or proficiency in English. (As in all such surveys, there is a small percentage of the population who do not respond, or who respond inappropriately to certain questions, which is why the figures do not always total 100%.) There are many immigrants from English-speaking countries, but nearly all adult migrants who speak a language other than English also speak English at varying levels of proficiency. On the basis of the 1996 census DIMA (2001) reports that, of the 15% of the population who spoke a language other than English at home, 12% also spoke good English, while the remaining 3% spoke English poorly. This means that there are a large number of people who speak English as a second language well. Of the

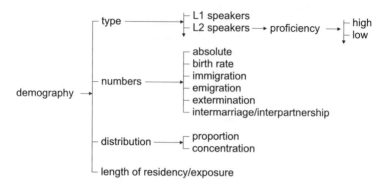

Figure 4.7 Demographic variables

Australian-born population (sometimes referred to in this book as 'the second generation') around 6% reported using a language other than English in the home. Almost all members of the Australian-born population speak English fluently.

In Sydney, 27% of the population reported using a language other than English at home – more than in any other part of Australia. For comparison, only 5% of the New South Wales population outside Sydney reported speaking a language other than English at home.

The number of Australian residents who reported using Spanish at home was 86 910, or nearly 0.5% of the Australian population over the age of 5. This makes Spanish the ninth most-used language in Australian homes. The percentages and numbers are given in the Table 4.5, which is drawn from AusStats (1999).

The number of people living in Spanish-speaking homes, including children below the age of 5, is 91 254 according to Clyne & Kipp (1997a). Within the Spanish-speaking community, there are speakers from most Spanish-speaking countries. The biggest Hispanic community by far has its origins in Chile, followed by Spain then Argentina, and nearly half of all Spanish speaker originate from the southern cone. Table 4.6 gives the figures for first-generation migrants. Not all of these migrants continue to speak Spanish at home. The table should be read from left to right to obtain a picture of when particular communities arrived in Australia.

Turning to speakers of Spanish as a second language, there are no census figures available on this issue. Since such people would mostly have acquired the language through instruction, some idea of the numbers can

Table 4.5 Languages spoken at home[a], Australia, 1996 (language speakers over the age of 5)

Language	Number of speakers (in thousands)	% born in Australia	As % of the Australian population
English	**13498.0**	**83.7**	**81.9**
Italian	367.3	40.7	2.3
Greek	259.0	46.7	1.6
Cantonese[b]	190.1	12.9	1.2
Arabic	162.0	37.8	1.0
Vietnamese	134.0	12.6	0.8
German	96.7	18.9	0.6
Mandarin[b]	87.3	6.4	0.5
Spanish	**86.9**	**17.6**	**0.5**
Macedonian	68.1	34.9	0.4
Tagalog (Filipino)	67.3	5.0	0.4
Croatian	66.7	32.4	0.4
Polish	61.0	16.2	0.4
Maltese	44.7	27.9	0.3
Turkish	42.2	31.3	0.3
Netherlandic	40.2	12.4	0.3
All other	696.8	20.0	4.4
Total speakers of languages other than English	*2470.2*	*26.0*	*15.4*

(a) Languages with more than 40,000 speakers aged five years and over.
(b) People who specified Cantonese or Mandarin have been separately classified; people who specified another Chinese language (e.g. Hokkien) or simply wrote 'Chinese' are included in 'All other'
Source: 1996 Census of Population and Housing (DIMA, 2001)

be drawn from the figures discussed in the section on education. From these it seems likely that 0.5% or less of the Australian population have studied Spanish as a second language. These low numbers for second language speakers do little to support the language in Australia.

Table 4.6 Birthplace and year of arrival[a] (overseas-born usual residents aged 5 years and over)

	Year of arrival						Total
	Before 1986		1986–1990		1991–1996		
Birthplace	*No.*	*% [b]*	*No.*	*% [b]*	*No.*	*% [b]*	
Spain	12 171	90.0	530	3.9	441	3.3	13 516
South & Central America & Caribbean							
Argentina	7 734	72.4	1 619	15.2	1 114	10.4	10 680
Chile	15 383	64.8	6 106	25.7	1 754	7.4	23 744
Uruguay	8 404	86.5	740	7.6	422	4.3	9 717
El Salvador	1 691	17.2	5 229	53.3	2 638	26.9	9 809
Other	11 618	55.1	4 322	20.5	4 554	21.6	21 095
Total Sth & Central America & Caribbean	*44 830*	*59.7*	*18 016*	*24.0*	*10 482*	*14.0*	*75 045*
Total:	57 001		18 546		10 923		88 561

(a) Includes year of arrival not stated and people who said they would be resident in Australia for less than one year.
(b) Percentage of total overseas born aged 5 years and over born in that group.
Source: 1996 Census Customised Matrix Table CS072 (Dima, 2001)
Usual residence basis – excludes overseas visitors

Birth rate

Since birth rate affects the size of communities, it has a direct impact on the numbers of speakers. One may also need to compare birth rates with other language groups. Giles *et al.* (1977) mention a tactic ('*La revanche des berceaux*'– the revenge of the cots) used in the nineteenth century by French Canadians of having large families to counteract the demographic effects of the flow of English-speaking immigrants.

Unlike the USA, where some ethnic groups have higher fertility rates than the general population, in Australia it seems that by the second generation there is generally little difference between groups. Abbasi-Shavasi writes:

Overall there was no significant difference between the fertility of the second generation of immigrant groups, and that of native-born women … Second generation 'migrants' have mostly experienced similar social institutions and economic conditions to the general Australian population, and therefore are expected to have similar fertility to Australian women. (Abbasi-Shavasi, 1998: 37)

The only information we have found on Spanish speakers comes from the analysis of the 1991 census statistics by the Australian Bureau of Statistics, Queensland (1994), and this showed that first-generation Chilean women had the same fertility rate as the total Australian population. The exact figures for the number of confinements per 1000 women are: birthplace Chile, 1835; total Australian population, 1831; Australian born, 1809. There is no real difference between these figures, and they seem to demonstrate that comparative birth rate is not significant in Spanish maintenance.

Immigration

Based on broad projections, in 2002, the Australian population was around 19.5 million. The last available census, that of 1996, showed a total Australian population of 17 753 770, of whom 16 488 751 were aged over 5. The strong migrant character of Australia can be seen in the fact that around a quarter of the Australian population was born overseas (23.5% of the Australian population reported being born overseas, 73.1% reported being born in Australia, and 3.4% did not state their birthplace). The effect of recency of immigration is discussed later under the heading of length of residency, but it is worth remarking that immigration from Spanish-speaking countries at the time of writing is low, and has never been a large component of Australian immigration.

The impact of immigration upon languages can be seen in the loss of indigenous mother tongues in countries such as the USA and Canada, where most native Americans no longer speak their mother tongue. The same is also true of Australian Aborigines.

Emigration

If an entire community leaves, taking its language with it, then that language is lost to the wider society. If members of a community leave then the reduction in numbers may affect the long-term viability of the language. Australia tends to be a country of immigration rather than emigration, although some emigration occurs. For instance, there are studies of returnees to Uruguay from Australia.

An interesting example of the effects of emigration is the Portuguese-based creole of Macau. Many of the predominantly Eurasian speakers of this language left the island and migrated to the West coast of the United States. The language has almost disappeared in Macau, but the community maintains its language to some degree in the USA, producing a newspaper and engaging in language-maintenance activity. As intermarriage and acculturation take their toll, it is possible that the language will disappear.

Extermination

This is not a fate that has befallen Spanish in Australia. However, in Tasmania the Aboriginal varieties spoken previously have almost disappeared along with their speakers as a consequence of imported diseases and deliberate extermination. Similarly Yiddish in Poland has almost disappeared, partly as a result of emigration, but mostly because of extermination of its speakers by the Nazis. Violence may combine with language-planning decisions to suppress a language along with its community, as is the case with Kurdish in some places. Disease, too, may decimate a community, thereby affecting the viability of its language variety.

Distribution

Proportion

If speakers of a language form a large majority, all else being equal, this supports their language because it can be used with many other people (but it may be worth remembering that there can be oppressed majorities – they are common in countries that are or were part of empires). On the other hand, members of a small minority, unless they live close together (see *concentration* below), will often find themselves having to use the majority language for everyday communication.

As we have already seen, Spanish speakers are a small proportion of the Australian population at large. Even within Sydney they are less than 1% of the population. This means that they are a small minority, particularly in comparison with the 82% of Australians who use only English at home. The weight in favour of English is strong, but there is limited support for Spanish.

Concentration

The factor at play here is whether speakers of a particular language live together or apart. If they live close together they increase the possibility of using their language in day-to-day life, and of establishing businesses and institutions such as clubs where the language is a viable means of communication. This may be enhanced by *cohesion* – the preference to mix with members of one's own community.

Australia has few ghettos of the kind found in other countries. The second generation of most minority groups tend to disperse. The Spanish speaking community in Australia is mostly concentrated in New South Wales. Table 4.7 shows the state distribution of Spanish according to Clyne and Kipp (1997a).

The figures in Table 4.7 reveal that 53% of Spanish speakers live in New

Table 4.7 Spanish speakers in Australia

New South Wales	Victoria	Queensland	Western Australia	South Australia
48 577	22 648	8 468	5 088	3 143
Australian Capital Territory	Tasmania	Northern Territory	Australia	
2 490	523	317	91 254	

South Wales, and in fact 43 902 (48%) live in Sydney. This would seem to indicate a fairly high concentration of Spanish speakers. Examining the figures for local government areas, Spanish appears to be quite widely distributed through Sydney, although the concentration is highest in the Fairfield/Cabramatta area.

Clyne (1982: 16) gives a method for calculating the concentration of languages within cities, but demonstrates that in Australia at least, this factor plays only a marginal role in language maintenance, perhaps because high-concentration ghettos do not exist.

Length of residency/exposure

Demographic status, and to a lesser extent other societal variables, take time to have their effect. A community that has recently migrated will begin with the language that its members brought with them. If the dominant language of their new country is different, it will take time for all the societal variables associated with a dominant language to change the language proficiency and language behaviour of the new arrivals. Equally, when indigenous minorities first encounter the language of new neighbours or invaders, it takes time for them to be affected by it (since they were resident in the country before this, it might be better to speak of length of exposure, rather than residency). The length of exposure to a particular socio-cultural context is related to changes in language proficiency (see Wong-Fillmore, 1991 for more detail). An important aspect of length of residency as it applies to communities, is whether the person was born in the country or overseas, often referred to as *first or second-generation* bilingualism, although migration below the age of 5 years is probably similar in its effects to being born in the host country (see for instance Silva-Corvalán, 1991).

English in Australia is certainly affected positively – DIMA (2001: Figure 4) shows a strong relationship between length of residence and the English proficiency of people who migrate to Australia speaking a language other than English.

With regard to Spanish in Australia, in Table 4.6 the information on the 'Year of arrival' reveals the different waves of Spanish-speaking migration into Australia that are a consequence of the factors discussed in the 'Political history' section earlier in this chapter. Migration from Spain occurred mainly in the late 1940s and the 1950s – 90% of the migration took place before 1986. Migration from the southern cone of South America (Chile, Argentina and Uruguay) took place mainly in the 1970s and 1980s. This can be seen in the higher figures for migration in the 1986–1990 period. Subsequent Hispanic migration has tended to come from Central America, as can be seen in the data for El Salvador, but figures in Clyne & Kipp (1997a: 8) show that the Spanish-speaking population increased by only 0.9% between 1991 and 1996, which would indicate that migration has slowed and almost ceased. This is probably a negative factor for language maintenance, since continuing migration refreshes the 'language pool' with speakers who are dominant in the most recent version ('temporalect') of the minority language.

These waves of migration mean different lengths of residency. The issue is, does this in turn affect levels of language shift? Looking first at the first generation, it seems to affect language shift among communities that integrate rapidly into Australian society, particularly those from Northern Europe. In the Spanish-speaking communities this profile is less apparent. Information in Tables 4.8 and 4.9 is drawn from Clyne and Kipp's (1997b) analysis of 1996 census data. Language shift is identified among those people who come from non-English speaking countries, who stated that they spoke only English at home.

The sharp rise in language shift in the 25–34 age group may be a product of marriage/partnership with non-Hispanics, and the consequent need to use English in the home – see the section on intermarriage (below).

Of particular interest in Table 4.9 is the sudden rise in language shift in the people aged over 35, whose parents had migrated before the 1970s. What this probably reflects is the change in the 1970s from a very small community to a much larger one. The Australian population born in Latin America quadrupled from 12 879 in 1971 to 53 640 in 1986, and rose again to 71 955 in 1991, which is near the current population (Bureau of Immigration Research Statistics Section: Queensland, 1994). Clyne and Kipp (1997b: 26) suggest that Chileans (among other communities) before 1981 were 'relativey few in number, and often isolated from speakers of their language. Many were in exogamous marriages'. Once the growth in population had taken place, and community had reached some form of 'critical mass', the rate of language shift to English among first-generation Chilean migrants

Table 4.8 Percentage of the **first** generation from Spanish-speaking countries who have shifted to English

Age/Birthplace	5–14	15–24	25–34	35–44	45–54	55–64	65+
Chile	9.8	8.1	17.5	9.1	6.4	5.4	6.8
Other Latin America	16.7	13.9	23.9	17.9	14.5	11.3	16.7
Spain	29.7	23.9	36.1	36.6	16.2	12.5	12.0

Table 4.9 Percentage of the **second** generation from Spanish-speaking countries who have shifted to English

Age/Birthplace	5–14	15–24	25–34	35–44	45–54	55–64	65+
Chile	40.0	30.9	45.2	83.3	69.4	85.7	94.4
Other Latin America	50.0	40.9	72.7	80.3	89.1	91.5	96.3
Spain	68.5	50.7	56.5	79.7	88.5	91.9	92.4

slowed substantially. Clyne and Kipp present this information in the form of Table 4.10.

These figures show the need to take into account the complex interactions of variables, but they also show clearly that larger numbers can assist in minority-language maintenance, affirming the basic demographic principle mentioned at the beginning of this section on Numbers.

Intermarriage/Interpartnership

These terms refer only to partnerships between people of different language backgrounds. In a country such as Australia, if a person from one language background marries or establishes a partnership with someone from a different language background, it is likely that the couple's only common language will be English, leading to the use of English in the home. Furthermore, in such a home, children will probably grow up speaking mostly English. The same pattern can be found in other societies where a dominant lingua franca serves as the shared language of partners from different language backgrounds. An example is the development of a community of native speakers of *Bahasa Indonesia* (or, more accurately, *Bahasa Jakarta*) in Jakarta where previously there were almost none, in part as a consequence of marriages between people with different mother tongues.

Clyne and Kipp (1997b) refer to a mixed partnership as 'exogamous', and a partnership within the language community as 'endogamous'. They

Table 4.10 Language shift by year of arrival

Birthplace	Pre 1981	1981–1986	1986–1991	1991–1996
Chile	14.3	6.7	4.5	4.7

Table 4.11 The effect of intermarriage on language shift in the second generation

Birthplace of parent(s)	Language shift (%)		
	Endogamous	Exogamous	All
Austria	80.0	91.1	89.7
France	46.5	80.4	77.7
Germany	77.6	92.0	89.7
Greece	16,1	51.9	28.0
Hong Kong	8.7	48.7	35.7
Hungary	64.2	89.4	82.1
Italy	42.6	79.1	57.9
Japan	5.4	68.9	57.6
Korea	5.4	61.5	18.0
Lebanon	11.4	43.6	20.1
FYR of Macedonia	7.4	38.6	14.8
Malta	70.0	92.9	82.1
Netherlands	91.1	96.5	95.0
Poland	58.4	86.9	75.7
PR China	17.1	52.8	37.4
Taiwan	5.0	29.2	21.0
Turkey	5.0	46.4	16.1
Chile	**12.7**	**62.3**	**38.0**
Other Latin America	**15.7**	**67.1**	**50.5**
Spain	**38.3**	**75.0**	**63.0**

Source: 1996 Census of Population and Housing (Dima, 2001)

provide the information in Table 4.11 drawn from the 1996 census (Dima, 2001), which has been modified to highlight Spanish-speaking countries.

The impact of intermarriage is highly salient (particularly for Spanish) in the data in Table 4.11, which show convincingly that this variable is a substantial weight in the scale against the maintenance of minority languages.

Institutions

There is a fast-developing field of 'institutional sociolinguistics' which looks at language behaviour in institutions. Here we are interested in the broad area of language use within the institution, which can be a consequence of both official and unofficial decisions. Institutional use is important because it offers a domain of use for the language, affecting both the amount of use of the language (see Chapter 5), and attitudes towards it (see Chapter 7), particularly if the approval is official.

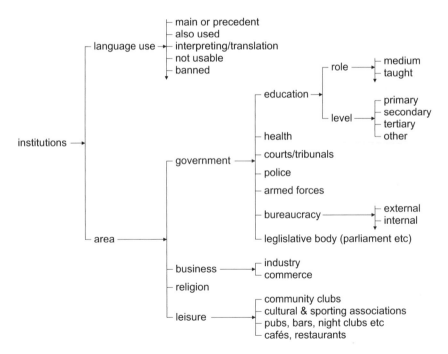

Figure 4.8 Institutions

Language use

The issue here is how the candidate languages can be used in various institutional settings. The array of types of language used in Figure 4.9 (based on Kloss, 1966) is not complete, but it gives an idea of the possibilities. For practical reasons, in most institutional contexts there is one working language, which may not be the same as that used for social purposes in the institution. Normally only one language is used for internal record keeping. However, there are institutional contexts where two or more languages are used for a full range of purposes, such as in Canadian federal institutions and European Union bureaucracy. A more common circumstance is where there is a main language, but one or more other languages are 'also used'. An interesting example is the Malaysian legal system where, if the case is run mainly in Bahasa Malaysia, the documentation is done in Bahasa Malaysia with summaries in English; if the case is run mainly in English, there are summaries in Bahasa Malaysia. However, English is precedent, in that if there is a dispute over the wording of legislation or regulations, the English version takes precedence over the Bahasa Malaysia version (for more detail see Gibbons, 2003). In Australia, English is the main and precedent language of almost all institutions.

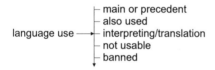

Figure 4.9   Language use and status

If another language is not used internally in an institution, translation or interpreting may be available for external contact with the public. This is essentially the case for languages other than English in Australia, including Spanish, in all government institutions other than education. Other languages are almost never used internally, and the primary language of external communication is English. However, interpreting or translation into most of Australia's many languages is usually available by means of a system of community interpreting/translation, which allows government agencies to communicate with people whose English is not sufficient for the purpose. Documentation may also be to some degree available in translation, for instance the South West Area Health Service in Sydney has brochures on a range of health issues available in many languages. In the legal system, while there is no right to an interpreter, in federal courts and in most Australian states if judges use their discretion not to employ an interpreter for a second-language speaker, they must be able to justify this decision. Australia has well-developed system to accredit interpreters and translators in up to a hundred languages, including Spanish.

It may be the case that there is no way that the language can be used in an institution, or it may be actively banned. For instance local languages may be banned in some educational institutions – in some countries schools even have a hat that must be worn by any child who uses a language other than the official medium of instruction, until the child finds another offender to pass the hat on to. In most states of the USA, there is legislation that bans the use of languages other than English in public institutions.

Looking briefly at some individual institutions, there may be unexpected language situations with consequences for bilingualism/biliteracy. In Iran, the internal language of record keeping in the *health* service is English. This means that almost all medical professionals in Iran are to some degree biliterate in Farsi and English. In Hong Kong it is assumed that all *police* (even expatriates) can speak Cantonese but, given the numbers of non-Chinese in some parts of Hong Kong, it is also desirable to have some English-speaking police. Such police officers wear red tags to indicate their bilingualism. The language of the *armed forces* in Singapore is Malay. This means that all those who do national service (most of the population) are to some degree bilingual in Malay. If the *bureaucracy* of a nation uses a partic- ular language for internal purposes, this means that government employ- ment (coveted in some countries) depends upon fluency in the language of the administration. For instance in New Guinea, where the spoken lingua francas are Tok Pisin and Hiri Motu, government servants need to know the internal language of bureaucracy – English – and many will also know at least one indigenous language, meaning that trilingualism is normal among Papua New Guinea government servants. It is common for govern- ment servants to communicate with the wider community (*externally*) in other languages. In Singapore, where English is the internal language of the bureaucracy, one is entitled to use any one of the four official languages to communicate with government departments. Although only a few people are likely to become members of a *legislative body*, the choice of language(s) used has great symbolic importance. In many newly-independent countries the choice of a local language for this purpose enhances its prestige. In Australia, in all these institutions other than educational ones, English is the main and precedent language in Australia. There is translation/interpreting available for Spanish. This provides strong support for English, and is perhaps neutral for Spanish (since the language is not actively prohibited).

Religion can be a powerful force for language maintenance and learning: some paradigm examples are:

(1) the survival of Hebrew for more than a thousand years without a community of first-language speakers, and its eventual revival as the language of Israel;
(2) the continued use of Sanskrit in Hindu religious practice;
(3) the learning of Arabic by Moslems around the world.

Churches, mosques, synagogues and temples may serve as focuses of social activity, and may develop their own communities: later we quote one of our interviewees stating that a major site for her use of Spanish is with the community and in the social activities of her church. In Australia the Greek Orthodox Church is normally recognised as playing a key role in the unusually high rates of maintenance of Greek (Clyne, 1991). As for Spanish in Sydney, an Internet search uncovered weekly Christian services in Spanish in six non-Catholic denominations, mostly in the Campbelltown and Fairfield areas.

In the *leisure* area, an important arena for interaction in language other than English is the community club: in Australia there are many of these in the main cities, and many of them sponsor sports teams. Indeed, many of Australia's professional soccer teams have emerged from such clubs. In the Sydney region there are more than 10 Hispanic community clubs, including three Chilean clubs, and the particularly large and active *Spanish Club* and *Uruguayan Club*. These clubs all have clubhouses, and most of them have a range of activities. There are a range of commercial Latin American night clubs (we found 12 in 2002, 5 of them long established), and other clubs that have regular salsa nights. Latin dance music is available every night of the week. Some of these clubs are family oriented, and have participants from all generations; others are more targeted at younger people. There are also more than 20 established Hispanic folkloric dance groups in Sydney, and 14 professional Latino bands. All these indicate lively Hispanic cultural vitality in Sydney, with a particular focus on music.

With regard to cafés and restaurants, food and drink often have strong symbolic significance – sometimes as the main remnant of a pre-existing culture. However, while cuisine may play a significant cultural role, linguistically it may be less important. Cafés and restaurants may be a place where people are comfortable to speak a minority language, but the amount of language involved in interacting with restaurant staff will not normally be great. It is part of a range of commercial interaction that may take place in a minority language (particularly shopping) where the volume of interaction is low, and is therefore likely to be of minor significance in language (as compared to cultural) vitality.

In Sydney there are relatively few Anglo food outlets, apart from pubs and American fast food. Most restaurants and cafes serve other cuisine. In virtually all however English is spoken, sometimes along with the language that matches the cuisine. Liverpool Street in the City has both the Spanish Club and around five Spanish restaurants, as well as a Spanish delicatessen. Spanish can be used in these places. The South American equivalents are mainly found western Sydney, but tend to be bakeries and cake shops with an attached café. In the Fairfield area there are many shops catering to the local South American community where Spanish is spoken.

Education

Education is handled separately from other institutions, since it usually has more impact on the lives of the general population and more influence on language than other institutions.

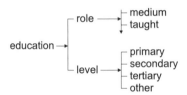

Figure 4.10 Education

Educational medium

The two possible roles of languages in education are to act as a medium, or to be taught (ignoring for now the language of internal communication in the school and the 'playground language'). If a language is a medium, it is used to teach subjects other than language, for instance in the bilingual programme reported in Gibbons *et al.* (1994) science was taught through the medium of Arabic, while social studies was taught through the medium of English. The use of a language as a medium of education has the potential to strongly influence the development of language proficiency. The well-known Canadian immersion programmes (see Genesee, 1987, for one account among many) have demonstrated unequivocally that educational immersion in a language can be a powerful means of inculcating that language in students. Similar evidence from a range of countries is given in Johnson and Swain (1997). Bilingualism and biliteracy are strongly supported when two languages are used effectively as media – bilingual education in its full sense. The use of a language as a medium may also affect the status of the language in the wider community, granting it a measure of prestige and respect that might otherwise not exist.

With regard to bilingual education in Spanish and English, there are some success stories where both languages are acquired (Lindholm-Leary, 2001). However there is comparatively little bilingual education in Australia (Gibbons, 1997) and even less in New South Wales. As far as the authors know, there is no bilingual education involving Spanish in that state. There was a short-lived programme at a Roman Catholic primary school in western Sydney, but that programme has now disappeared. Almost all school education in New South Wales takes place in English only, which explains in part why second-generation children from non-English speaking homes generally have a higher proficiency in English than in their mother tongue by the end of primary school (for evidence of this see Slade & Gibbons, 1987).

The lack of Spanish-as-medium educational programmes, and the almost exclusive use of English, are among the most important single factors discussed in this chapter. The educational system places a large weight in the scales in favour of English. It places a negative weight against Spanish for several reasons. As discussed in Chapter 2, mainstream education is likely to be the only place where 'high' and 'academic' registers of Spanish will be learned. Without considerable commitment and effort, the Spanish of the second generation is likely to be limited to the everyday and the domestic. Another negative factor for Spanish is that if the home language is ignored by the education system, this sends a clear message to students about the value given to languages other than English in the wider society, and helps to create the attitudes that make this situation self perpetuating. If the language that the child brings to school is not recognised and used by the school, it is depreciated.

Language taught
One factor in language learning is language instruction. Language instruction varies considerably in its effectiveness, as a result of programme characteristics (particularly the amount and concentration of time), resources, social context, and the attitudes of students, among other factors. It often seems to be more effective when, rather than being the only access to a language, it is part of a range of language-learning opportunities. Rarely does language instruction alone lead to a high level of proficiency. At the institutional level, language instruction can form part of mainstream schooling. We have not found information on the national

availability of Spanish in mainstream education in Australia, but we have figures for school students who study for their School Certificate (the school-leaving examination taken by most secondary school students) in New South Wales (home to a third of the total Australian population, and most of the Spanish-speaking community). Students who take a Spanish unit in this examination would mostly have achieved a functional command of Spanish. In the year 2000, 80 716 students sat for the examinations, of whom 303 took a Spanish unit, around 0.38%. The figures from previous years are 414 for 1998, and 346 for 1999 – below 0.5%, or one in two hundred. Many of these students would be from Spanish-speaking backgrounds, in other words they are not true second language speakers. The proportion of students studying Spanish in high schools in other states of Australia is usually lower. For universities the latest figure that we have obtained is that each year fewer than two thousand students complete a unit in Spanish in Australia. The support for Spanish in mainstream education is therefore very low.

English, by contrast, is strongly supported in mainstream education. There is compulsory instruction in English as a mother tongue or as a second language in all schools, universities often seek evidence of English proficiency as an entry requirement, and almost all offer English tuition to second language speakers. The degree of support from English instruction in Australian education is high.

There are also extra-curricular forms of study available in many countries. In Indonesia, for instance, there are very many private institutions that teach English, and quasi-governmental bodies such as the Indonesia Australia Language Foundation. There are also foreign-government-funded language institutions around the world such as the Goethe Institute and the Instituto Cervantes. There may also be subsidised instructions in evening colleges. Finally, there may be private tuition available – in South Korea, for example, this is widespread.

In Australia several bodies receive government funding to teach English as a second language through the Adult Migrant Education programme, and colleges of Technical and Further Education (TAFE).

The Australian government's response to the demand from communities for minority language instruction for their children was the establishment and continuing funding of the so-called 'ethnic' or 'Saturday' schools. Given the extraordinary number of community languages in Australia, this type of schooling is part of an appropriate response to this demand, although there are clear benefits to mainstreaming some community languages in regular schooling. These ethnic/Saturday schools run outside normal school hours and the mainstream curriculum, and are to some degree dependent on the input of minority language communities.

The Instituto Cervantes is not represented in Australia, although the Spanish government funds some Spanish teachers to run free Spanish courses in major cities. Spanish instruction is also available in evening classes and private language schools, as well as through private tuition.

The consequences of these low rates of availability of Spanish in mainstream education for our sample of Spanish speakers are discussed in Chapter 6.

Media

There are many other more subtle means of categorising the 'media' (means of communication with the public) than that given in Figure 4.11, but it gives a useable summary. Each medium that uses a particular language permits access to and experience of that language, and enhances its status. Particularly minority-language communities can benefit from access to material in their language, which can extend the range of registers available and keep them in touch with language developments elsewhere, including source countries. Here we are discussing the simple existence of media. The importance or 'weight' of each medium depends to a large degree on the number of people that make use of it, and the amount of use by these people, the contact arena discussed in the next chapter.

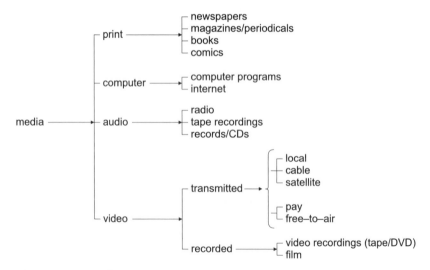

Figure 4.11 Media

Print media

In Australia the media place most of their weight in favour of English, which is not surprising given the role of English as mother tongue of the majority, and lingua franca of the remainder. There are many more print publications available in English than in other languages. Outside the major cities there is almost no *print* material available in languages other than English. However, according to a recent survey, a Chinese language newspaper has the fourth rank in sales in Sydney. Inner city newsagents in Sydney sell local newspapers in an astonishing range of languages. Currently in Australia there are more than 150 publications in languages other than English covering 38 different languages.

Regular Spanish newspapers with national circulation are: *The Spanish Herald*, published twice a week, with sales figures of around 12 000; *El Extra Informativo*, published weekly, selling 25 000 copies (50% in New South Wales); and *El Español en Australia*, published weekly, selling 24 000 copies (60% in New South Wales). In total, these newspapers sell 100 000 copies a week, to a Spanish-speaking population of around 80 000 people, which indicates that they are widely read in the community. Through the Internet there is access (for instance through the *Españanet* website) to many Spanish and Latin American newspapers, and some (such as *El País)* are available in small numbers in Australia.

In public libraries, while the overwhelming majority of books are in English, there are also substantial holdings of Spanish-language books, particularly in areas where there is a higher density of Spanish speakers. Cabramatta Public Library has the largest holdings, with 4750 items in Spanish, including the following: 2455 fiction books, 1526 non-fiction books, 20 cassettes, 140 videos for adults, 32 periodicals, 558 children's books, 8 children's videos, and 10 children's kits. The holdings in other parts of Sydney are smaller, but these numbers illustrate how minority languages, even those with a relatively small population, are supported in Australian public institutions.

Electronic media

As with the print media, there are far more public resources available in English than in other languages. However the government-sponsored *Special Broadcasting Service* (*SBS*) has a television channel that broadcasts in a range of languages, including news and current affairs from overseas broadcasters in Cantonese, Mandarin, Japanese, Indonesian, Italian, German, French, Spanish (from both Spain and Chile), Hungarian, Ukrainian, Russian, Greek and Arabic. It predominantly broadcasts non-English documentaries, programmes and films in their original languages (subtitled in English) from around the world. *SBS* has also recently set up a news channel in languages other than English, but no more information is available at the time of writing.

In addition to free public broadcasting, for Spanish there is cable access via TARBS to television from Spain (*Radio Televisión Española*) and Chile (*Televisión Nacional de Chile*). There is also a subscription *World Movie* cable channel that provides some films in Spanish. We also know of at least four video shops that specialise in Spanish-language material. Much of their stock is telenovelas (soap operas) in Spanish, but there are also films made in Spanish, and Hollywood movies and children's cartoons dubbed into Spanish.

SBS also has three radio stations in Sydney, which every day broadcast local one-hour radio programmes in more than 30 languages, including Spanish. For our teenage interviewees, there is a weekly programme on Sundays called *Gente Joven*, run by and for young Hispanics. This plays the latest Latino music, gives news of relevance to young people from the Spanish-speaking world and the Australian Hispanic community, and runs interviews in Spanish with local young people. Australia is probably unique in the range of minority languages catered for in the public media.

There is subscription access to *Radio Austral,* which is a 24-hour Australian Spanish language satellite radio station. Previously this could only be received via special receivers, but it now has a local licence to broadcast in the suburbs of Sydney with the highest concentrations of Spanish speakers: Fairfield, Cabramatta and Liverpool. Other local stations are *Radio Rio,* which broadcasts in Spanish every day until 10 pm, and *Radio Ritmo* and *Radio La Bomba,* which broadcast two hours each week in Spanish.

With the Internet, the dominant language is still English. It is quite difficult at the time of writing to avoid arriving at an English-language website, even if one begins in another language. Nevertheless there has been rapid development of material in other languages, and one of the strongest of these is Spanish. While computer programs are mostly available in Spanish versions, these are hard to access in Australia, where the overwhelming majority of material is in English only. Nevertheless, as we shall see in the next chapter, some computer programs are used in their Spanish versions in the Sydney Hispanic community.

The issues that arise when we examine media are the extent to which these resources are actually used by second-generation teenagers, and the effect that use can have on language proficiency. This will be addressed in the next chapter.

Conclusion

When the total societal picture is examined, many forces that act to sustain or suppress bilingualism emerge, as do potential areas of language use. No two countries will be exactly alike. It is very difficult to sustain a language over generations if there is no societal support, and the language is used purely within the home (Fishman, 2000). It should be noted, however, that these societal factors generally affect the *accessibility* of the language: with the possible exception of education, they do not guarantee that people will avail themselves of the possibilities. Even in Australia, with its overwhelming majority language, we noted that around 3% of the population speak it poorly.

The weights in the scales favouring English in Australia weigh heavily. For almost all practical purposes, English is sufficient. Spanish in Australia is much less favoured: a person who speaks only Spanish is severely disadvantaged, and is alienated from many mainstream activities. The demographic minority status of Spanish leads to lack of official recognition and use in governmental agencies. Nevertheless, as we explored the many avenues of availability of Spanish in the media, we were agreeably surprised. Partly as a consequence of its position as a major world language, there is a remarkable range of these. The overall societal situation in Australia makes the future of Spanish precarious. It is balanced between Fishman's (1991) stages 5 and 6, where the survival of a language is neither assured nor denied. Only if opportunities are exploited, and attitudes are strongly in favour of the language, will it survive within the community, the family and the individual.

One possibility is action at the national and local levels to modify the societal picture, so that it provides more support for minority languages in the ways suggested by Fishman (1991). Action available to the Hispanic community in Australia includes support for and establishment of Spanish-language media; and favouring the use of Spanish in local institutions, for instance in restaurants, shops and religious services. In terms of political action, it was partly political pressure by language minority groups that led to the establishment of the system of 'ethnic' language schools. If as a next step ideological resistance to bilingual education were overcome, this would place another substantial weight in the scales.

Societal Variables: The Interviewees

This section provides socio-demographic information on our Sydney interviewees, and looks at any resulting proficiency effects.

Age

Basic language development takes place mainly in the early years of life, although people continue to accumulate vocabulary and in many cases to refine their grammatical proficiency. Register, however, to the extent that it is tied to literacy and technicality, is likely to continue to develop for much longer, throughout education, since exposure to academic register in a particular language comes through learning school subjects in that language, and perhaps in adulthood through particular literate work contexts. We would therefore predict that entirely English-educated students would show age-related development of academic register in English, while Spanish-educated students would show age-related development of academic register in Spanish. These predictions are borne out by the results displayed in Table 4.12.

These figures show that, for the Australian educated, there is a significant relationship between age and both scores on the English tests, and on the Spanish C-test. This appears to show that the development of written English and of Spanish grammar and vocabulary is related to age, but other aspects of Spanish are not. The picture is reversed with those partly educated in a Spanish-speaking country, where it is the development of register that is very strongly related to age (such significances on a sample

Table 4.12 Correlations of age with test results

	Entirely Australian educated		*Partly educated in Spanish-speaking country*		*All Sydney interviewees*	
	Corr	*p*	*Corr*	*p*	*Cor*	*p*
English cloze: water	0.19	0.1040	0.47	0.0537	0.17	0.1113
English cloze: hibernation	0.24	**0.0371**	0.05	0.8457	0.18	**0.0880**
English cloze total	0.25	**0.0328**	0.27	0.3052	0.20	*0.0571*
Spanish basic literacy	-0.02	0.8975	-0.43	0.0879	-0.05	0.6359
Spanish C-test	0.48	**<0.0001**	0.31	0.2230	0.48	**<0.0001**
Spanish self rating	0.15	0.1882	0.14	0.6084	0.23	**0.0291**
Spanish history cloze	0.05	0.6517	0.74	**0.0004**	0.16	0.1293
Spanish science cloze	0.07	0.5802	0.30	0.2486	0.12	0.2669
Spanish cloze total	0.06	0.5810	0.76	**0.0002**	0.15	0.1396
	Observations = 75; missing values = 9		Observations = 17; missing values = 3		Observations = 93; missing values = 13	

of only 17 are surprising). These findings lend support to the propositions put forward in Chapter 2: first, that the acquisition of academic register in a language is strongly related to education through that language, and second that it is a developmental phenomenon.

Another issue that arises from Table 4.12 is that age is not significantly related to the self-rating of proficiency in either of the two groups, but it is significant when the groups are combined. This might lead us to suspect that the major difference in self-rated proficiency is between the two groups. This impression is confirmed by a comparison of the mean scores of the two groups, which shows approximately a one-standard-deviation advantage for the Spanish-educated group, and lower minimum assessments for the Australian-educated group – see Table 4.13.

Table 4.13 Self assessment: Basic statistics

	Entirely Australian educated	*Partly overseas educated*
Mean	26.345	32.800
Standard deviation	5.867	6.023
Standard error	0.640	1.347
Minimum	13.000	17.000
Maximum	40.000	40.000
Observations	84	20
Missing values	2	0

Because of the number of missing values, the oral scores were correlated separately with age. The results are in Table 4.14.

Table 4.14 shows that there is a relationship between oral performance in Spanish and age. There are various possible interpretation of this. First, there is the likelihood that oral language continues to develop among teenagers, particularly in the areas of fluency and accent – teenagers becoming more articulate as they mature. Second, however, we note that this is more strongly marked among those educated in a Spanish-speaking country – the basic correlations are strong, despite the lower significances produced by the small size of the group. The Australian-educated group show this phenomenon considerably more weakly in general, probably because there are other factors (such as the proficiency balance between their two languages, and limited development of Spanish in general) that affect the issue in addition to age factors.

Table 4.14 Correlation of age with Spanish oral performance

	Entirely Australian educated		Partly educated in Spanish-speaking country		All Sydney interviewees	
	Corr	p	Corr	p	Corr	p
Oral fluency	0.31	**0.0151**	0.58	**0.0088**	0.38	**0.0003**
Oral accent	0.35	**0.0046**	0.48	**0.0354**	0.40	**0.0001**
Oral idiomaticity	0.18	0.1660	0.57	**0.0093**	0.31	**0.0047**
Oral mixing	0.16	0.2118	0.43	0.0692	0.24	**0.0313**
Oral total	0.30	**0.0174**	0.59	**0.0065**	0.39	**0.0002**
	Observations = 62; missing values = 22		Observations = 19; missing values = 1		Observations = 82; missing values = 24	

Sex

As noted in Chapter 1, there were 63 females and 43 males in our study. We obtained this information by asking interviewees to click a button either M or F, below the caption:

sexo/sex

We assume that our interviewees recorded their biological sex, although we can also assume a strong relationship with their cultural gender. T-testing revealed no major differences in language proficiency.

Education

The level of parental education was obtained by asking the following question about the level of education of the father and the mother.

Highest level of education completed by your father (*Choose one box*)
Nivel de educación más alto de tu padre (*Selecciona una casilla*)
1   Primary/primaria
2   1–4 years secondary/1–4 años secundaria
3   more than 5 years of secondary/5+ años secundaria
4   Vocational training/capacitación vocacional
5   Bachelor degree/bachiller o licenciatura
6   Postgraduate degree/posgrado

Where necessary, the interviewer could help out with the categorisation. (The same question was also asked about the level of education of other caregivers, see below.) It should be noted that this is the claimed level of education, and there may be some small inflation in these claims.

Table 4.15 Father's educational level

		Frequency	%
1	Primary	26	24.5
2	1–4 years secondary	15	14.2
3	5+ years of secondary	20	18.9
4	Vocational training	21	19.8
5	Bachelor degree	20	18.9
6	Postgraduate degree	4	3.8
	Total:	106	100.0

Observations = 106; missing values = 0; mean = 3.057; standard deviation = 1.560

Table 4.15 and Figure 4.12 show that around a quarter of the fathers of our interviewees have had only primary education. On the other hand a large proportion (42.5%) have post-secondary education. This confirms that our sample is fairly representative of the first-generation Hispanic community in Australia, which includes a large group of poorly-educated economic migrants, and a large group of well-educated refugees who fled political persecution from various regimes in Latin America.

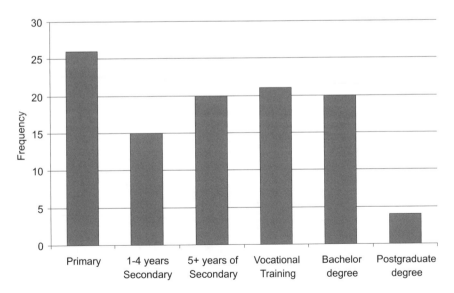

Figure 4.12 Father's educational level

Table 4.16 Mother's educational level

		Frequency	%
1	Primary	19	17.9
2	1–4 years secondary	19	17.9
3	5+ years of secondary	19	17.9
4	Vocational training	23	21.7
5	Bachelor degree	23	21.7
6	Postgraduate degree	3	2.8
	Total:	106	100.0

Observations = 106; missing values = 0; mean = 3.198; standard deviation = 1.489

The profile of the mothers' education in Table 4.16 and Figure 4.13 is slightly different in that the mothers are better educated in general, with 17.9% having only a primary education, and 46.2% having post-secondary education, nearly a quarter with degrees.

When assessing any influence of the caregiver's education on the language development of the interviewees, it is clearly important to check that the primary caregiver was a parent, and to include information on the

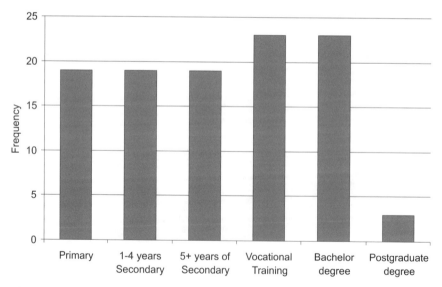

Figure 4.13 Mother's educational level

Table 4.17 (a) Primary caregiver

Value	Frequency	%
Mother	90	84.9
Grandfather	2	1.9
Grandmother	14	13.2
Total:	106	100.0

(b) Education of primary caregivers other than the mother

		Frequency	%	Valid %
1	Primary	8	17.9	50.0
2	1–4 years secondary	7	6.6	43.8
3	5+ years of secondary	1	0.9	6.2
	Missing values	90	84.9	
	Total:	106	100.0	100.0

Observations = 16; missing values = 90; mean = 1.562; standard deviation = 0.629

level of education of other primary caregivers. We therefore included the following question on this issue.

Who looked after you most when you were a child?
¿Quién te cuidó durante más tiempo cuando eras niño/a?

mother / madre
father / padre
grandmother / abuela
grandfather / abuelo
other / otra persona

If the primary caregiver was not one of the parents, there a follow-up question asked about the level of education of the other caregiver, resulting in the information given in Table 4.17.

In our sample, fathers were never primary caregivers (the likely cultural interpretation of this is obvious). The only caregivers other than the mother in our sample were grandparents: 14 grandmothers and 2 grandfathers. The educational level of these grandparent caregivers is worth considering, since none of them have education beyond secondary level, and their average level of education is much lower. This probably represents general inter-generational differences in levels of education. It is also interesting to note that, in all cases where the primary caregiver was a grandparent, the mother had a tertiary education. One could speculate that the enhanced employment opportunities led some mothers to not adopt the primary caregiver role.

Occupation

Our information collection included questions about the occupation of the parents or other primary caregiver of our interviewees – partly as an indicator of our interviewees' socio-economic status (SES), or social class in traditional sociological models. The questions asked about these persons were the following, where [...] indicates father/mother/other caregiver:

What is/was your [...]'s job?
¿En qué trabaja/ba tu [...]?

The occupation of the parents/caregivers was coded as follows: unskilled manual = 1, skilled manual = 2; white collar and small business = 3; nurses, teachers, dental technicians = 4; other professions = 5; home duties or retired = 0. Home duties as a category is problematic, as (among other possibilities) it may indicate a prosperous home where the mother or father does not need to work, a home with conservative family values, or unemployment. To remove misleading effects it was recoded as a missing value and as a mean score, but this did not produce any significant changes in results.

Father's occupation

From Table 4.18 and Figure 4.14 it can be seen that two thirds of the fathers are employed in manual work. This is the reality of most migrant societies, that even well-educated and well-qualified migrants mainly work in manual employment, taking a step down the socio-economic ladder as a consequence of migration. The causes are complex, and this is not the place to describe them, but they include prejudice, lack of network connections, inadequate English proficiency for professional work, and an inappropriate work culture for the Australian context. It is important to notice this factor, however, because in our study we may find literacy practices and literate language that are not always associated with manual workers.

Mother's occupation

We previously noted the difficulty of assessing the socio-economic status of home duties, and the data in Table 4.19 and Figure 4.15 show that this is the occupation of 29.2% of the mothers.

Possibly in line with their higher levels of education, the mothers who are in employment outside the home have higher rates of white-collar work.

Table 4.18 Father's occupation

		Frequency	%	*Valid %*
0	Home duties or retired	2	1.9	2.1
1	Unskilled manual	30	28.3	30.9
2	Skilled manual	41	38.7	42.3
3	White collar and small business	12	11.3	12.4
4	Nurses, teachers, dental technicians	12	11.3	12.4
	Missing values	9	8.5	
	Total:	106	100.0	100.0

Observations = 97; missing values = 9; mean = 2.021; standard deviation = 1.010

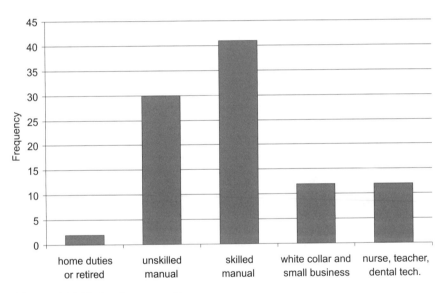

Figure 4.14 Father's occupation

Occupation of other caregivers

Not surprisingly the grandparents, as shown in Table 4.20, are overwhelmingly retired or involved in home duties. The two employed grandparents are a cleaner and shopkeeper. Little can be assumed about social and linguistic practices from these data.

Table 4.19 Mother's occupation

		Frequency	_%_	_Valid %_
0	Home duties or retired	31	29.2	30.7
1	Unskilled manual	26	24.5	25.7
2	Skilled manual	12	11.3	11.9
3	White collar and small business	21	19.8	20.8
4	Nurses, teachers, dental technicians	10	9.4	9.9
5	Other professions	1	0.9	1
	Missing values	5	4.7	
	Total:	106	100.0	100.0

Observations = 101; missing values = 5; mean = 1.564; standard deviation = 1.417

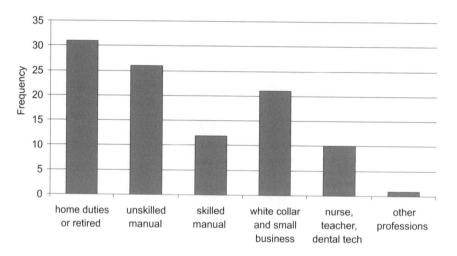

Figure 4.15 Mother's occupation

Relationship between family background and language proficiencies

In the light of the limited confidence that was placed in the notion of occupational status as it applies to this group, it is not surprising that there were few relationships between occupational status and the measures of English and Spanish proficiency. However, among our Australian-educated

Table 4.20 Occupation of other caregivers

		Frequency	%	Valid %
0	Home duties or retired	13	12.3	86.7
1	Unskilled manual	1	0.9	6.7
3	White collar and small business	1	0.9	16.7
	Missing values	91	85.8	
	Total:	106	100.0	100.0

Observations = 15; missing values = 91; mean = 0.267; standard deviation = 0.799

interviewees there was a consistent negative relationship between the father's occupation and the interviewee's oracy in Spanish, as shown in Table 4.21.

This negative relationship was unexpected, and we can only speculate on the reasons for the result. It is possible that the father's occupational level may be an indicator of homes where more English is used. As we saw earlier in this chapter, there is evidence of a direct relationship between occupational level and English proficiency in the Australian community. The father's occupational level may therefore be associated with English proficiency, and perhaps acculturation. It certainly means that it is possible to use English in the home, whilst in homes where the parental English proficiency is low, this is less easy. However, no correlation was found between the father's occupation and the English proficiency tests, so another speculative explanation may be that fathers with higher-level occupations spend less time talking to their children.

Table 4.21 Correlation between Spanish oracy and father's occupation

	Father's occupational level	
	Corr	p
Oral fluency	-0.25	0.0562
Oral accent	-0.27	0.0380
Oral idiomaticity	-0.33	0.0108
Oral mixing	-0.29	0.0233
Oral total	-0.35	0.0065

Observations = 60; missing values = 24

Perhaps more surprising was the lack of any relationship between parental education and language proficiency – it may be that there are intervening variables at play. This is not the case for the Chilean sample, as discussed later.

Conclusions

The finding that the overseas-educated have age-related variation on Spanish register measures, while the Australian-educated have age-related variation on English register measures has implications for both mainstream education and Saturday/ethnic schools in minority contexts. It is an indicator that, for formal purposes, the dominant language of the Australian-educated is English, and points to the need for more exposure to Spanish higher registers in both forms of education if age-appropriate register development is sought. The general lack of relationship between parental education/employment, and advanced language proficiency may reflect on our measuring techniques, but may also indicate that there really is little relationship, and that other factors are more important.

Societal Variables: The Santiago Sample

As we noted earlier, the Santiago sample consisted of girls aged around 13 years. We looked to parental education (Table 4.22) and employment (Table 4.23) to see whether there were any relationships with Spanish proficiency in this mainly Spanish monolingual group.

Table 4.22 Parental education: Santiago

	Mother	*Father*
Primary	1	1
1–4 years Secondary	4	3
5+ years of Secondary	28	13
Vocational training	16	18
Bachelor degree	29	39
Postgraduate degree	4	4
Missing values	14	23
Total:	82	77

Table 4.23 Parental occupation: Santiago

	Mother	*Father*
Home duties	25	0
Unskilled manual	3	7
Skilled manual	13	19
Nurses, teachers, white collar, small business	42	26
Other professions	6	25
Retired, dead, missing	5	19
Total:	65	77

Parental education

In Chile a substantial proportion of the older generation has only primary education. In our data we have a substantial number of missing values, but almost no reports of primary education. We therefore suspected that, in those cases where education was not reported, it would have been mainly to primary level, but respondents were reluctant to report this.

Parental occupation

It can be seen from these data that the parents of the Santiago respondents are engaged mainly in middle-class occupations. The large number of home duties (mainly recorded as 'ama de casa' *housewife*) poses the same problem as the Australian sample, and reduces the usability of the mother's occupation as a predictor.

Relationship between family background and language proficiencies

Our initial processing showed no statistical relationship between the proficiency measures and parental education or occupation. Importantly, there is no relationship between family background and control of grammar as measured by the C-test, confirming results from many other studies. It is worth noting that occupation, a traditional indicator of social class in sociological models, showed no relationship with the language proficiency measures. With regard to education, it seemed possible that the large number of missing values may have affected the result. When educational 'missing values' were replaced with 'primary education', significant relationships emerged with the multiple-choice cloze tests only (Table 4.24). Obviously this procedure is questionable, but we believe the finding is worth recording.

Table 4.24 Correlations of parental education with cloze measures: Santiago

	History m/c cloze		Science m/c cloze		Total of cloze scores	
	Corr.	p	Corr.	p	Corr.	p
Mother's education	0.19	0.0613	0.18	0.0816	0.24	**0.0170**
Father's education	0.17	0.0990	0.18	0.0891	0.23	**0.0275**
Sum of parental education	0.20	0.0529	0.20	**0.0492**	0.26	**0.0100**

Observations = 5; missing value = 1

The data shown in Table 4.24 indicate a weak relationship between parental educational levels and the scores on the register clozes, predictably indicating higher levels of command of academic register amongst teenagers in more educated families. Parents with a higher level of education are more likely to have a higher proficiency in academic register, and therefore to be able to transmit it to their children. However, as we shall see in Chapter 6, there may be mediating factors involved, particularly literacy practices.

Conclusions: The Two Samples

Both the Santiago and the Sydney samples have a reasonable spread of educational levels and occupational levels among parents, although the occupational levels in Sydney are somewhat depressed by the migration experience. Despite the substantial literature on the effects of social class on language achievement, our study offers little support for such a view. Recent discussions of social class have defined it in terms of social practices and resources rather than occupational or educational categories. In the chapters that follow we will examine practices and resources in the home, particularly with regard to literacy, and a more refined portrayal will emerge.

Chapter 5

Interpersonal Contact

THE ISSUES

Introduction

Language acquisition and maintenance occur through contact between an individual and a language. Contact can be interpersonal (as in normal daily interaction), or it can be non-interactive, watching television for instance. It is through such exposure and use that language develops and is maintained. The societal variables we discussed in the previous chapter create many such opportunities, and attitudes and beliefs shape the way that the individual seeks out and utilises contact, but it is the contact itself that is an essential element in language development and maintenance. Therefore it is important to analyse the amount and the nature of such contact, in order to see how it influences and interacts with the level and the nature of language proficiency. Some writers, particularly Li (1994), treat this as an issue of code choice. However, this may not reflect the reality of the experience of all bilinguals. First, the bilingual may be less powerful than others (for example, in the family hierarchy children may have less control than parents), which means that they may not be free to choose their preferred code. An important element of this is the language used in institutions, which is the result of language-planning decisions of the type discussed in the previous chapter, over which the bilingual often has no control. Second, interlocutors may be monolingual, or have a limited proficiency in one of the candidate languages, so communicative efficiency pushes code choice in the direction of their stronger language (this seems to often be the case with grandparents in minority-language communities – see for instance Ng & He, forthcoming). Third, the bilingual's proficiency may be stronger in certain areas in one of her/his languages. There is a chicken-and-egg effect here, in that dominance in domains is a product of contact, but it also affects contact.

Interpersonal contact can be examined in terms of a person's social networks, while non-interactive contact can be examined primarily through media use. This division is not absolute however, since one type of social network is education, which can include some one-way communication, while computer games and crossword puzzles are to some degree interactive, if not interpersonal. Interpersonal contact is examined in this chapter, and non-interpersonal contact with a language is the subject of Chapter 6.

Social Networks

Hamers and Blanc (2000: 111) define social networks as: 'the sum of all the interpersonal relations one individual establishes with others over time.' Interpersonal interaction takes place within what Fishman refers to as domains, such as family life, commercial transactions (e.g. shopping), or education. This in turn takes us back to the notion of register field, implying that, if some of these domains are accessed in only one language, then the registers appropriate to these domains are likely to be less developed in the other language – bilinguals may develop a form of functional specialisation in their languages. Various attempts have been made to examine the impact of social networks on bilingualism and biliteracy.

An early example was the Heidelberg Pidgin-Deutsch project (Klein & Dittmar, 1979), which examined the level of development of German syntax among 48 'foreign workers' from Spain and Italy, and attempted to relate it to two groups of factors, personal factors, and what they called the 'social environment'. The personal factors were sex, mother tongue, age at migration, length of residency in German (all had been there more than three years), length of study, and job qualification on migration. The 'social environment' factors consisted of social network variables: contact with Germans at the workplace, and contact with Germans in leisure time (domestic arrangements were also indirectly examined). Table 5.1 shows the only factors that were significantly related to German proficiency, in descending order of importance.

The most important variables in Table 5.1 are age on arrival (the younger they were, the more German they learned) and the social contact variables – contact with Germans in leisure time and at work. The researchers point out that none of the interviewees who entered Germany at an early age had little contact with Germans. They also mention that the people who had the best German often had a German partner, and some of them were integrated into the community, belonging to the local soccer team and drinking at the neighbourhood bar. The other factor that assisted them was their social-class origin, as manifested in type of employment and education before migration. Skilled workers seemed to have achieved a higher level of German than unskilled workers, perhaps because they were on a more equal social footing with German workers (what we refer to as the 'power relationship' in what follows). Sex and mother tongue did not have a signif-

Table 5.1 Factors related to German proficiency, in descending order of importance

	Variable	*n*
1	Contact with Germans in leisure time	0.64
2	Age on arrival	-0.57
3	Contact with Germans at work	-0.53
4	Job qualification on migration	0.52
5	Years of education	0.35
6	Length of residency	0.28

icant effect. It is noticeable that, beyond three years, length of residency, which one might predict to be an important predictor of contact, is actually of limited importance. Possible reasons for this are given in Wong-Fillmore (1991) and Schumann (1978), who both show, from different perspectives, that it is possible to have lengthy periods of residence with very limited contact with local language speakers.

These findings demonstrate the potential importance of interpersonal contact. They were supported by the subsequent ZISA project (Clahsen *et al.*, 1983), but unfortunately this latter study suffered methodological problems (Hudson, 1993).

More sophisticated ways of examining the role of social networks were taken from sociological theory and applied to language by Milroy (1980). In a remarkable study she demonstrated the relationship between dialect features and social networks in Belfast. Her methodology was observation allied to tape recording to obtain her data, and both qualitative and statistical analysis. In association with Li Wei, her description was later extended to bilingual communities, particularly the study of the Chinese bilingual community in Newcastle, UK, reported in Milroy and Li (1995), Li *et al.* (1992) and Li (1994).

LePage & Tabouret-Keller (1985) provide an expanded understanding of how such network ties act to shape the language behaviour of individuals, and also show how individuals have some degree of control over their language behaviour.

Modelling social networks

The following description of networks is based on Milroy (1980), but has been changed slightly in the light of experience. The model operates on the

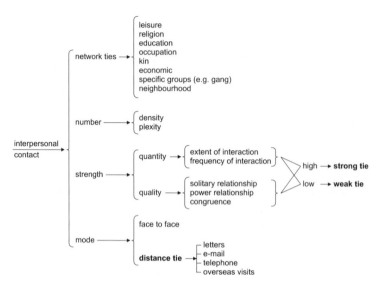

Figure 5.1 Interpersonal contact

basis that types of social contact establish *network ties*. Some major network ties are given in Figure 5.1.

It is no coincidence that the network ties in Figure 5.1 correspond closely to some of the *domains* that Fishman *et al.* (1971)had earlier identified as important in bilingual maintenance, and that they are the personal experience of some of the societal structures discussed in the previous chapter. However, in this case we are not discussing the overall societal availability of a language, but the individual's experience of it. For instance, the fact that there are church services available in Spanish in Western Sydney does not mean that a Spanish speaker in a distant centre is able to visit the church and establish Spanish network ties in the religious domain.

Milroy also suggested ways of assessing how these ties work together to influence the language of the individuals in the network. If person X has a number of network ties with another person – for instance they are cousins (*kin*), they work together (*occupation*), and live nearby (*neighbourhood*) – that other person is in a position to have a strong influence on X's language. This relationship is referred to as *multiplex*. Furthermore, if the people whom X knows all know each other then they are likely to establish a community of practice (Wenger, 1998). These two aspects of network ties are shown in Figure 5.2.

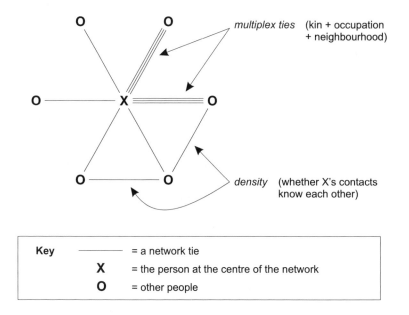

Figure 5.2 Density and plexity of network ties

Milroy (1980) provides a formula for calculating the influence of network ties, based on their density and plexity. Another factor is the strength of each individual tie. Milroy suggests that the more equal the power relationship between individuals, the stronger the tie.

Milardo (1988) distinguishes 'exchange' and 'interactive' networks. The exchange type refers to those networks in which people develop close relationships, in which favours and support can be exchanged. Family and close friends are typical exchange networks. Interactive networks are those in which, despite regular contact, the participants do not develop any type of support or dependence. A typical example would be the tie to the person from whom one buys a newspaper. Granovetter (1982) refers to a similar phenomenon by the more accessible terms 'strong' and 'weak' network ties, which we will use in this book. The difference between the two types seems to have two elements, the quantity and the quality of contact. In terms of quantity, one is likely to have much more extended interaction with kin than with the newspaper seller and, if one is living with kin, much more frequent interaction. Josiane Hamers (personal correspondence) also suggests that the quality of contact is important – the relationship with kin will tend to have greater value, to have emotional force and to be taken seriously; but kin relationships can be negative or positive: in social-psychological terms, this is solidarity. Hamers has encountered cases where adolescents have rejected the language associated with a hated father. It is at this point that contact shades over into attitudes.

Milroy and Li (1995) and Li (1994) suggest a third type of network, one that consists of 'passive ties'. These are distance contacts with people that one values, usually kin overseas. If significant family members such as grandparents are resident in another country, then the need to maintain contact with them in their own language may be an important form of contact, and perhaps a motive in language maintenance. Some possible forms of distance contact are presented in Figure 5.1. The trend to improved and much cheaper distance communication, including e-mail and long-distance telephone calls, along with the more widespread use of video phones, will probably increase the importance of this type of contact in future. We refer to such ties as 'distance ties'.

Schumann (1978) adds another piece to this complex picture, suggesting that, particularly at initial contact, congruence may affect contact. This congruence may be cultural congruence: a Hungarian and a Romanian may find contact and interaction facilitated by the shared elements of their cultures (their cultural congruence), while contact with a Khond tribal person from India may be more problematic. Linguistic congruence would similarly favour interaction between a Romanian and a Spaniard (who both speak Romance languages) over interaction between a Hungarian and a Spaniard. Over time, such congruence can be negotiated – one can learn about other cultures, or learn other languages/varieties. This is Schumann's 'acculturation' effect on language development.

The methodology associated with network studies is typically ethnography, or participant observation. This probably provides the most accurate form of data collection. However Hamers (1994) has also shown that is possible to gather data on this topic by questionnaire and interview methods.

Returning to our concern with the development of register, it is clear that the different classes of contact outlined above will create the contexts for the development of different register features. Looking at the 'leisure' element, for instance, unless one experiences commentary upon and discussion of soccer in a particular language, one is unlikely to learn technical terms such as 'offside'. Similarly, if a people experience a language only in informal contexts, and never in more formal contexts such as religion or work, they are unlikely to develop more formal register. If experience is limited to contexts where only speech is used, such as with neighbours or in a gang, development of written register features is unlikely. Since forms of contact are associated with different register features, they are likely to influence both the level and the nature of bilingual proficiency. A critical context for the development of higher register is education, which will be discussed in the next chapter.

Media use does not involve language production by both parties (in this sense it is not interactive). Interactive distance media are emerging at the time of writing (particularly through the Internet), but currently they tend to limit the user to sets of closed comprehension choices, and so remain essentially one way communication. The various types of media are given in Figure 4.11 in Chapter 4. Their role in language development and maintenance is discussed in Chapter 6.

THE STUDIES

Strong Network Ties

In this part of the research, we attempted to examine the interviewees' strong network ties. The people selected were family members and another 'important person' (which in practice was usually a friend or a boy/girl-friend). As with the other questions, there were open questions first, then a series of closed questions, then open questions in which students were asked to reflect on what they had just done. The interviewees typed in their own responses, so errors in spelling etc. are their own. As already noted, there were 5 questionnaire/test instruments, each of which had a number of items. The questionnaire/test is indicated by a hash symbol (#), and the question number by **Q**. So questionnaire 4, question 75 is referred to as **#4 Q75**.

Open questions

In Questionnaire 4, the following open questions were asked about strong network ties.

#4 Q2

These questions are about whether you use Spanish or English with people who are important in your life.
Estas preguntas son acerca del uso del español o el inglés con gente importante en tu vida.

Which people are particularly important in your life?
¿Qué personas son particularmente importantes en tu vida?

#4 Q3

Which people do you like or love the most?
¿Quiénes son las personas que más aprecias o quieres?

#4 Q4

Who do you use Spanish with?
¿Con quién hablas español?

Some examples of responses to the 'importance' question follow. As with all these open questions, the interviewees typed in their responses, which are reproduced here in their original form, including spelling, punctuation and use of capital letters. English translations of Spanish comments are given in italics.

MOTHER AND FATHER

Primero mi familia despues mis amigos
first my family, then my friends

mis familiares (padres, mi hermana y flia), mis amigos, la familia en Argentina -abuelos, tíos, etc
my family members (parents, my sister and family), my friends, the family in Argentina – grandparents, aunt and uncles

MUM DAD SISTER GRANDMA AUNTY FAMILY AND FRIENDS

Mis padres, hermanos y amigos de la escuela.
my parents, siblings and school friends

papá, mamá
dad, mum

las personas importantes en mi vida son mis padres mi abuelita,mis tios y tias.
the most important people in my life are my parents, my granny, my uncles and aunts

god,mum,dad,famliy,friends

parents,brothers,friends,relatives

my mother my family and my close friends

MY PARENTS, BROTHERS, GRANDPARENTS, FAMILY, FRIENDS, FAMOUS CELEBRITIES THAT I LIKE, TEACHERS (UNFORTUNATELY), AND PEOPLE OF INFLUENCE.

MUM, DAD, STEPDAD, BROTHERS, SISTERS, AND FAMILY

parents, sister, relatives, boyfriend, friends, people that i care for and that i want to be around to help them in whatever they need.

MY FAMILY, GOD, MY BEST FRIEND, AND ME

MY MUM, AUNTY, GRANDMA AND MY FAVORITE TEACHER WHOM I WRITE TO BECAUSE SHE LEFT OUR HIGH SCHOOL.

MADRE, PADRE, HERMANA, TIAS Y TIOS, NOVIO, AMIGAS Y AMIGOS, TODA LA FAMILIA– COMO PRIMAS ETC
mother, father, sister, aunts and uncles, boyfriend, friends, all the family – like cousins etc

These examples include some of the more unusual responses. It is noticeable that many of the responses are ranked for importance, beginning mostly with the mother, then father, then siblings, then other people (the last response is a good example). This corresponds to the numbers of mentions of each participant in Table 5.2, giving a reasonably clear idea of the relative importance of various people in the lives of the interviewees.

Answers to **Q3** (Which people do you like or love the most?), however, make this even clearer. The answers were in many cases similar to the previous, but tended to focus more on the nuclear family. Some examples of responses (including more unusual ones) follow.

my parents, my friends

padres, hermanos
parents, siblings

TODA LA FAMILIA INCLUSO MAS LEJANA
all my family including the more distant

PADRES Y HERMANO (AMIGOS SIGUEN EN IMPORTANCIA)
parents and brother (friends are next in importance)

MI PAPA Y MI MAMA
my dad and my mum

I love my mum, I sort of love my dad, I really really like my boyfriend, but I don't know whether I love him

ME,THEN MY FAMILY

family and friends i can share things with

my mother and family and all my close friends

MY MUM,SISTER AND DAD

MIS FAMILIARES (PADRE , MADRE , HERMANOS)
my family (father, mother, siblings)

The last quote would seem to demonstrate that at least some of the interviewees mean 'nuclear family' when they use the word 'family'.

The following are some examples of answers to **Q4**, the core question, 'Who do you use Spanish with?'

CON TODOS LOS ADULTOS EN LA FAMILIA
with all the adults in the family

LA FAMILIA, AMIGOS (A VECES)
family, friends (sometimes)

con toda mi familia espanola. padre portugues
with all my spanish family, portuguese with father

mi hermano mi familia unos amigos mis profesores de espanol y mis padres
my brother my family some friends my spanish teachers and my parent

mis padres y casi nunca con mi hermano
my parents and almost never with my brother

un poco con mi familia
a little with my family

TODOS DE MI FAMILIA
all my family

IMMEDIATE FAMILY, RELATIVES, AND SPANISH SPEAKING FRIENDS.

MUM,DAD,FAMILY,BROTHERS ,SISTERS,(SOME FRIENDS)

I speak spanish with my grandmother as she only speaks spanish and sometimes with my parents

PERANTS , RELETIVIES OVER SEAS AND SOME OF MY PERANTS FRIENDS

MY MUM,MY AUNTY, MY GRANDMOTHER, MY OHTER GRAND-MOTHER, MY SISTERS, MY FRIEND KATTY, MY GRAND- MOTHER, MY OTHER AUNTIES, UNCLIES AND MY OTHER FAMILY WHO AT THE MOMMENT LIVE IN MEXICO AND AT SPANISH CLASS.

The people mentioned in these responses were different in interesting ways from the previous replies. There was a greater focus on the older generation, and many interviewees specified 'some friends' or 'Spanish-speaking friends'. Spanish classes also appear.

The number of mentions of various types of people in answer to the questions is given in Table 5.2. These figures provide a range of information. It is evident (as one might expect) that parents are the most important and most loved people in the interviewees' lives. When parents are not mentioned specifically, it is likely that they are referred to as '(my) family' instead, meaning that they are included by almost all interviewees (apart from those like the interviewee who put only 'me' in all three columns!). Not all of our interviewees have siblings, but siblings receive frequent mention. Next in importance come friends, and then grandparents. In cases where grandparents are not resident in Australia, some of our interviewees will have had comparatively little contact with them.

Comparing the numbers for **Q2** and **Q3**, when the emotional and affective element is introduced, the main difference in responses is a reduction in unspecified 'friends', and more focus on close friends, and particularly girl/boyfriends. Most of the minor participants at the bottom of the table are eliminated. Moving to **Q4**, which introduces the use of Spanish, the main difference is the halving of the sibling figure (probably indicating that around half of our interviewees use English with their siblings), and the disappearance of cousins. These two facts may indicate generational language shift in progress, where the minority language is used with older generations, but is used less with peers and younger generations. The friends with whom Spanish is used are specifically narrowed down to Spanish-speaking friends, as one would expect. However, it is important to note that English is used with other friends:

I use English the most with my friend

I use English most of the time as my friends are Australian.

Table 5.2 Participants mentioned in the responses to **Q2, Q3** and **Q4**

	#4 Q2 *important*	#4 Q3 *love most*	#4 Q4 *speak Spanish*
Family (not further specified)	45	40	46
Spanish-speaking family			1
Relatives	7	3	1
Relatives/family overseas	2	1	3
Parents	57	59	57
Siblings	37	35	18
Grandparents	15	12	13
Aunts/uncles	13	5	11
Cousins	8	4	
Nephews/nieces	2	1	1
In-laws	1		
Friends	37	18	16
Girl/boyfriend	2	7	2
Close/good/best friends	2	9	
Some friends (probably Spanish speaking)			10
Spanish-speaking friends			3
Friends of my parents/family			11
School friends	3		
Teachers	3	1	
(Fellow) students of Spanish			2
Spanish teachers			6
Spanish classes			4
Neighbours			1
God	2	1	
Me	2	3	1
Godfather		1	
Pets	1		
Famous celebrities	1		
People of influence	1		
Step dad	1		

Note: spaces indicate no mention

Spanish instruction (mainly in 'ethnic' or Saturday schools) also emerges as an important site for Spanish use – this is developed in the next chapter. It is interesting on occasions to compare the responses to all three questions. One interviewee gave the following responses to the three questions, showing a generational difference in Spanish use.

[Q2] THE MOST IMPORTANT PEOPE IN MY LIFE ARE MY FAMILY.

[Q3] I DONT ACTUALLY LOVE ONE OF THEM BETTER THAN ANOTHER SO I'D SAY I LOVE ALL OF THEM THE SAME.

[Q4] MY GRANDMA AND MY GRANDFATHER

The open questions following the closed questions were:

#4 Q75
Is there anything else you wish to say about who you speak Spanish with?
¿Quieres agregar algo sobre las personas con las que hablas español?

#4 Q76
Is there anything you want to say about these questions?
¿Quieres comentar sobre estas preguntas?

94 interviewees did not reply or replied 'no' to **Q75** (including 'no gracias', 'nope' and 'not really'). However, a handful of responses that contained interesting additional information.

voy a algunas tiendas en que hablo espanol
I go to some shops where I speak Spanish

This response indicates that there are weaker network ties (in this case economic) that might need to be considered.

Unas veces cuando voy a las fiestas latinas conozco a una gente que no habla ingles entonces TENGO que hablar en espanol.
Sometimes when I go to latino parties I meet a people (sic) who does not speak English then I HAVE TO speak in Spanish.

i mainly speak spanish with those who do not understand english,

[#1 Q29] When mum doesn't understand what I am saying and I have to explain in Spanish

These comments point to our interviewees using Spanish when forced to do so with people who do not speak English. It is not universal however – one interviewee commented in the reverse:

[#1 Q43] Hablo espanol donde es posible pero donde no se pueda tengo que hablar ingles.
I speak Spanish wherever possible but where I cannot I have to speak English.

This type of proficiency-based code choice is well established in the literature on code switching (see for instance Gibbons, 1987).

Question **Q76** elicited no comments other than:
interesting

Q28 and **Q29** in Questionnaire 1 (about the interviewees' life history and domains of language use) also elicited information about this topic. These questions were asked after a series of questions about the interviewee's educational and migration experiences, but before the more targeted questions that we have just discussed.

#1 Q28

Is there anything else in your life history that might have affected your knowledge of Spanish and English?
Has experimentado algo más en tu vida que pueda haber influído tu conocimiento del español o del inglés

my parents speak spanish all the time

I have a grandmother that can only speak Spanish. I have visited Uruguay many times to see all my relatives over there. I have no relatives here, so I have to go to Uruguay if I want to see them.Having a mother that works I nthe travel department , makes me use Spanish mostly at home. Also, to communicate with my parents we use Spanish. My parents speak English but it is easier for them to speak Spanish.

yes that at the beginning when i was younger i didn't really want to learn , untill later i realised that if i didn't learn i wouldn't be able to communicate with my family.

MY GRANDMOTHER LIVES IN AUSTRALIA AND DOESN'T SPEAK ENGLISH SO I HAVE TO TALK SPANISH WITH HER

1. MIS PADRES CUANDO ME TUBIERON, NO HABLABAN INGLES. 2. ESTUBE DE VACACIONES EN URUGUAY POR DOS MESES 3. MI ABUELA Y TIA, NINGUNA DEL LAS DOS HABLAN MUCHO INGLES. *1. When my parents had me they did not speak English. 2. I was on holiday in Uruguay for two months. 3. My grandmother and aunt, neither of them speak English.*

My parents and family have brought me up speaking Spanish and usually it is the only language that I speak at home

ABLO ESPANOL PORQUE QUIERO ABLAR CON MI FAMILIA
I speak Spanish because I want to speak to my family

OUR GRANDMOTHER LIVES WITH US, BUT SHE DOESN'T UNDERSTAND ANY ENGLISH SO WE HAVE TO TALK WITH HER IN SPANISH. MY FIRST LAUNGUAGE WAS SPANISH.

PERUVIAN GRANDPARENTS VISITED FREQUENTLY FOR HOLIDAYS (EVERY 2 YEARS) WHEN I WAS YOUNG.

have a lot of Spanish friends , I go to places where they speak Spanish

when I was growing up I went to a dancing school where everyone spoke

Spanish even the teacher. my parents talk to me both in English and Spanish,but my brother talks to me in English

I also have the privelige to speak spanish at home.

no hablo espanol en casa pero hablo con mis abuelos cuando vienen de visita.

I don't speak Spanish at home, but I speak it with my grandparents when they come and visit.

These extracts give small portraits our interviewees' use of languages. Some usually speak Spanish at home, others do not. Generational differences in language use emerge clearly, as does the importance of contact with family who live in the source country. Indeed in some of these extracts this emerges as a main motive for language maintenance. The same themes emerge in the responses to **Q29**.

#1 Q29 Speech Domains / Ámbitos de uso del idioma hablado

These questions are about the parts of your life where you use Spanish or English. In these questions, 'use' means either speak or listen.

Estas preguntas son acerca del uso del español o inglés en tu vida diaria. En estas preguntas el 'uso' se refiere a hablar o escuchar.

Where do you use Spanish?

¿En dónde usas el español?

CON LA FAMILIA (EXTENDIDA)
with the (extended) family

AT GRANDMOTHER's HOME

en la casa de mi hermana, con las amigas (ellas hablan con padres en español)
in my sister's house, with [female] friends (they talk to parents in Spanish)

With my grandparents or other relatives who are not living in Australia. Also, when I am with my parents and their spanish When mum doesn't understand what I am saying and I have to explain in Spanish

cousins houses

As my grandmother only speaks Spanish, we would be unable to communicate with her if we hadn't learnt the language. Also, to communicate with my parents we use Spanish. My parents do speak English

when we go to relatives houses

at home, speaking to my grandmother ,

FAMILY GATHERINGS

en casa de los padrinos
in my godparents' house

amigos espanoles
Spanish friends

Con mis amigas latinoamericanas
with my Latin American friends
With my grandparents or other relatives who are not living in Australia.
Also, when I am with my parents and their spanish friends. When I speak
to my speaking friends. When mum doesn't understand what I am saying
and I have to explain in Spanish
CON ALGUNOS AMIGOS DE HABLA HISPANA
with some Spanish speaking friends

In the answers to **Q28** and **Q29** there our interviewees frequently mention being obliged to use Spanish with grandparents who do not speak English. The picture of our interviewees using Spanish with 'some' friends and English with others also emerges clearly. There is also mention of Spanish use with Spanish-speaking friends, because our interviewees can speak Spanish only with Spanish-speaking friends: English is the lingua franca of schools, and most friends made at school will not speak Spanish.

Conclusion

These qualitative data give major support to the notion of the importance of strong network ties in language development and maintenance. As a next step, however, we wished to obtain quantitative data that would permit comparison with other factors, and correlation with our proficiency measures, so that their impact on the nature and amount of language proficiency could be assessed.

Closed questions

The importance of strong network contacts was examined using the questions shown on the next page. The score awarded to closed-question responses is given on the left (the higher the score the greater the contribution to contact). As with all closed questions, the interviewee responded by clicking a box on the computer screen. The questions were of three types. One type asked about opportunities for contact with these people: if they were alive (for the older generation), or if the interviewee had such a person in his/her life (e.g. cousins or older siblings), the frequency with which the interviewee contacts that person, whether the person lives with or near the interviewee; and whether the person goes to the same club, church etc. as the interviewee. This group of questions therefore focused upon the quantity of contact. The second type of question focused on the language most used with these people – English or Spanish. The third type of question dealt with the quality of the contact, the degree to which the contact was important and pleasant. This type of question was included at the suggestion of Josiane Hamers.

In the next questions, please pick one box which best says your answer.
Para las próximas preguntas, escoje el casillero que mejor refleje tu respuesta.

MATERNAL GRANDMOTHER / ABUELA MATERNA

These questions are about one of your grandmothers – your mother's mother.
Do you understand?
Estas preguntas son sobre una de tus abuelas – la madre de tu madre.
¿Entiendes?

Item 1

Is this grandmother still alive?
¿Todavía vive esta abuela?

2   yes / sí
1   no

Item 2

How often do (did) you see this grandmother?
¿Con qué frecuencia ves (veías) a esta abuela?

5   more than once a day / más de una vez al día
4   more than once a week / más de una vez a la semana
3   more than once a month / más de una vez al mes
2   more than once a year / más de una vez al año
1   almost never / casi nunca

Item 3

What language do (did) you use with this grandmother?
¿En qué idioma hablas (hablabas) con esta abuela?

5   almost always Spanish / casi siempre español
4   mostly Spanish / mayormente español
3   Span and English about equally/tanto español como inglés
2   mostly English / mayormente inglés
1   almost always English / casi siempre inglés

Item 4

Does (did) this grandmother live with or near you?
¿Esta abuela vive o vivía contigo o cerca tuyo?

1   no
2   near / cerca
3   with / con

Item 5

Does (did) this grandmother go to the same church, club or organisation as you?
¿Esta abuela concurre o concurría a la misma iglesia, organización o al mismo club que tú?

2   yes / sí
1   no

Item 6

How important to you are (were) your contacts with this grandmother?
¿Cuán importante para ti es o era el contacto con esta abuela?

1   no importance / de ninguna importancia
2   little importance / de poca importancia
3   average importance / de mediana importancia
4   much importance / de mucha importancia
5   very great importance / de suma importancia

Item 7

How pleasant for you are (were) your contacts with this grandmother?
¿Cuán agradable es o era el tiempo que pasas/pasabas con esta abuela?

5   very pleasant / muy agradable
4   fairly pleasant / bastante agradable
3   neither pleasant nor unpleasant/ni agradable ni desagradable
2   fairly unpleasant / bastante desagradable
1   very unpleasant / muy desagradable

These questions were asked about the following people: all four grand-parents, mother and father, older siblings, younger siblings, cousins, any other important person in the interviewee's life. Two interviewees did not access the questionnaire, so their data are not included in the processing, and all figures are based on 104 interviewees, of whom 84 are entirely Australian educated.

As with the other variables that we examined, the network contact variable was examined for its possible effect on the level of development of Spanish. The interpersonal contact issue addressed in this chapter is concerned with oral interaction. One would therefore predict a strong relationship with oracy, including pronunciation, idiomaticity, vocabulary and grammar. However, we will also examine other aspects of language – basic literacy and literate register – to see whether they too are affected by interpersonal contact.

Item 3: Language used

A basic question of interest is what language our teenage interviewees use with family members, since the family is a primary domain for trans-mission and maintenance of minority languages. Table 5.3 provides this basic information – remembering that 5 means 'almost always Spanish' while 1 indicates 'almost always English'.

Table 5.3 shows that our interviewees nearly always use Spanish with their grandparents. They use it a little less often on average with their parents, even less with siblings, more with cousins, and least of all with the other important person, usually a friend, boyfriend or girlfriend. There is a small tendency to use more Spanish with older siblings than with younger ones. We see here the type of change in language use across generations from a minority to a majority language described in Gal (1979). Thus change may reflect the language proficiencies of the interlocutor, since bilinguals tend to use both languages in their repertoire with fellow bilinguals.

Looking in more detail, it is noticeable that nearly a third of our interviewees use mostly English or 'almost always' English with their siblings. The effect of cousins may be explained by the fact that some of these cousins reside in Spanish-speaking countries, and may have limited English. There also appears to be a small and statistically insignificant effect for gender in the difference between grandmother and grandfathers, and between mother and father, with less Spanish used with men. This may reflect the fact that men are more likely to be in the full-time workforce, and are therefore to have a higher proficiency in English (this pattern is supported by

Table 5.3 Descriptive statistics for Item 3

	1 *Almost* *always* *English*	*2* *Mostly* *English*	*3* *Spanish* *and* *English* *about* *equally*	*4* *Mostly* *Spanish*	*5* *Almost* *always* *Spanish*	*#* *Missing*	*Mean*	*SD*
Maternal grandmother	0	0	0	10	94	0	4.904	0.296
Paternal grandmother	6	0	2	6	90	0	4.673	0.980
Maternal grandfather	1	1	2	6	94	0	4.837	0.593
Paternal grandfather	6	0	2	5	91	0	4.683	0.978
Mother	3	4	31	20	46	0	3.981	1.079
Father	6	4	27	19	48	0	3.952	1.186
Older siblings	13	18	25	1	7	40	2.547	1.167
Younger siblings	13	16	23	2	2	48	2.357	0.999
Cousins	11	16	22	8	46	1	3.602	1.451
Other important person	23	10	15	1	5	50	2.167	1.270

Observations = 104; missing values = 2

census data). For the interpretation of the data it is important to note that 40 interviewees do not have older siblings, 48 do not have younger siblings, and only 54 include a significant other.

We also asked the caregiver to complete some of the same questions in order to check the reliability of the reports from our interviewees. Table 5.4 gives the figures for two core items: Item 2 (How often do you see X?) and Item 3 (What language do you use?).

It can be seen from Table 5.4 that the responses are very close. The differences arise mostly from missing values – those few examples where the caregivers did not complete the questions. Looking for example at the figures for contact with the mother, the difference in the means was produced by different scores for only two interviewees. For the father, it was three. These results indicate that the information provided by the interviewees is generally reliable.

Table 5.4 Comparison of responses of caregivers and interviewees: Frequency of contact and language use

	Perceived frequency of contact				Perceived language use			
	Caregiver		Interviewee		Caregiver		Interviewee	
	Mean	SD	Mean	SD	Mean	SD	Mean	SD
Maternal grandmother	1.860	1.463	1.981	1.475	4.930	0.432	4.904	0.296
Paternal grandmother	1.370	0.960	1.519	1.149	4.760	0.842	4.673	0.980
Maternal grandfather	1.320	0.963	1.413	1.120	4.780	0.824	4.683	0.978
Paternal grandfather	1.290	0.856	1.385	0.885	4.980	0.141	4.837	0.593
Mother	4.920	0.563	5.000	0.000	4.350	0.968	3.981	1.079
Father	4.740	0.928	4.702	0.934	4.300	1.078	3.952	1.186
Older siblings	4.576	1.024	4.609	0.936	2.621	0.989	2.547	1.167
Younger siblings	4.925	0.549	5.000	0.000	2.434	0.747	2.357	0.999
Total:	25.001		25.609		33.155		31.934	

The differences between the interviewees and the caregivers are interesting. For example on the frequency of contact with the father, the missing values in the caregiver data sometimes occur where the interviewee reports little contact with the father. In this case the caregiver may feel some embarrassment in reporting a separation or divorce of the parents (remembering that many of our families are of Roman Catholic origin). Overall the interviewees report marginally higher contact with grandparents, and marginally less use of Spanish – our feeling is that the second difference is produced more by wishful thinking by the caregiver than inaccuracy in the reporting by the teenagers.

Relationship between language used and proficiency

Perhaps unsurprisingly, of all the network variables, the language used has the most important relationship with language proficiency. Table 5.5 contains correlations between four proficiency measures and the data from item 3 on language use. The correlations with the figures for grandparents were not highly significant, and we found only limited relationships between contact with grandparents and proficiency. One reason for this was that around 84% of grandparents did not live near the interviewees – many presumably were in the country of origin – and in only 4% of cases did the grandparents live with the family. Our interviewees therefore lived

Table 5.5 Correlations between preference for Spanish (Item 3) and oral measures: Grandparents

		Maternal grandmother	*Paternal grandmother*	*Maternal grandfather*	*Paternal grandfather*
Fluency	Corr	0.14	0.24	0.00148	0.23
	p	0.1887	**0.0280**	0.9893	**0.0381**
Accent	Corr	0.19	0.22	-0.07	0.21
	p	0.0818	**0.0409**	0.5267	**0.0486**
Idiomaticity	Corr	0.12	0.23	-0.05	0.19
	p	0.2558	**0.0369**	0.6679	0.0774
Mixing	Corr	0.05	0.35	-0.11	0.34
	p	0.6737	**0.0008**	0.3198	**0.0014**
Total	Corr	0.15	0.31	-0.07	0.29
	p	0.1740	**0.0040**	0.5537	**0.0076**

Observations = 85; missing values = 19

mainly in nuclear families, and contact with grandparents was in most cases so sparse as to not much affect language proficiency.

In the case of the language used, this effect was exacerbated by the fact that language use with grandparents is almost always Spanish meant that there was insufficient variation to establish correlations with the Spanish proficiency measures. (The correlations used throughout are Fisher's R to Z, generated by the *Statview* package. These correlations are conservative – when some of the data were reanalysed using Spearman rank order correlations, significances were often much higher.)

The only area affected was oracy, as is shown in Table 5.5. (All interviewees were used as there are many missing values in the oracy data – the correlations for the Australian educated alone were almost the same, but with reduced p values as a consequence of lower numbers). We have no explanation as to why paternal grandparents have more effect than maternal grandparents.

It is clear from Table 5.6 that the language used within the family is significantly related to oral proficiency. It is interesting to note that it is older siblings that affect younger siblings. Various authorities note that there is a tendency within migrant families for the second generation to

Table 5.6 Correlations between preference for Spanish (Item 3) and oral measures: Non-grandparents (Australian-educated only, $n = 84$)

		Mother	Father	Older siblings	Younger siblings	Cousins	Important other
Fluency	Corr	0.38	0.23	0.35	0.32	0.34	0.07
	p	0.0019	0.0649	0.0262	0.0740	0.0058	0.7083
Accent	Corr	0.36	0.36	0.39	-0.03	0.38	0.28
	p	0.0037	0.0030	0.0110	0.8726	0.0022	0.1185
Idiomaticity	Corr	0.48	0.30	0.40	0.25	0.45	0.31
	p	<0.0001	0.0152	0.0098	0.1594	0.0002	0.0802
Mixing	Corr	0.40	0.52	0.32	0.31	0.37	0.14
	p	0.0011	<0.0001	0.0384	0.0791	0.0026	0.4355
Total	Corr	0.49	0.43	0.45	0.26	0.47	0.23
	p	<0.0001	0.0004	0.0029	0.1416	<0.0001	0.2000
Missing values		21	21	43	51	22	51

speak the community language with older generations, but English with their peers. Older siblings can play a particularly important role in language shift by introducing English into the home environment of younger siblings. However, younger siblings do not have the same effect on the older siblings. These findings incidentally make causal flow clear, since presumably if it were language proficiency that affected the language used, there would be no difference between older and younger siblings. Since the 'significant others' use little Spanish, they do not seem to have a significant impact on the development of the language

In the case of the non-oral measures, the effect of grandparents was not significant, but language choice with other family members did correlate with the measures (Table 5.7).

In these findings, as in others, the reliability of the self-assessment measure is open to question, since it shares a subjective element with the contact measures. What it may show is that greater use of Spanish in the family increases confidence in using the language. This part of the research focused on the use of the spoken language, so it is predictable that there is no relationship on any contact measure with the basic literacy measure. The strong relationships between the use of Spanish with various family members and the other measures are of interest. It is clear that grammar and vocabulary, as measured by the C-test, are related to use of Spanish

Table 5.7 Correlations between preference for Spanish (Item 3) and proficiency measures: Australian-educated interviewees (*n* = 84)

		Mother	*Father*	*Older siblings*	*Younger siblings*	*Cousins*	*Important other*
Basic literacy	Corr	-0.17	-0.09	0.09	0.15	-0.03	0.00207
	p	0.1535	0.4586	0.5300	0.3827	0.8120	0.9905
C-test	Corr	0.25	0.13	0.44	0.18	0.42	0.16
	p	**0.0264**	0.2666	**0.0016**	0.2754	**0.0001**	0.3628
Cloze total	Corr	0.26	0.05	0.26	0.15	-0.06	0.09
	p	**0.0209**	0.6718	*0.0768*	0.3715	0.5963	0.6165
Self assessment	Corr	0.45	0.31	0.51	0.49	0.51	0.18
	p	**<0.0001**	**0.0063**	**0.0001**	**0.0013**	**<0.0001**	0.2964
Missing values		8	8	35	46	8	48

Table 5.8 Correlations between preference for Spanish (Item 3) and proficiency measures: All interviewees (n = 84)

		Mother	*Father*	*Older siblings*	*Younger siblings*	*Cousins*	*Important other*
Basic literacy	Corr	-0.10	-0.10	0.09	0.17	0.05	-0.08
	p	0.3215	0.3364	0.5202	0.2338	0.6222	0.5856
C-test	Corr	0.28	0.27	0.45	0.21	0.34	0.15
	p	**0.0057**	**0.0072**	**0.0003**	0.1297	**0.0006**	0.2853
Cloze total	Corr	0.28	0.13	0.31	0.13	-0.02	0.12
	p	**0.0052**	0.2156	**0.0177**	0.3410	0.8438	0.4015
Self assessment	Corr	0.46	0.35	0.61	0.49	0.44	0.20
	p	**<0.0001**	0.0004	**<0.0001**	**0.0001**	**<0.0001**	0.1579
Missing values		5	5	45	50	6	53

with family members. The use of Spanish with the mother is strongly related to proficiency in the language.

Because a sizeable proportion of our sample did not have older or younger siblings, the number of usable responses was low, so we repeated the analysis with the whole sample (Table 5.8).

In the larger sample, there is stronger evidence of the importance of language use with the father and older siblings. For this reason, in the remainder of this section, the whole sample will be used.

The association of scores on the register clozes with use of Spanish with the mother and older siblings may reflect literacy practices in the home – the mother and older siblings interacting with the younger siblings over Spanish texts.

The lack of influence of younger siblings on the Spanish of older siblings may indicate that older siblings tend to lead the shift to English in the home. Education for our interviewees takes place entirely in English, so it is more convenient to use English to refer to that educational experience. English is also the language of child culture (Opie & Opie, 1959) and of youth culture in Sydney – for instance the magazine *Viva* (which is targeted at young Australian Latinos, and describes itself as 'The only lifestyle Australian magazine about the Latino world') is written entirely in English. Our figures reflect this reality, since a possible interpretation of the results is that older siblings' language use influences that of younger siblings, and thereby influences their language proficiency, but that younger siblings do not exert such influence on older siblings. Again the 'important others' do not seem to have a significant impact on the development of the language.

In general the choice of Spanish rather than English with intimates is strongly related to oracy and general proficiency in Spanish.

Item 2: Frequency of contact

Another variable that seemed to play a role in language proficiency was the frequency of contact with people (see Item 2, above).

Beginning with grandparents, there is a majority (77.4%) of grandparents whom our interviewees 'almost never' meet (Table 5.9). In most cases we believe this is because the grandparents are resident overseas, mainly in the family's country of origin.

It should be noted that only 21 interviewees see their paternal grandparents more than once a year – 83 almost never see them. The figures for the maternal grandmother are stronger, but they are even worse for the paternal grandfather. These low levels of contact mean that there are insufficient interviewees who have regular contact with grandparents to allow us to uncover influence from them. In consequence there is no significant relationship between frequency of contact with grandparents and the results of the proficiency test. This holds true for all grandparents, and for any combination of grandparents. The lack of influence by grandparents on proficiency is probably a result of lack of contact. Studies of other communities where grandparents are in regular contact seem to show strong influence on the grandchildren's minority language proficiency.

Turning now to frequency of contact with other family members, and the 'other important person', Table 5.10 provides the raw data.

Table 5.9 Frequency of contact with grandparents

	Maternal grandmother	*Paternal grandmother*	*Maternal grandfather*	*Paternal grandfather*	*% of total*
Almost never	66	83	83	90	77.4%
More than once a year	9	4	10	1	5.8%
More than once a month	6	7	4	4	5.0%
More than once a week	11	4	6	2	5.5%
More than once a day	12	6	1	7	6.3%
Total	104	104	104	104	100%

Table 5.10 Frequency of contact with nuclear family members and important person

	Father	Mother	Older siblings	Younger siblings	Cousins	Important other
Almost never	5	0	3	0	48	2
More than once a year	1	0	0	0	7	2
More than once a month	1	0	2	0	28	7
More than once a week	6	0	9	0	17	22
More than once a day	91	104	50	54	3	21
Total	104	104	64	54	103	54

Contact with nuclear family members is very frequent, apart from 6 or 7 interviewees who appear to be separated from their fathers, and perhaps also from their older siblings. This means that there is little variation in the amount of contact with family members that can be used in statistical analysis. In fact, since all 54 interviewees saw their mother and younger siblings every day, in their case there was no variation at all. So only the variation in the language used or the pleasantness of the contact is likely to be statistically related to language proficiency. This was confirmed by preliminary analysis. The only likely exception was 'cousins' but no positive relationship was found here.

Items 6 and 7: Quality of contact

The next variable we wish to examine is the area of *quality* of contact, as measured by Items 6 and 7, on the importance and pleasantness of contact respectively. The correlations that follow are derived by adding the figures from the two measures, and using it as a variable in correlation analysis (the individual items reveal almost the same pattern, but the volume of data makes the tables difficult to read). Despite our predictions, the quality of contact with parents and grandparents did not reveal any relationship with language proficiency. Table 5.11 shows the effect of the quality of contact with the people mentioned upon the proficiency scores of our interviewees.

It appears that development of higher registers is related to the quality of the relationship with older siblings and the significant other, while basic

Table 5.11   Effects of quality of contact ($n = 104$)

		Basic literacy	C-Test	Register clozes	Self assessment	Missing values
Older siblings	p	0.4790	0.2208	**0.0395**	**0.0479**	45
	Corr	0.09	0.16	0.27	0.26	
Younger siblings	p	**0.0069**	0.4419	0.9343	0.3506	50
	Corr	0.36	-0.11	0.01	-0.13	
Cousins	p	**0.0421**	0.5132	0.2487	0.7340	6
	Corr	0.21	0.07	-0.12	0.03	
Other important person	p	0.7733	0.3209	**0.0320**	0.4533	53
	Corr	-0.04	0.14	0.30	0.11	

literacy is related to the quality of the relationship with younger siblings. This can be explained in part by the relative stage of language development of the contactee. Normally older siblings will be at a more advanced stage of language development than the interviewee, so quality contact with them could support development of high register. Friends are likely to be of a similar age, and they may even work on homework together, again fostering the development of academic language. In contrast, younger siblings are normally at a lower stage of language development, so contact with them may support only basic literacy. The topics discussed with cousins may not be primarily academic. The positive role played by the significant other is an unusual finding.

Combined contact variable: Language used and quality of contact

When we began this study, we intended to combine the three types of measure (language used, quantity and quality of contact) into a single contact measure. However, as we have seen, the quantity of contact varies little, so it is unlikely to contribute much to statistical analysis, rather it may muddy the waters. We therefore constructed a joint contact variable, by adding the responses of Items 6 and 7 (quality of contact) (giving a score out of 10) and multiplying them by the responses to Item 3 (the amount of Spanish used, doubled to also give a score out of 10).

This combined contact variable was then correlated with the proficiency measures. First the results for the oral measures are given in Tables 5.12 and 5.13 (grandparent figures were not significant). The full data set was used to avoid low numbers.

Table 5.12 Correlations of combined contact variable with oral measures: Nuclear family (*n* = 104)

	Mother		Father		Older siblings		Younger siblings	
	Corr	*p*	*Corr*	*p*	*Corr*	*p*	*Corr*	*p*
Fluency	0.36	**0.0006**	0.23	**0.0334**	0.46	**0.0006**	0.23	0.1126
Accent	0.26	**0.0145**	0.40	**0.0001**	0.53	**<0.0001**	0.02	0.8949
Idiomaticity	0.43	**<0.0001**	0.32	**0.0027**	0.60	**<0.0001**	0.22	0.1219
Mixing	0.43	**<0.0001**	0.47	**<0.0001**	0.38	**0.0052**	0.19	0.1911
Total	0.44	**<0.0001**	0.42	**<0.0001**	0.60	**<0.0001**	0.20	0.1712
Missing values	21		21		55		57	

Table 5.13 Correlations of combined contact variable with oral measures: Cousins and important other (*n* = 104)

	Cousins		*Important other*	
	Corr	*p*	*Corr*	*p*
Fluency	0.30	**0.0061**	0.07	0.6236
Accent	0.26	**0.0164**	0.19	0.1995
Idiomaticity	0.36	**0.0008**	0.30	**0.0402**
Mixing	0.36	**0.0007**	0.10	0.4820
Total	0.38	**0.0003**	0.19	0.2013
Missing values	21		21	

When a high quality of contact with intimates is combined with a preference for Spanish, it is very strongly related to Spanish oral proficiency. The exception here are the 'important others', simply because Spanish is rarely used with them. However, when Spanish is used we see a slight effect on idiomaticity.

Turning now to the other proficiency measures, these too reveal some relationship with the joint quality/language used variable. This is displayed in Tables 5.14 to 5.16.

The strong relationship between the self-assessment of Spanish proficiency and the contact measures is probably in part a result of the variation shared by subjective measures (in contrast to the other objective proficiency

Table 5.14 Correlations of combined contact variable with proficiency measures: Grandparents ($n = 104$)

	Maternal grandmother		*Paternal grandmother*		*Maternal grandfather*		*Paternal grandfather*	
	Corr	*p*	*Corr*	*p*	*Corr*	*p*	*Corr*	*p*
Basic literacy	0.06	0.5577	0.13	0.1907	0.06	0.5416	0.17	0.1027
C-test	0.05	0.6097	0.20	**0.0497**	0.03	0.7865	0.21	**0.0410**
Self assessment	-0.06	0.5493	0.20	**0.0490**	0.12	0.2327	0.28	**0.0049**
Span cloze total	0.03	0.7720	-0.13	0.1912	-0.03	0.7360	-0.11	0.2734
Missing values	7		7		7		7	

measures). It may also indicate that better contact with Spanish speakers enhances confidence in one's Spanish abilities.

Looking briefly at the individual results, the results on the C-test and self-assessment are significant for the paternal grandparents, but not for the maternal grandparents. We are not sure why this occurs. Contact with the mother and the older siblings is significantly related to the development of both grammar and vocabulary, and literate register, but contact with other family members affects vocabulary less. For the reasons we explored earlier, contact with younger siblings is related only to the development of basic literacy. Interestingly, the language used and the quality of contact with cousins is also a significant indicator of development of

Table 5.15 Correlations of combined contact variable with proficiency measures: Nuclear family ($n = 104$)

	Mother		*Father*		*Older siblings*		*Younger siblings*	
	Corr	*p*	*Corr*	*p*	*Corr*	*p*	*Corr*	*p*
Basic literacy	0.05	0.5897	-0.10	0.3445	0.10	0.4317	0.30	**0.0253**
C-test	0.29	**0.0040**	0.20	**0.0444**	0.44	**0.0004**	0.15	0.2753
Self assessment	0.46	**<0.0001**	0.33	**0.0008**	0.63	**<0.0001**	0.43	**0.0011**
Span cloze total	0.28	**0.0045**	0.14	0.1695	0.35	**0.0060**	0.11	0.4243
Missing values	7		7		47		57	

Table 5.16 Correlations of combined contact variable with proficiency measures: Cousins and important other ($n = 104$)

	Cousins		Important other	
	Corr	p	Corr	p
Basic literacy	0.12	0.2506	-0.12	0.4195
C-test	0.34	**0.0005**	0.15	0.2976
Self assessment	0.44	**<0.0001**	0.23	0.1075
Span cloze total	-0.08	0.4564	0.19	0.1769
Missing values	8		55	

grammar and vocabulary. This finding may be a signpost to use of Spanish outside the nuclear family.

Finally, we multiplied the frequency, quality and language use measures for each type of strong contact other than grandparents, and added them to give a total measure of strong Spanish contact. The results are in Table 5.17.

This affirms the general picture we have seen. It should be noted that the

Table 5.17 Correlation of total of strong contact with proficiency measures

Fisher's R to Z		
	Corr	p
Basic literacy	0.08	0.4523
C-test	0.27	**0.0086**
Self-assessment	0.40	**<0.0001**
History cloze	0.18	0.0841
Science cloze	0.20	0.0564
Spanish cloze total	0.21	**0.0420**
English cloze water	-0.18	0.0775
English cloze hibernation	-0.10	0.3267
English cloze total	-0.16	0.1158

Observations = 96; missing values = 8

correlation with the C-test is robust, indicating that strong contact aids the development of grammar and vocabulary. There is also some impact on the development of literate register as measured by the register clozes, probably reflecting the effect of the mother and older siblings just mentioned. Once more there is a strong relationship with self assessment of proficiency. The relationship with the English measures is not significant, but it is negative.

Conclusions

The questions asked in this survey examined three elements of contact with intimates – the language used, the frequency of contact, and the quality of contact. Although it seems likely that frequency of contact plays a role, the lack of variation on this parameter meant that it could not be analysed statistically. By far the most important variable in our analysis was the language used – whether Spanish or English was used more in the language contacts with intimates. Of less importance, but making a contribution, was the quality of these contacts. The correlations that emerge from this analysis are in many cases robust, which appears to support the general view that strong networks play an important role in language development and maintenance. They place a substantial weight in the scales. This affirms that families, even when there is little support from the wider social context, can play a significant role in maintaining a minority language.

However, although contact contributes to language development, it is only one in a range of factors. In essence, contact provides the *opportunity* for language development, but does not secure it. Other factors (such as the nature of language used in such contacts), other forms of contact with language (such as media and reading), and above all attitudes to the language (whether the opportunity to use it is warmly embraced, rejected, or something in between) also play their roles in the maintenance and loss of minority languages.

Distance Network Ties

We did not include this area as part of our original research design – an omission that in retrospect we would like to have corrected. At the time of the data collection email had not become widely used as a medium, but we suspect it would now play a significant role. Contact with family overseas can be a motive for maintaining Spanish, since some of these overseas contacts will be monolingual in Spanish, and the lack of Spanish proficiency is a barrier to communication. The responses to the open questions comment on the use of both oral and written distance communication with family and friends overseas as a significant use of Spanish.

Oral communication

#1 Q 28

escribo cartas a mi familia en espana.
I write letters to my family in Spain
WE ALSO CALL UP OUR FAMILY IN MEXICO WHEN THEY HAVE A
BIRTHDAY.

#1 Q29

EN EL TELEFONO CUANDO ABLO CON MI FAMILIA
on the telephone when I speak to my family

#4 Q 75

I NORMALLY TALK TO THEM OVER THE PHONE.

#1 Q43

hablo por teléfono con mis familiares
I speak with my relatives over the phone

manteniendo conversaciones telefonicas
having telephone conversation

Written communication

#1 Q98

les escribo a mis familiares en Australia en español –hermana, 37 años
I write to my family in Australia in Spanish – sister 37 years old

cuando escribo en espanol es mas frecuente cuando escribo a mi familia en
espana.
When I write in Spanish its more frequent when I write to my family in Spain

yo escribo a mis primos en espana por las vacaciones
I write to my cousins in Spain in the holidays

siempre escribo cartas a mi familia en espana
I always write letters to my family in Spain

I HAVE A PENPAL IN SPAIN AND I WRITE TO HER IN SPANISH.

solo escribo en espanol cuando escribo a la familia en espanol.
I only write letters in Spanish when I write to the family in Spanish.

TENGO AMIGOS HISPANOS EN PERU Y CANADA A QUIENES LES
ESCRIBO CARTAS EN ESPANOL . ESCRIBO UNA CARTA AL MES.
*I have Hispanic friends in Peru and Canada to whom I write letter in Spanish. I
write one letter a month.*

CUANDO RECIBO CARTAS DE PRIMO/AS DE COLOMBIA
When I get letters from cousins in Colombia

The writing of letters in Spanish is a literacy practice of the type
discussed in Chapter 6.

Weak Network Ties/Domains

Rather than attempt the type of detailed questioning that we examined for intimate relationships, we examined this area in terms of domains of use, such as visits to the doctor and cafés. As is usual in our research we used both open and closed questions.

Open questions

The opening question about this area was **#1 Q29 (#1 Q28**

#1 Q29 Speech Domains / Ámbitos de uso del idioma hablado

These questions are about the parts of your life where you use Spanish or English. In these questions, 'use' means either speak or listen.
Estas preguntas son acerca del uso del español o inglés en tu vida diaria. En estas preguntas el 'uso' se refiere a hablar o escuchar.

Where do you use Spanish?
¿En dónde usas el español?

There was also a closing question:

#1 Q43

Is there anything else you wish to say about where you use Spanish?
¿Quieres agregar algo más sobre donde hablas español?

There were also some replies to other questions relevant to this topic. Many of the responses to these items (not surprisingly) referred to areas of strong contact with parents, grandparents, siblings, friends and family overseas. These are discussed in the previous section, on strong contact. There was one general reference to Spanish domains.

si voy a un lugar que sea espanol pues hablo espanol
If I go to a place that is Spanish then I speak Spanish

One interviewee mentions use in the Spanish community generally:

hablo español en casa y con la comunidad española
I speak spanish at home and with the Spanish community

and use within Spanish community clubs and parties is also mentioned.

CLUB FAMILIAR
family club

el club espanol
the spanish club

club uruguayo
uruguayan club

En el club espanol
in the spanish club

CUANDO VOY AL CLUB URUGUAYO– LOS FIN DE SEMANAS.
When I go to the Uruguayan Club at the weekend
YES I USE SPANISH WHEN I GO TO SPANISH CLUB

fiestas del club espanol.
Spanish Club parties
at parties
en las fiestas Colombianas
at Colombian parties
SPANISH SOCIAL EVENTS
EN FIESTAS SURAMERICANAS
at South American parties
IN PARTIES,
I HAVE ALSO ENCOUNTERED SPANISH AT FAMILY GATHERINGS
WITH FRIENDS THAT ALSO SPEAK THE LANGUAGE.

There were two mentions of use of Spanish in Spanish-speaking nightclubs:
NIGHTCLUBS(SPANISH)
AT ALOT OF NIGHTCLUBS

and one in restaurants:
resturants

Some interviewees spoke of using Spanish when dancing (presumably folk or Latin American dance):
en el baile (danza española)
at dancing (spanish dancing)
DANCING
AEN EL GRUPO DE DANZAS
in the dances group
when iwas growing up i went to a dancing school where everyone spoke spanish even the teacher
i speak spanish in other places with family and friends especially at my dancing group [tierra colombiana].

One interviewee also mentions rehearsals ('el ensayo') but does not say for what. Another mentions basketball, but there were only two other mentions of sporting events:
SPORT ALSO.
SOCCER,

This small number of mentions surprised us since sports clubs (particularly soccer clubs) may be run by minority communities in Australia (as some were originally in Chile).

The use of Spanish in shops was mentioned a number of times:

voy a algunas tiendas en que hablo espanol
I go to some shops where I speak Spanish

cuando voy a un negocio donde hablan español
when I go to a shop where they speak Spanish

#1 Q51
SOME SHOPS I VISIT USE SPANISH, TEO CECINA, CASTRO, ETC
EN FAIRFIELD CUANDO VOY A LOS COMERCIOS
In Fairfield when I go to the shops
in ethnic shops.

There were also mentions of the use of Spanish in religious observance:

a veces hablo espanol en misas en la escuela
sometimes I speak Spanish in (Catholic) masses at school

YO USO ESPANOL CUANDO CONVERSO CON GENTE EN LA
COMUNIDAD DE LA IGLESIA EN QUE MI FAMILIA Y YO ASISTIMOS.
*I use Spanish when I talk to people in the community of the church that my family
and I attend*

One interviewee mentioned hearing people speaking Spanish in the street:

#1 Q51
CUANDO UNO ANDA POR LAS CALLES SE PUEDE ESCUCHAR A LA
GENTE HABLANDO EN ESPANOL
when one walks along the street people can be heard speaking in Spanish

Other comments have to do with media and music, discussed in Chapter 6.

'Secret language' use

One interesting sidelight from the open questions was that Spanish is used by our interviewees as a secret language (Halliday, 1978), so that they can speak without others understanding.

EN CLASE CON COMPANERAS PARA QUE LOS OTROS NO SEPAN QUE
DECIMOS
in class with classmates so that the others won't know what we're talking about

en la escuela cuando quiero que otras personas no entiendan
at school when I do not want other people to understand

i use it with my friends when i don't want the other person to know what i'm talking about

I TALK IN SPANISH WHENEVER I AM IN A BAD MOOD WITH A
TEACHER AT SCHOOL. BUT I DO NOT SWEAR IN SPANISH.

The closing question to this section on domains (**#1 Q44**) was:

Is there anything you want to say about these questions?
¿Quieres hacer algún comentario sobre estas preguntas?

Altogether, 98 interviewees answered 'no' or did not respond. There were four critical comments:

They need more detail.

I THINK THAT SOME OF THE QUESTIONS ARE IRRELEVANT. THE SAME QUESTIONS HAVE BEEN REPEATED SEVERAL TIMES.

THIS QUESTION SEEMED TO BE A BIT PERSONAL. AN EXAMPLE IS THE QUESTIONS ABOUT MY PARENTS WORK.

SOME OTHER QUESTION MAY BE ASSOCIATED WITH THE PERSONS WAY OF LIFE AND HOW IT INTERRACTS WITH THE LANGUAGE.

Four other comments were supportive:

Estan bien.
They are good

very interesting ones =)

INTERESTING

OJALA QUE SEAN MUY UTILES. MUY BUENAS PREGUNTAS.
I hope they will be very useful. Very good questions.

Closed questions

The closed questions followed the following format.

#1 Q30

Please pick one box which best says your answer.
Escoje el casillero que mejor refleje tu respuesta.

What language do you use outside of class with schoolmates (not ethnic school)?
¿Qué idioma usas con tus compañeros fuera de la clase (excluyendo la escuela étnica)?

5   almost always Spanish / casi siempre español
4   mostly Spanish / mayormente español
3   Span and English about equally/tanto español como inglés
2   mostly English / mayormente inglés
1   almost always English / casi siempre inglés

The same question was asked about the following possible interactions:

teachers at school (not ethnic school) / tus profesores/as en el colegio (excluyendo la escuela étnica)?
friends of your family / los amigos de tu familia?
neighbours / tus vecinos?
for shopping / cuando vas de compras?
at the doctors / cuando vas al médico?

The education questions were aimed at the use of Spanish in mainstream education. We also wished to see whether institutions such as ethnic clubs, churches, and cafés and restaurants had any impact. However, some of our interviewees would visit these little if at all, so a question concerning recency as well as language use was included, leading to a two-part question. (We wish to acknowledge the help of Gordon Wells and Rodrigue Landry in the construction of these questions.)

#1 Q36

How recently have you gone to a café or restaurant?
¿Cuándo fue la última vez que fuiste a un café o restaurante?

5   within the last 24 hours / en las últimas 24 horas
2   within the past week / en la última semana
3   within the past month / en el último mes
4   within the past year / en el último año
5   almost never / casi nunca

#1 Q37

What language do you use in cafés and restaurants?
Qué idioma usas cuando vas a un café o restaurante?

5   almost always Spanish / casi siempre español
4   mostly Spanish / mayormente español
3   Span and English about equally/tanto español como inglés
2   mostly English / mayormente inglés
1   almost always English / casi siempre inglés

The same format was used to ask about:

a church, synagogue or temple / la iglesia, sinagoga o templo?
a club, association or organisation / un club, asociación u organisación?

Results

The results of this section were somewhat disappointing. The basic statistics concerning the use of Spanish in Table 5.18 show clearly that Spanish is used little outside the home by those who were wholly Australian educated. Only with family friends is there much use of Spanish, and there is some use in churches/synagogues/temples and in clubs/associations/organisations.

These are important findings, because Fishman (1991, and elsewhere) has made a strong case that maintaining discrete domains for the use of minority languages is an important factor in their survival. This does not augur well for the maintenance of Spanish in this group.

The relationship between weak networks and oral proficiency in Table 5.19 is what one might predict (it is worth remarking at this point that the two types of data were entirely independent of each other). It does seem

Table 5.18 Use of Spanish in various domains (*n* = 84)

	Mean	*SD*	*Minimum*	*Maximum*
School mates	1.643	0.786	1	4
Teachers	1.298	0.773	1	5
Family friends	3.643	1.083	1	5
Neighbours	1.452	0.827	1	4
Shops	1.607	0.919	1	4
Doctor	1.833	1.325	1	5
Café & restaurant (language)	1.786	0.983	1	5
Church etc. (language)	2.643	1.510	1	5
Club etc. (language)	2.369	1.306	1	5

that in those areas of weak contact where Spanish is used, there is a relationship with oral proficiency.

We did not include in this analysis those interviewees who had been brought up in Spanish-speaking countries. When they were added, the same pattern emerged, but correlations were strengthened. These results show convincingly the relationship between use of Spanish in everyday life and the development of oral proficiency in the language.

Some weak correlations were also found between some of the other proficiency measures, and teachers, schoolmates and family friends and 'all weak ties', but significances were generally low. The picture was clarified somewhat by using less-demanding Spearman correlations (Table 5.20 – only significant correlations are shown).

The self-assessment figures probably reflect to some degree the interviewee's confidence in using Spanish in these domains. The only network ties that appear to influence grammar, vocabulary and basic literacy are those of schooling and family friends, and there is a case for viewing these as strong rather than weak network ties. This adds weight to Fishman's views of the importance of sustaining strong domains of use in both languages to support bilingualism. The association between the school domain and basic literacy is predictable. The teachers who use Spanish would be mainly teachers at Saturday/ethnic schools, despite the attempt in the question wording to avoid this. Overall the main effect of using more Spanish in various domains (as revealed by the correlation of the sum of the

Table 5.19 Correlations of oral measures with weak networks

	Fluency		Accent		idiomaticity		Mixing		Oral measures total	
	Corr.	p	Corr.	p	Corr.	p	Corr.	p	Corr.	p
Schoolmates	-0.03	0.8003	0.02	0.8823	-0.01	0.9074	-0.02	0.9042	-0.01	0.9090
Teachers	0.03	0.8263	0.18	0.1508	0.17	0.1830	0.21	0.0933	0.17	0.1685
Family friends	0.26	**0.0372**	0.31	**0.0109**	0.35	**0.0038**	0.29	**0.0184**	0.37	**0.0025**
Neighbours	-0.02	0.8619	0.13	0.3153	0.17	0.1739	0.01	0.9387	0.08	0.5190
Shopping	-0.02	0.9046	0.09	0.4933	0.14	0.2848	0.01	0.9611	0.06	0.6300
Doctors	0.18	0.1586	0.11	0.4062	0.16	0.2092	-0.10	0.4258	0.10	0.4107
Cafés & restaurants	0.00118	0.9926	0.14	0.2599	0.10	0.4229	0.07	0.5924	0.09	0.4744
Churches etc	0.15	0.2452	0.26	**0.0359**	0.25	**0.0478**	0.11	0.4052	0.23	0.0702
Clubs etc	0.00351	0.9780	0.04	0.7807	0.03	0.8108	0.09	0.4746	0.05	0.7074
All weak ties	0.14	0.14	0.29	**0.0190**	0.30	0.0147	0.15	0.2472	0.26	**0.0356**

Observation = 65; missing values = 19

Table 5.20   Spearman correlations of weak contacts with proficiency measures

	Basic literacy		C-test		Self assessment	
	Rho	p	Rho	p	Rho	p
Schoolmates	0.280	**0.0128**				
Teachers	0.277	**0.0139**	0.272	**0.0157**	0.286	**0.0092**
Family friends			0.346	**0.0021**	0.429	**<0.0001**
Cafés & restaurants – language used					0.263	**0.0165**
All weak ties					0.282	**0.0101**

Observations = 79; missing values = 5.

domain scores with self rating) is on confidence in using the language (as measured by self assessment, and on oral proficiency).

We entered the sums of the weak networks and the strong networks as independent variables into stepwise multiple regressions, with the C-test, cloze total and self assessment as dependent variables. In each case the strong network was entered as a significant variable, but the weak network was not. This affirms the general picture of strong network contacts being far more important than weak ones. Weak network ties place only small weights in the scales.

Time spent in Spanish-speaking countries

Since time spent in countries where a language is spoken usually provides large amounts of contact – indeed immersion – this contributor to contact is worth examining for its impact. It also a variable where directionality is not in question – our interviewees had little choice about visiting the source country with their parents, so the effect is one of the experience on the language, not the language on the experience.

In our sample 13 interviewees had never visited Spanish-speaking countries. There appears to be a natural division between the interviewees who have spent less than three years in a Spanish-speaking country, and the remainder. It is clear from Table 5.21 that the most have spent less than three years in a Spanish-speaking country.

Open questions

In their replies to **#1 Q28** concerning their life history, a number of inter-

Table 5.21 Time spent in a Spanish-speaking country

(a) All interviewees

Months	No.	Months	No.
0	13	40	1
1	5	48	2
2	2	49	2
3	1	50	1
4	3	60	3
5	3	68	1
6	1	72	6
8	1	73	3
9	1	76	1
12	10	82	1
14	2	108	3
15	2	114	3
21	1	120	2
24	17	132	1
36	13	144	1
Subtotal	75	*Subtotal*	*31*
		Total	**106**

(b) Australian-born interviewees

Months	No.	Months	No.
0	13	40	1
1	5	48	1
2	2	60	3
3	1	72	5
4	1	73	2
12	5	108	2
14	1	120	2
24	14	132	1
36	10	*Subtotal*	*17*
Subtotal	52		
		Total	**69**

viewees specifically mentioned residence in Spanish-speaking countries as affecting their knowledge of Spanish.

> when I went to Colombia I studied for a year, I learnt a lot there
>
> I was born in El Salvador and came at the age of nine so that was what influenced my Spanish.
>
> SOLO CUANDO ME FUI A ARGENTINA.
> *Only when I went to Argentina*
>
> i have gone to South America a few times because I have many relatives over there,
>
> I have visited Uruguay many times to see all my relatives over there. I have no relatives here, so I have to go to Uruguay if I want to see them.
>
> VISITANDO A MI FAMILIA EN EL ECUADOR 2 ANOS ATRAS
> *Visiting my family in Ecuador 2 years back*
>
> when i go to espana or estoy con familia
> *when I go to Spain or am with family*
>
> I went to school in Chile when II was ten years old.
>
> When we went to Ecuador & Argentina in 1993 I needed to speak Spanish
>
> en Argentina el español me posibilitó hablar con familiares, eso me hizo sentir la importancia/necesidad del español (escribir y hablar)
> *in Argentina Spanish made it possible for me to speak to my relatives, that made me aware of the importance/necessity of Spanish (speaking and writing)*
>
> HE VIVIDO EN UN PAIS EL CUAL LA LENGUA ES EL ESPANOL
> *I have lived in a Spanish speaking country*
>
> ALGUNOS AMIGOS DE HABLA HISPANA HAN VIAJADO Y HAN TRAIDO EXPRESIONES DE LUNFARDO
> *Some Spanish speaking friends have travelled and have brought back Lunfardo expressions*

There are two categories of experience reflected in these comments – pre-migration learning, and visits. The fact that these arose spontaneously without elicitation is evidence of the importance that the interviewees attach to them. The last comment is also interesting because it indicates freshening of the language pool by the visits of *others* to Spanish-speaking countries, and also it refers to the acquisition of non-standard language forms, in this case the Argentinian argot Lunfardo, which has many influences from Italian.

Closed questions

We noted earlier a flaw in our research design that did not allow us to isolate time spent in a Spanish-speaking country from education. In an attempt to get round this problem, when we limited our data to the Australian educated there was a Spearman correlation with the C-test (corrected

$\rho = 0.251$; $p = 0.0219$), but no relation to other measures, including oracy. These results would seem to support the common view that periods of residence in a country where a language is spoken to some degree affect grammar and vocabulary. However, as one might expect, residence without schooling seems to do little to enhance literate register, although it may encourage literacy practices, as we shall see when we come to this topic. The relative weakness of this effect may be a result of the problems with our data on this topic. However, it is noteworthy that this finding parallels that of the limited effect of residence in the Heidelberg Pidgin-Deutsch project discussed in the first part of this chapter, perhaps reaffirming the importance of quality rather than quantity of contact.

Conclusions

Methods

The methods used here proved their worth. The comments given by the interviewees in response to the open questions are a rich source of qualitative data. In general they affirm the closed questions, since they raise exactly the same issues. However, the open responses also provide additional and quite unpredictable information, such as the use of Spanish as a secret language, as well as a rounded portrayal of the interviewees' interpersonal contacts with Spanish speakers.

The closed questions were of value in that they gave quantitative information on the amount of our interviewees' contact, and also permitted correlations with the proficiency measures which gave a clear picture of what aspects of proficiency are associated with interpersonal contact, and the relative strength of different forms of contact. This was not possible using only qualitative data.

Findings

In general we found that network contact is associated with oral proficiency, grammar and vocabulary development, and confidence in using the language. As one would expect, oral interaction is associated most strongly with the development of oral proficiency, and has a limited impact on biliteracy. This is an important finding, because there has been a tendency in much bilingualism research to focus on the spoken language. Other approaches to biliteracy may be needed. In fact there were some tentative indications that home literacy practices, and the mother's language use may be associated with the development of basic literacy and literate register. These possibilities are examined using different data in the next chapter. The strong network ties were clearly of much greater importance than the weak ones.

Chapter 6

Education, Media Use and Literacy

THE ISSUES

Chapter 5 looked at the development and maintenance of the spoken form of two languages. This chapter has a complimentary focus – the written language, and more generally the issue of biliteracy.

The Nature of Biliteracy

Literacy is a complex and multifaceted phenomenon. In reading it involves an interactive relationship between recognition of the ideological base (including background knowledge) of both reader and writer, knowledge of text types or genres, language knowledge, and knowledge specific to the written language (such as sound–symbol relations, punctuation and pausing, whole word shapes and concepts of print). The interaction between these so-called top-down and bottom-up elements is mediated by a range of literacy skills and strategies. Writing is similar, but involves productive deployment of these, as well as motor skills. Beyond literacy abilities lie literacy practices and their role in society.

An in-depth survey of this fascinating but complex area is beyond the scope of a book such as this. We will therefore limit ourselves to outlining some major aspects and then relating these aspects to the biliteracy issues that they raise (references to other work are also provided, so that readers can explore issues further if they wish). Older definitions of literacy, and the origins of the word itself, are limited to the ability to produce and understand written texts. This definition is quite restrictive (literacy is understood more broadly in this book). This older view of literacy is also widely shared by members of the public. While almost everyone develops a spoken or signed language, a significant proportion of the world's population is not literate in this sense of being able to read and write. In developed countries between 5% and 15% of the population are estimated to be functionally illiterate. For most people literacy is acquired initially through formal education rather than through exposure and use like spoken language, although significant contributions may come from the home. This has meant historically that this type of narrowly defined literacy has been a central issue in a range of educational traditions including the Western, Islamic and Chinese.

Biliterate transfer

Some fifty years ago UNESCO became convinced (UNESCO, 1953) that it is easier to acquire initial literacy in one's mother tongue. The breakthrough to literacy, developing the understanding that marks on paper can represent the spoken language, is not always easy to achieve. This breakthrough will come more easily in the language the person knows best. This is a strong argument for beginning education in the mother tongue, and there is substantial evidence that where this is possible and practical, it is more effective (see for instance the various cases discussed in Coulmas, 1984).

Furthermore, if literacy can be easily transferred from the mother tongue to a majority language, this rather indirect route via mother-tongue literacy may be the more efficient way for minorities to acquire literacy in the majority language. In the following sections we will examine the potential for transfer of various aspects of literacy between languages, but there is a question as to whether this happens in fact. As long ago as the 1970s, research reported in Skutnabb-Kangas (1981) demonstrated that children from Finnish-speaking homes in Sweden performed substantially better in Swedish if their home language was supported. Cummins has been a significant figure in developing what he calls the 'linguistic interdependence hypothesis' (Cummins, 1979). Cummins and his associates have performed substantial research in this area, working with both Japanese and Portuguese-speaking children in Canada. Cummins *et al.* (1987) showed that maintenance of Portuguese in Canada supported the development of English as a second language. Cummins' theories also include the notion that literacy and the language of schooling in particular develop more rapidly in a second language if they are developed initially in the mother tongue. Similarly, Cummins and Nakajima (1987) found a strong association in a sample of Japanese heritage students between the development of literacy in Japanese, and the development of literacy in the second language – English. Landry and Allard (1991) likewise write 'educational support in the mother tongue was found to be an essential factor in the promotion of an additive type of bilingualism for the minority Francophone students'. Cummins (1984) also makes the point that children who have been educated in the mother tongue before migration and have attained substantial literacy appear to do better in school. With regard to writing, Edelsky (1982) found that children in an elementary school bilingual programme applied what they knew of writing in their mother tongue to writing in the second language. Concerning more advanced writing skills, Jones and Tetroe (1984) found that writers transferred the planning process from their first language to their second. The substantial literature on language transfer (see, for example, Gass & Selinker, 1983) seems to show that, while there is only limited transfer of low level lexico-grammatical form from one language to another, higher level and more abstract areas of language behaviour may transfer. Even in the less ideal situation where initial literacy is acquired in the second language, there is still the possibility of transfer to literacy in the mother tongue. In order to develop fuller model of literacy, we will now examine various aspects of literacy and will briefly note their potential for transfer.

Basic literacy

Basic literacy initially entails grasping the notion that language can be realised in a graphological as well as a phonological form (sometimes referred to as the 'concept of print'). It also involves developing a concept of oneself as a writer/reader. This might be called the initial breakthrough. Simultaneously with the 'breakthrough' a reader/writer must learn the written symbols by which language is graphologically realised. Alphabetic writing systems are parasitic on the phonological form, but mainly ideographic systems, such as Chinese or early Egyptian hieroglyphs, mostly are not. Nevertheless, both alphabetic and modern ideographic systems involve the literate in recognising links between sounds and symbols, between spoken words and whole word symbols/symbol clusters, and between information structure and punctuation/format/graphic conventions.

In most European languages that use the Roman alphabet (including English and Spanish), the written form represents an earlier rather than a current pronunciation. In English this difference is highly marked, and the writing is to some degree inconsistent even historically. In Spanish the written form corresponds much more consistently to the spoken, as one interviewee wrote:

that i notice that spanish is really easy to read or sound out the word

However, written Spanish maintains features that have been lost in most varieties of the spoken language, such as initial *h-*, the contrast between *b* and *v*, and in South American and Southern Spanish varieties the contrast between *s, z* and soft *c* (all pronounced [s]). Those areas where there is a lack of correspondence between pronunciation and writing commonly cause both comprehension and spelling problems.

Turning to the issue of biliteracy, once the initial breakthrough is achieved, it applies to other languages. Where the two languages involved use the same alphabet, this knowledge transfers from one language to the other. However, the phonological value of the letters is not identical across languages. In languages that share the Roman alphabet, the rough correspondence between the sounding out of letters, as well the close similarity in the use of punctuation and format, means that basic literacy in such languages has a high degree of transferability, although the transfer is not problem free.

The development of biliteracy is made more difficult if two different alphabetic scripts are involved – for example the subcontinental child learning both the Roman and the Devanagari or Arabic scripts. The learner can transfer the understanding of a correspondence between letter and sound, but the letters used are different. This difficulty is increased for people who wish to be biliterate in languages where one is alphabetic and the other is mainly ideographic (for instance German and Chinese). In this case, transfer of basic literacy is limited to concepts of print, particularly the understanding that symbols can represent sounds, and some punctuation and formatting correspondences (a German reader may be able recognise which parts of a Chinese newspaper are advertisements, lead stories, headlines, readers' letters and editorials on the basis of their format). Nevertheless as we noted earlier, Cummins and Nakajima (1987) found considerable flow through from Japanese literacy to English.

Background knowledge

This term is used to denote both cultural and real-world knowledge. The process of writing and reading involves in part an attempt by the writer to have the reader share some element of his/her world view, whether real or imagined (perhaps one's world view is always somewhere in between). This emerges from the total world view of the writer, and to make sense must fit to some degree with world view of the reader. To give an obvious example, if the text that mediates between writer and reader consists of instructions on how to use a washing machine, it will not be intelligible to a reader who has no concept of a washing machine (unless it includes far more of the writer's knowledge base than a text written for a culture where washing machines are taken for granted). In some older references on literacy this is referred to as the issue of 'knowledge schemas'. But this term can be somewhat misleading since persuasive texts may try to get the reader to view existing knowledge in a new way, and likewise educational texts may attempt to have readers reconfigure and reconceptualise existing information.

However, our knowledge base includes conflicting understandings of reality, and most people (other than fanatics) live with this form of uncertainty, even though their understandings of the world are loosely systematic. Reading for basic meaning can involve an attempt to grasp the writer's world view without necessarily integrating this into one's own world view. Critical literacy involves matching the writer's world view against the reader's world view to reveal disagreements. It may also involve the attempt to uncover the writer's world view and assumptions, in part by unpacking the linguistic means used, as well as by readers examining their own world view in the light of the text.

It is this aspect of literacy that licenses such expressions as 'television literacy' where the viewer is encouraged to examine the values that underlie a programme, and the techniques used to put them across.

Effective communication (in speech or writing) demands an understanding of the communication partner's world view (remembering that any two human cultures will have substantial shared areas or common ground). This means that biliterates need an understanding of the cultural communities with which they communicate. This need not involve fully integrating and accepting two world views, but does require an understanding and ability to operate within them. In summary, to this limited extent, biliteracy requires biculturalism.

In so far as transfer is concerned, there will be shared knowledge in bilingual contexts, and more importantly the skill of deploying that knowledge to enable both reading and writing can be transferred.

The consequences of different resources

The two modes, speech and writing, are very different in their communicative possibilities. Speech is far richer, in having a wide range of non-verbal resources including (perhaps most importantly) intonation, but also overall pitch, loudness, syllable length, pace, voice qualities (such as croaky or laughy), and non-verbal segments (umms, intakes of breath, teeth-sucking and so on). The equivalents in spoken language are variations in font such as italics, bold and underlining, font size and overall text layout, but these resources communicate much less than their oral equivalents.

While the written form suffers from expressive deficits, it has powerful advantages. It developed initially as a means of storing information – it is no accident that the earliest cuneiform writings are records of the storage and exchange of goods. While orate societies often have extraordinarily-developed techniques for memorisation of oral text, the volume of information and the stability of that storage are greatly enhanced by writing. The volume of storage has subsequently expanded exponentially with the development of new technologies (Ong, 1982), firstly with the development of the printing press, and subsequently with electronic storage. For the literate, access to this information can be much easier than consulting human memories of text – see for instance Haley's (1976) description of consulting a 'griot'. This whole notion of independent storage of text means that writing need be only loosely connected to the context in which it was composed – reduced 'context embedding' in linguistic terms.

While it is possible to store longer texts in oral form (the *Iliad*, the Norse sagas and earlier parts of *The Bible* were probably all originally oral texts), the nature of the writing process makes it far easier to plan text, move chunks long distances within a text, and revise extensively. Therefore, as we saw in Chapter 2, written texts can more readily be planned and carefully and coherently constructed. Linguists, particularly Halliday (1985), have noted the continuum, running from least planned and highly contextualised to most planned and context reduced: the 'mode continuum' discussed in Chapter 2. In Chapter 2 we also noted the linguistic consequences of the fact that written language need not be produced in real time, which leaves an opportunity for editing.

Other aspects of written texts, particularly those used for schooling, as mentioned in Chapter 2, are first that the language tends to be impersonal, since it is often written for people whom the writer does not know personally. Second, it may be specialised, involving concepts that are not part of everyday knowledge or everyday language. These two aspects are known as 'tenor' and 'field' respectively in Hallidayan register analysis.

This register notion extends our understanding of literacy beyond the comparatively low-level mastery of the graphological system, and narrows the focus of 'applied background knowledge'. The language knowledge involved in literacy extends beyond grammar and vocabulary to the particular type of language used for literacy purposes, in other words the written register.

Mastery of register, particularly mode, is acquired slowly and with increasing difficulty as the language comes less and less to resemble the conversational form. It is also deeply implicated in educational practice, not only because literacy is a core educational concern in its own right, but also because formal education includes the transmission and reproduction of knowledge in written form. This type of literacy is therefore crucial for effective education, and is usually a product of it.

Biber (1988) has shown that similar contextual demands and constraints have produced similar outcomes across languages, but with some differences produced by the differences between the grammatical resources available in different language, as we saw in Chapter 2. For the biliterate, this means that the more abstract underpinnings of register are transferable, but the detailed lexico-grammatical resources involved will have to be learned in both languages. There is evidence that the learning of literate register in the mother tongue assists its development in the other language (Cummins & Nakajima, 1987), perhaps by transfer at this abstract level. In the research discussed in this book, one major objective is to explore the degree to which our Hispanic teenagers acquire register aspects of literacy in two languages.

Genres

There is one other aspect of literacy that merits attention here. Part of the planning of texts involves the sequencing of elements so that the text can do its job. In a narrative, this means that the 'story line' must be presented in a way that the reader can grasp. In an argument text, planning involves the logical sequencing of points. Over time, cultures tend to develop a consensus on the best way to sequence elements to attain a particular end (within the framework of the culture and contextual physical constraints). These structured text types are often referred to as 'genres'. Christie (1990: 3) writes 'To be literate in the contemporary world is to understand the very large range of written forms, text types or – as I shall call them here, *genres* – which we all need for both the reading and writing essential to participation in the community'. Genres are particularly useful for organising written or spoken texts, and for prediction when reading or listening. Although genres are not universal, in bilingual contexts many are likely to be shared.

Skills and strategies

There is a range of skills and strategies that make effective reading and writing possible. These include prediction and planning, skimming and scanning, making inferences, and whole-to-part and part-to-whole checking of comprehension and comprehensibility. They also include the conscious (rather than unconscious) deployment of some of the elements of literacy already discussed.

For the biliterate these elements are not identical from one language to another, but they are very similar, so they can be transferred with minor adaptation rather than fresh learning.

Literacy practices

This was a major area of research activity in the 1990s (see particularly Baynham, 1995). In contradiction of previous understanding, it was shown that reading and writing are often joint activities rather than individual activities. For instance members of a family may jointly reach an understanding of a newspaper article and their reaction to it, if sections are read aloud and discussed. Likewise the production of a letter may involve a number participants contributing to and jointly negotiating its content and wording. This type of process needs to learned – it is an aspect of literacy in its own right. But it is also an apprenticeship into other aspects of literacy, such as understanding, handling and developing a critical approach to background knowledge issues and decoding and producing formal written register. Indeed, it is probably literacy practices that offer the greatest possibility outside formal education of acquiring literate register: both joint and individual practices provide natural contexts for their development.

In a context (particularly a home or educational context) where two languages are in use in literacy practices, this provides a supportive environment for the learning of literacy practices in both languages, and for the development of other aspects of literacy through them. In a minority-language context, there may be problems with this, however. There can be no guarantee of high levels of literacy in either the minority language or the majority language in bilingual communities, so these contexts may be absent. A more likely scenario for second-generation descendants of migrants is that older family members are dominantly literate in the minority language. Moreover, the literacy resources needed for literacy practices in the minority language may be in short supply – for instance, it may be difficult to obtain common home literacy resources such as cookbooks or teenage magazines in the minority language.

If bilingual education is available (see below) literacy practices in two languages are likely. If a monolingual education in a majority language is provided to minorities, then exposure to certain types of literacy practice in the language of education is probable, but informal literacy practices in the majority language are not so likely. The minority language may have the reverse profile – a lack of formal literacy practices, but use of informal ones. The implications of this for the development of formal and informal register are evident, although there is no direct mapping (informal practices may be applied to formal registers, and vice versa). Literacy practices may be to some extent language specific (the practices involved in Quranic study, for instance), but most should be transferable. Their deployment to the languages involved will be a critical variable in the development of biliteracy.

The Role of Education

One of our major concerns, the development of higher register, will occur primarily through use of the language as an educational medium. For other reasons, education is a significant factor, since a substantial proportion of language contact during the critical years for language development (childhood and adolescence) takes place at school: it would be difficult to over estimate the importance of this form of language contact. This means that careful analysis of educational language use is needed, language both as medium and as a curriculum subject. A full understanding of educational language contact includes the language used both inside and outside the classroom, between students, between students and teachers, and in educational media of all types. One would also need to consider all forms of education, primarily mainstream education, but also extra-curricular study such as evening schools, private lessons, and bodies such as the Goethe Institute or the Instituto Cervantes.

There is substantial evidence that the educational medium is one of the most effective means of promoting bilingualism and particularly biliteracy – witness in particular the remarkable successes of Canadian immersion education (Swain & Lapkin, 1982; Genesee 1987). In more traditional minority situations it can also be highly effective (Lindholm-Leary, 2001). But there is also considerable evidence that poor bilingual education (like any poor education) is ineffective, both as a means of producing bilingualism in students and as a way of promoting their learning of other subjects such as science or geography (Cziko, 1992). One of the factors that distinguishes good from poor bilingual education is the type of language experience that the education provides. Some forms of bilingual education do not provide substantial amounts of education in the weaker language, or do not make the contact comprehensible and engaging for the learner. This may occur in classrooms where the teacher mixes or alternates the two languages to the point where only one if them is needed for comprehension (Wong Fillmore, 1985), so the other is largely ignored. Wong Fillmore (1985) also mentions classrooms where one language is used mainly for classroom management rather than for core learning. This may in effect be bi-orate but monoliterate. Neither of these forms of contact is likely to produce the potential register and literacy results that come from use as an educational medium. With regard to use outside the classroom, Baetens Beardsmore (1995: 60–64) describes the particular value for language acquisition of student–student interaction. To summarise therefore, the use of a language within education can provide substantial support for that language(s), and the development of literacy in it. Bilingual education can be a major factor in the development of biliteracy.

Media

There are means of language acquisition and maintenance that do not involve face-to-face contact. For instance one of the authors stayed with a multilingual Rumanian doctor who had achieved a working knowledge of English almost entirely through watching cable television. As one would predict, his comprehension was far better than his productive capacity, but he could communicate. Some forms of media are presented in Figure 4.11 in Chapter 4.

The capacity to use distance communication and media is often referred to as 'literacy', as in 'computer literacy' and 'media literacy'. When the word is used in an unmodified form, it normally refers to the ability to understand and produce written language, mainly in print media. The ways in which people engage with print media are can be analysed in terms of literacy practices.

THE STUDIES

Our interviewees, as we shall see below, have not had the benefit of bilingual education; the Australian-educated have been educated entirely in English, so a major concern in the area of language maintenance is the degree to which they have developed literacy in Spanish. Our proficiency measures in particular look at basic literacy and the development of literate register – Cummins' cognitive academic language proficiency, the development of which has not been extensively studied in minority languages. The factors that might play a role in the development of literacy in Spanish include education (particularly any formal education through the medium of Spanish), the study of Spanish in mainstream schooling, and the study of Spanish at an ethnic/Saturday school. Other possible influences are the use of written media and home literacy practices and resources. These will be examined in turn for their influence. We also include in this chapter other forms of non face-to-face contact in the form of media such as radio, television and film.

Spanish-medium Education

In Chapter 4 we observed that our sample included some teenagers who had been educated in a Spanish-speaking country. These are the only interviewees who had experience of Spanish-medium education, since none of our interviewees had experienced Spanish-medium education in Australia, reflecting the paucity of bilingual education in this country, particularly in New South Wales (see Gibbons, 1997). Before the time of data collection there had been one bilingual Spanish/English programme in New South Wales (in Sacred Heart Catholic Primary School, Cabramatta; since discontinued), but none of our interviewees had attended it. It is difficult therefore to separate the effects of residence in a Spanish-speaking country, and the effects of educational medium.

Open questions

Only one interviewee (in response to **#1 Q28**) mentioned studying through the Spanish medium:

when I went to Colombia I studied for a year, I learnt a lot there

Closed questions

A likely interpretation of these figures is that the partly Spanish-educated students in general have much more confidence in their Spanish ability than the wholly Australian-educated.

Exploring this more, we examined the number of months over the age of 5 years spent in a Spanish-speaking country, which is a rough indicator of months of Spanish-medium education. This figure was then correlated with various of the proficiency measures (using Spearman correlations, since the data were strongly ranked), see Table 6.1.

The results in Table 6.1 provide evidence of the effectiveness of the educational medium in producing control of more literate aspects of Spanish. It is noticeable that the correlations are stronger with the Spanish register and grammar measures, and less strong with basic literacy and oral proficiency – the reverse of the effects of the teaching of Spanish described below. The relationship with English proficiency may reflect the phenomenon discussed earlier in this chapter (see for example Cummins, 1984),

Table 6.1 Basic statistics on the relative Spanish self ratings of the two groups

	Partly Spanish educated	*Australian educated*
Mean	82.000	65.863
Standard deviation	15.057	14.667
Standard error	3.367	1.600
Count	20	84
Minimum	42.5	32.5
Maximum	100	100
Missing	0	0

Table 6.2 Spearman rank correlations: Months of education in a Spanish-speaking country prior to migration by tests

	Basic literacy	C-test	Spanish cloze total	Oral total	English cloze total
Sum of squared differences	119655.0	111704.5	128011.5	71053.5	127154.0
ρ	0.303	0.349	0.336	0.353	0.259
p	**0.0024**	**0.0005**	**0.0006**	**0.0011**	**0.0095**
Missing values	5	5	1	19	5

that minority-language children who have a firmly established mother tongue generally obtained a higher level of proficiency in their second language.

The Study of Spanish in Mainstream Education

Of our 59 Australian-born interviewees, 29 (one half) had received no Spanish-language instruction at school, and another 11 had received less than one year of Spanish-language instruction. In other words 68% of our sample had received little or no formal Spanish instruction at school, and nearly all substantial instruction had been obtained during periods outside Australia. Only one interviewee, in response to **#1 Q29**, mentioned.

At school I use Spanish in Spanish class

This lack of support for minority languages in mainstream education is normal in New South Wales. Spanish instruction in school therefore had little effect on the Spanish of our Australian educated interviewees. The only significant correlation, interestingly, was with basic literacy (correlation = 0.33; p = **0.0023**; observations = 80; missing values = 4), which corresponds to the primary school stereotype of instruction in basic spelling and writing skills.

The Study of Spanish in Ethnic/Saturday Schools

There is a system of so-called 'ethnic' or Saturday schools in Australia, funded by the federal government, where minority-language students of both primary and secondary school age can obtain minority language instruction.

Open questions

Many of the interviewees mentioned Saturday school as an important influence upon their Spanish proficiency. In answer to **#1 Q28** (Is there anything else in your life history that may have affected your knowledge of Spanish and English?), these were some of the comments.

GOING TO SATURDAY SCHOOL HELPS BECAUSE I USE SPANISH WITH SCHOOL MATES]

I also learn Spanish at Saturday school (Liverpool Girls H/S) for two hours

ATTEND SATURDAY SCHOOL OF LANGUAGES (SPANISH)

LOS SABADOS.
Saturdays.

However, not all the comments were positive – in the following comments one interviewee expresses the alienation caused by being forced to attend Saturday school.

MAMA ME QUITA LAS GANAS PORQUE ME SIENTO OBLIGADO A IR LOS SABADOS A ESCUELA
Mum takes away my motivation because I feel obliged to go to school on Saturdays.

In answer to **#1 Q29** (Where do you use Spanish?) a large number of interviewees mentioned Saturday school. Some of the comments follow.

CON AMIGOS DE HABLA HISPANA (ESCUELA DE ESPANOL)
With Spanish speaking friends (Saturday School)

en ashfield en una clase de espanol para el hsc
in ashfield in a spanish class for the hsc [Higher School Certificate]

en la escuela espanol
in spanish school

en casa y escuela de espanol
at home and spanish school

en el colegio de espanol
in spanish school

en la escuela de espanol.
in spanish school.

every saturday at spanish school

I ALSO USE SPANISH WHEN I'M AT SPANISH SCHOOL.

In answer to **#1 Q79** some interviewees added:

I USE SPANISH ... AT SPANISH SCHOOL WITH MY CLASSMATES AND TEACHER.

I MOSTLY USE SPANISH WHEN I AM AROUND SPANISH SPEAKING FAMILY AND FRIENDS AND WHEN I ATTEND SPANISH SCHOOL

SOLO EN CASA Y EN EL COLEGIO DE ESPANOL.
Only at home and in Spanish school.

In answer to **#1 Q98** on literacy practices:

I READ AND WRITE SPANISH WHEN I AM AT SPANISH CLASS ON SATURDAYS.

MY READING AND WRITTING SKILLS HAVE VASTLY IMPROVED BOTH IN ENGLISH AND SPANISH THANKS TO THE SPANISH CLASSES I HAVE BEEN TAKING.

COMO YO ME CRIE EN AUSTRALIA ME DEMORO UN POCO PARA LEER Y HABLAR ESPANOL,AUNQUE EN COLEGIO DE ESPANOL ME A AYUDADO.
As I was raised in Australia I was a bit late in reading and speaking Spanish, although Spanish school has helped me.

Closed questions

Altogether, 72 interviewees had received little or no instruction in this manner (children may drop out after minimal attendance). The figures for years of attendance are in Table 6.3.

Attendance at Spanish Saturday school seems to strongly benefit basic literacy, and to a lesser extent oracy, and grammar/vocabulary, as is shown

Table 6.3 Ethnic / Saturday school attendance (*n* = 106)

Years of attendance	Number of interviewees
1	1
2	1
3	3
4	2
5	4
6	7
7	4
8	5
9	4
10	2
11	1
Total	**34**
Missing	72

in Table 6.4, which displays the correlations between the amount of ethnic school Spanish instruction and scores on the tests discussed in Chapter 3.

There is no relationship with the acquisition of higher register proficiency as measured by the Spanish register tests. This conforms to a pattern in which language instruction generally does not affect the acquisition of academic register unless it is specifically designed to do so. Saturday schools have their strongest effect on basic literacy, and a lesser effect on grammar and vocabulary as measured by the C-test. We note that the effect on oracy is mainly greater fluency and less mixing, rather than improved accent. This may have implications for the curriculum of Saturday schools. It is interesting to note that English proficiency measured on one of the tests is also related to attendance at Saturday school, confirming a general

Table 6.4 Correlations of ethnic/Saturday school attendance with various language measures (Australian-educated interviewees only)

	Corr	*p*
English cloze: water	0.28	**0.0181**
English cloze: hibernation	0.09	0.4527
English cloze total	0.22	0.0718
Basic literacy	0.45	**<0.0001**
C-test	0.30	**0.0108**
Self rating	0.12	0.3265
Spanish history cloze	0.08	0.5206
Spanish science cloze	0.01	0.9507
Spanish cloze total	0.05	0.6726
Oral fluency	0.34	**0.0114**
Oral accent	0.16	0.2477
Oral idiomaticity	0.23	0.0910
Oral mixing	0.32	**0.0176**
Oral total	0.33	**0.0152**

Observations = 69; missing values = 15.
Oral measures: observations = 54; missing values = 30

pattern of relatedness of English and Spanish proficiency. When the whole sample was used, some of the p-values increased owing to the larger sample size, but the correlation coefficient mostly decreased, showing that ethnic schools are more important for the Australian-educated than for those who migrated later in life.

Literacy Practices

The objective of this part of the interview was to discover how often various literacy practices occurred that might involve the use of Spanish, and to discover which language (Spanish or English) was used.

Open questions

The opening and closing open questions about media use were the following.

#1 Q44 Media / Medios de comunicación
These questions are about the media you use in Spanish and English.
Estas preguntas son acerca de los medios de comunicación en español e inglés que utilizas.

Through what media (radio, tv etc) have you mainly encountered Spanish?
¿A través de qué medio de comunicación has tenido más contacto con el español? (radio, tv, etc)

#1 Q51
Is there anything else you wish to say about where you have encountered Spanish?
¿Quieres agregar algo más acerca de los contextos en que has sido expuesto al español?

These questions elicited some comments on print media. The number of mentions of specific print media were:

- newspapers: 26
- magazines: 7
- books: 3

Specific comments of interest are given below.

Newspapers

#1 Q44
MI ABUELITA ME LE DE SU PERIODICO ESPANOL
my grannie reads to me from her Spanish newspaper
A TRAVES DE LIBROS Y PERIODICOS EN ESPANOL *through books and newspapers in Spanish*

#1 Q51
EN EL DIARIO ESPANOL QUE MIS PADRES COMPRAN
In the Spanish newspaper that my parents buy

Books/Magazines

A TRAVES DE LIBROS Y PERIODICOS EN ESPANOL
through books and newspapers in Spanish

#1 Q51
en libros de leccion que me mandan mis tios.
In reading books that my aunts and uncles send me.
libros
books
LECTURA DE LIBROS
reading books

Other

#1 Q51
POR MEDIO DE LA COMPUTADORA
by means of the computer.
IN LETTERS ,
juego con cartas espanolas e inglesas
Spanish and English card games

The last comment may be a reference to fantasy gaming using cards, which are popular among some teenagers in Sydney. As with speaking, some interviewees commented on the need to write Spanish to Spanish monolinguals.

#1 Q85
To write messages to people who only read Spanish.

After the closed question on literacy practices, there an open question asking for additional comments. There were a number of comments about writing letters to family – these are quoted in the section on 'Distance Network Ties' in Chapter 5. The following are some other comments, many of them to do with proficiency in literacy.

#1 Q85
tengo que leer novelas de espanol este ano para la escuela.
I have to read novels in Spanish this year for school.
I READ AND WRITE SPANISH IN SPANISH SCHOOL,AND I TEND TO READ A BIT OF SPANISH AT HOME.
en cartas a mi famila
in letters to my family

EN REALIDA NO ME ATREN MUCHO LOS LIBROS PERO CADA VEZ QUE HE LEIDO UNO EN ESPANOL ME DESPIERTA UN SENTIMIENTO ESPECIAL . CAPAS POR QUE ES MI PRIMERA LENGUA Y LOGRO ENTENDER CON MAS DETALLES Y FACILIDAD PERO PRINCIPALMENTE POR QUE ENTIENDO O ME IDENTIFICO AT SATURDAY SCHOOL

I really don't like books much but every time that I have read a book in Spanish it arouses a special feeling. [Perhaps?] because it is my first language and I can understand in more detail and more easily, but mainly because I understand or I identify more at Saturday School.

READING SPANISH IS HARD ASWEL BECAUSE I SOMETIMES SAY IT IN AN ENGLISH MANNER.

I'M VERY SLOW IN WRITING AND READING IN SPANISH

I STARTED READING A BOOK IN SPANISH BUT IT GETTING HARDER SO EVENTUALLY I STOPPED.

I find that I can read pretty well in Spanish but my spelling is awful.

usually the books read are for school purposes.

LEO LAS NOVELAS EN ESPANOL DEL COLEGIO.

I read books from school in Spanish.

CUANDO TENGO QUE ESCRIBIR ALGO SOBRE ALGO EN ESPANOL.

when I have to write something about something in Spanish.

Once again these comments give a rich picture of Spanish use.

Closed questions

The two aspects, the frequency of use of literacy practices and the language used, could not easily be covered in a single question for each possible literacy practice. During consultation with Gordon Wells, the possibility developed of a two-part structure for each literacy practice: a question concerning the recency of the literacy practice, and a second question concerning the balance between the languages in the use of the literacy practice. Furthermore, in discussion with Rodrigue Landry, the point was raised that a question framed in the form of 'how often do you ...' is considerably more vague than a question framed as 'when did you last ...' which involves the memory of the most recent use. Any accidental recent uses would be washed out in a fairly large data set such as that discussed here. The form of the questions is shown below, with the score to the left.

*Sample question: Recency of literacy practices (**Item 1**)*

How **recently** have you consulted an **encyclopaedia**?
¿Cuando fue **la última vez** que consultaste una **enciclopedia**?

5   in the last 24 hours / en las últimas 24 horas
4   in the last week /en la última semana
3   in the last month / en el último mes

2   in the last year / en el último año
1   almost never / casi nunca

Sample questions: Language of literacy practices (Item 2)

Which language do you use most often to consult an **encyclopaedia**?
¿En qué idioma están las **enciclopedias** que más consultas?

5   almost always Spanish / casi siempre español
4   mostly Spanish / mayormente español
3   Spanish and English about equally/tanto español como inglés
2   mostly English / mayormente inglés
1   almost always English / casi siempre inglés

The overall results for the recency of individual literacy practices are given in Table 6.5.

The means shown in Table 6.5 for the Australian-educated and those with overseas education are for all items within 0.1 of the means for the total sample, showing that the recency of literacy practices is not significantly different between Australian-educated and overseas-educated interviewees.

It can be observed from these figures that the most common literacy practices are reading stories to Spanish speaking children, reading comics, and writing letters or cards.

These figures reveal that there are few literacy practices where Spanish is used to any substantial extent. Most literacy events occur almost always in English, particularly the reading of encyclopaedias, religious texts, comic fiction, library books, the use of computers and diary writing. The maximum figures show that there are some literacy practices which not even the interviewees educated in a Spanish-speaking country perform primarily in Spanish, particularly library and computer use, and to a lesser degree the use of encyclopaedias. These probably reflect the relative availability of these resources. In Australia access to computer programs and Internet links, library books and encyclopaedias will be predominantly in English. Even in Spanish-speaking countries, people sometimes work in English on computers.

Narrowing down to the Australian-educated interviewees, Figure 6.1 is a chart that shows the ranking of the means shown above. The top six literacy practices in the chart, where Spanish is more likely to be used, are all socially interactive, while the bottom ten literacy practices, where Spanish is less used, are all individual. Essentially, anything that the interviewees do alone, for themselves, shows a strong preference for English. Spanish is used mainly in literacy practices where the interviewees are interacting with Spanish speakers, such as reading a story to a Spanish-speaking child, writing messages, cards and letters, or talking in the home.

Table 6.5 Recency of literacy practices in both languages ($n = 106$)

	Mean	*SD*
Encyclopaedia	3.274	1.047
Dictionary	3.217	1.211
Religious texts	3.679	1.134
Read story to a child	4.179	1.003
Newspaper	3.425	1.394
Magazine	3.387	1.377
Comic	3.962	0.985
Fiction	3.443	1.155
Library	3.170	0.990
Computer	3.689	1.390
Write messages	3.585	1.271
Write letters/cards	4.349	0.905
Write diary	3.868	1.122
Politics talk	3.792	1.232
Science talk	3.509	1.132
History talk	3.462	1.140

Range: minimum = 2; maximum = 5

In fact they seem to use Spanish when they have to, and English otherwise. So socially-interactive literacy practices are likely to make a larger contribution to Spanish proficiency. However, these figures, apart from literate talk, are so low that literacy practices are not likely to make a very large contribution to the development of Spanish literacy. Interviewees who break this pattern, and make substantial use of Spanish for private uses, are of course more likely to develop higher levels of literate register.

It is again unsurprising to note that, as is shown in Table 6.6, interviewees who were educated in a Spanish-speaking country are more likely to use Spanish in literacy practices (the difference between them and the entirely Australian-educated is significant on a T-test) but this difference is small in scale. This pattern is also evident in Table 6.7.

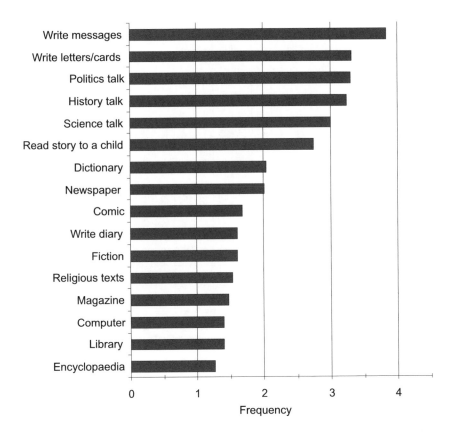

Figure 6.1 Use of Spanish in literacy practices among Australian-educated

Any impact of literacy practices on Spanish proficiency is likely to be a combination of the frequency with which the literacy practice occurs, and the extent to which Spanish is used in it. To examine this combined effect, the scores on the recency and language used variables were multiplied together to give a score out of 25. The scores are shown in Table 6.7.

These scores give a picture of which literacy practices are more or less commonly undertaken in Spanish. Essentially they confirm the pattern observed concerning the language of literacy practices described above.

Table 6.6 Language choice for literacy practices

	All Sydney subjects				Entirely Australian educated				Partly educated in Spanish-speaking country			
	Mean	SD	Min	Max	Mean	SD	Min	Max	Mean	SD	Min	Max
Encyclopaedia	1.349	0.618	1	4	1.262	0.494	1	3	1.476	0.814	1	4
Dictionary	2.010	0.955	1	5	2.036	0.937	1	5	2.238	0.889	1	4
Religious texts	1.821	1.217	1	5	1.536	0.937	1	5	1.762	1.179	1	5
Read story to a child	2.745	1.480	1	5	2.738	1.553	1	5	3.000	1.612	1	5
Newspaper	2.009	0.961	1	5	2.012	0.963	1	5	2.381	1.322	1	5
Magazine	1.509	0.808	1	5	1.476	0.814	1	5	1.619	0.669	1	3
Comic	1.736	1.132	1	5	1.679	1.055	1	5	2.095	1.375	1	5
Fiction	1.689	0.844	1	5	1.607	0.836	1	5	1.762	0.768	1	3
Library	1.396	0.612	1	3	1.405	0.623	1	3	1.476	0.680	1	3
Computer	1.377	0.639	1	3	1.405	0.661	1	3	1.571	0.811	1	3
Write messages	3.821	1.337	1	5	3.833	1.378	1	5	4.000	1.304	1	5
Write letters/cards	3.481	1.587	1	5	3.310	1.598	1	5	3.667	1.390	1	5
Write diary	1.708	0.995	1	5	1.607	0.905	1	5	1.952	1.244	1	5
Politics talk	3.472	1.462	1	5	3.298	1.471	1	5	4.000	1.342	1	5
Science talk	3.198	1.430	1	5	3.000	1.397	1	5	3.667	1.426	1	5
History talk	3.396	1.405	1	5	3.238	1.376	1	5	3.952	1.244	1	5
Number of respondents	106				84				21			

Almost always English = 1, almost always Spanish = 5

Table 6.7 Strength of Spanish literacy practices (recency * language choice)

	All subjects		Entirely Australian educated		Partly educated in Spanish-speaking country	
	Mean	*SD*	*Mean*	*SD*	*Mean*	*SD*
Encyclopaedia	4.443	2.747	4.119	2.236	4.952	3.154
Dictionary	6.623	3.912	6.369	3.948	6.952	3.640
Religious texts	6.858	5.753	5.667	4.587	6.381	6.523
Read story to a child	11.264	6.829	11.286	7.242	13.429	8.334
Newspaper	6.726	4.081	6.786	4.157	7.952	4.421
Magazine	5.198	4.100	5.083	4.116	5.333	2.834
Comic	6.717	4.627	6.571	4.266	8.095	6.115
Fiction	5.528	2.896	5.107	2.621	5.619	2.941
Library	4.415	2.333	4.298	2.210	4.714	2.473
Computer	5.104	3.283	5.095	3.299	6.000	4.405
Write messages	13.453	6.852	13.488	7.046	14.190	7.827
Write letters/cards	15.132	7.755	14.571	7.712	14.714	6.857
Write diary	6.594	4.527	6.226	4.328	7.476	5.446
Politics talk	13.179	7.224	12.833	7.475	16.524	7.208
Science talk	10.943	6.025	10.143	5.697	11.143	5.062
History talk	11.613	6.221	11.071	6.140	14.810	6.593
Number of respondents	106		84		21	

Comparison data from Chile

The nature of the Chilean interviewees was given in Chapter 4. We used the same instruments on the Chilean group in order to see how our Australian bilinguals compared with (largely) monolingual Chilean Spanish speakers (Table 6.8 and Figure 6.2).

The possible score for individual literacy practices ranged from 1 (almost never) to 5 (in the last 24 hours). The most recent (and therefore probably most frequent) literacy practices of the Chilean sample are news-

Table 6.8 Recency of some literacy practices: Chilean vs Australian-educated interviewees

	Chileans		*Entirely Australian educated*	
	Mean	*SD*	*Mean*	*SD*
Encyclopaedia	3.38	1.16	3.27	1.05
Dictionary	3.77	1.22	3.20	1.25
Religious texts	2.87	1.42	3.60	1.13
Newspaper	4.25	1.12	3.45	1.40
Magazine	3.91	1.05	3.40	1.36
Comic	3.26	1.33	4.03	0.95
Fiction	2.68	1.37	3.38	1.17
Library	2.27	1.05	3.08	0.93
Politics talk	2.89	1.58	3.85	1.22
Science talk	3.27	1.37	3.50	1.14
History talk	3.47	1.21	3.45	1.16
Overall mean	3.28		3.47	
Number of respondents	96		84	

paper reading and magazine reading. The use of dictionaries and encyclopaedias is also quite frequent. Library use is quite infrequent, mostly in the almost never to once a month area. Among the three topics for home discussion, politics is discussed least frequently, history most frequently and science falls in between.

When we compare this with the Australians, a different profile emerges. In the written media it is comics and religious texts that are most common. The ordering of the types of talk is reversed. This may reflect the recent history of Chile, where political talk was until recently somewhat risky. The Australians also seem to make much more use of libraries, perhaps reflecting the relative levels of development of the public library systems in the two cities.

Looking at the standard deviations for the Chileans, the large variance in the politics score would suggest that in the minority of homes where politics is discussed, it is discussed a lot. The pattern for religion is similar,

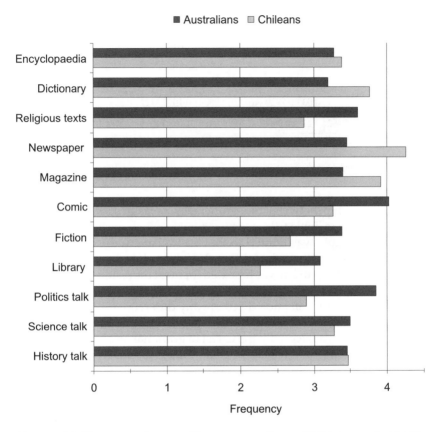

Figure 6.2 Recency of some literacy practices: Chilean vs Australian-educated interviewees

suggesting that among students from religious homes, religious texts are commonly read, whilst in other homes they are not – an unsurprising finding that indicates that these measures are working as expected.

Relationship between home literacy practices and proficiency

A major objective of this research was to see whether there is a relationship between home literacy practices and proficiency. It is important to remember that the 'recency' data include both English and Spanish, that the 'language' data represent the preferred language and, when the two are multiplied together, we get an idea of the frequency of Spanish literacy practices.

Table 6.9 Correlation of proficiency measures with literacy practice totals

	Basic literacy		C-test		Science cloze		History cloze		Cloze total		Self evaluation	
	Corr	p	Corr	p	Corr	p	Corr	p	Corr	p	Corr	p
Recency	-0.06	0.5921	0.03	0.7720	<0.001	0.9874	-0.10	0.3122	-0.05	0.6332	-0.06	0.5311
Language	-0.03	0.7492	0.44	**<0.0001**	0.20	**0.0488**	0.16	0.1219	0.20	**0.0500**	0.66	**<0.0001**
Total	-0.08	0.4524	0.40	**<0.0001**	0.19	0.0674	0.10	0.3221	0.16	0.1209	0.58	<0.0001

Observations = 97; missing values = 9

The relationship between the proficiency measures and the literacy practice scores is in Table 6.9.

When the sample was limited to the Australian-educated, the correlations were stable, but the reduced sample size produced a small reduction in significance. This pattern was repeated for most the results that follow, so the results concerning literacy practices will use the whole sample, and only when it is specifically noted is there any difference for the Australian educated. It can be seen from the above that the use of Spanish in literacy practices is also correlated with the C-test of grammar and vocabulary, and the self evaluation of language proficiency. Interviewees who use Spanish more in their literacy practices score more highly on the science cloze measures of the development of literate register, although the relationship is not strong. The history cloze did not correlate in these calculations, and did not contribute to improving the correlations when combined with the science cloze. The recency/frequency of the literacy practices did not play a role overall, and combining recency with language reduced the correlations rather than strengthening them. In general then, it is the use of Spanish in literacy practices rather than the recency/frequency of them that is related to Spanish acquisition. This may indicate that an overall orientation in favour of using Spanish is more important than the frequency of literacy practices.

Turning now to the scores on the oracy measures, the same pattern emerges in Table 6.10. It is the use of Spanish, rather than the frequency of literacy practices, that produces the difference in proficiency. The same pattern of significant correlations is found among the Australian-educated. This might therefore indicate that the use of Spanish in home literacy practices is part of wider orientation towards the use of Spanish generally in the home, since it correlates with oral proficiency.

Looking now at individual practices, as once might expect from the

Table 6.10   Correlation of oracy measures with literacy practice totals

	Oral fluency		Oral accent		Oral idiomaticity		Oral mixing		Oral total	
	Corr	p	Corr	p	Corr	p	Corr	p	Corr	p
Recency	0.05	0.6189	0.09	0.4252	0.04	0.6918	0.06	0.5826	0.04	0.6812
Language	0.42	<0.0001	0.52	<0.0001	0.60	<0.0001	0.36	0.0005	0.56	<0.0001
Total	0.38	<0.0002	0.50	<0.0001	0.53	<0.0001	0.33	0.0017	0.51	<0.0001

Observations = 87; missing values = 19

information given previously, there is little linkage between the recency of individual literacy practices and Spanish proficiency. However, when the language used was examined, there were a number of significant correlations, as can be seen in Table 6.11.

It is surprising to find so many relationships between individual literacy practices and proficiency. However, this should not be taken too literally – it is possible that there is a mediating factor of overall Spanish-literacy orientation that can help to explain the linkages. Particularly noteworthy in the individual results are the importance of reading fiction and newspapers in Spanish, of keeping a diary in Spanish, and the significance of serious talk within the home. We noted earlier that serious talk in Spanish was more common than other literacy practices, which may go some way to explaining its importance. Basic literacy shows almost no relationship with literacy practices except with comics, which may reflect the low literacy demands of comic books. Grammar and vocabulary as measured by the C-test relate to various literacy practices, as does the development of literate register.

When the figures for the entirely Australian-educated and the partly overseas-educated were compared, some differences emerged. Essentially the entirely Australian-educated seem to have stronger relationships between home literacy practices and proficiency than do the overseas-educated. This can be explained by the fact that the overseas-educated will have had many more opportunities to acquire Spanish outside the home, in particular its written aspects at school.

The reverse is the case when the oracy measures are used. In this case the relationship with the spoken language is weaker among the entirely Australian-educated, so the more conservative figures are used (Table 6.12). The figures are quite clear, in that the various measures of literate talk correlate strongly (as one would expect) with oracy. Other practices that

Table 6.11 Correlations of proficiency measures with preference for using Spanish in individual literacy practices

		Basic literacy	*C-test*	*Science cloze*	*History cloze*	*Cloze total*	*Self evaluation*
Encyclopaedia	Corr	-0.04	0.21	0.12	0.03	0.08	0.36
	p	0.7137	**0.0424**	0.2619	0.7445	0.4319	**0.0002**
Dictionary	Corr	-0.05	0.25	0.06	0.20	0.15	0.34
	p	0.6578	**0.0122**	0.5364	**0.0471**	0.1376	**0.0006**
Religious texts	Corr	-0.02	0.18	0.00165	0.02	0.01	0.35
	p	0.8250	0.0825	0.9872	0.8734	0.9190	**0.0004**
Story to a child	Corr	-0.05	0.16	0.07	0.13	0.12	0.19
	p	0.6135	0.1166	0.4665	0.2043	0.2586	0.0635
Newspaper	Corr	0.04	0.28	0.07	0.01	0.04	0.26
	p	0.7167	**0.0056**	0.4854	0.9458	0.6816	**0.0102**
Magazine	Corr	0.08	0.23	0.08	0.04	0.06	0.35
	p	0.4526	0.0241	0.4574	0.7056	0.5379	**0.0004**
Comic	Corr	-0.20	0.17	-0.04	0.04	0.01	0.16
	p	**0.0486**	0.1051	0.7185	0.6695	0.9537	0.1139
Fiction	Corr	0.00361	0.29	0.17	0.21	0.21	0.44
	p	0.9721	**0.0042**	0.0941	**0.0367**	**0.0342**	**<0.0001**
Library	Corr	0.06	0.06	0.02	0.01	0.02	0.12
	p	0.5543	0.5904	0.8336	0.9083	0.8579	0.2292
Computer	Corr	0.16	0.03	0.03	0.05	0.05	0.17
	p	0.1072	0.7842	0.7597	0.6202	0.6509	0.0984
Write messages	Corr	0.10	0.22	0.06	0.13	0.11	0.41
	p	0.3472	**0.0313**	0.5436	0.2082	0.2897	**<0.0001**
Letters/cards	Corr	0.06	0.43	0.15	0.04	0.10	0.50
	p	0.5708	**<0.0001**	0.1476	0.6967	0.3195	**<0.0001**

Table 6.11 *(continued)*

Write diary	Corr	0.04	0.26	0.23	0.16	0.22	0.45
	p	0.7336	**0.0105**	**0.0233**	0.1202	**0.0341**	**<0.0001**
Politics talk	Corr	0.11	0.29	0.20	0.14	0.19	0.54
	p	0.2817	**0.0033**	**0.0496**	0.1585	*0.0612*	**<0.0001**
Science talk	Corr	0.04	0.31	0.23	0.06	0.16	0.50
	p	0.7304	**0.0016**	**0.0213**	0.5318	0.1140	**<0.0001**
History talk	Corr	-0.01	0.35	0.22	0.11	0.18	0.54
	p	0.89944	**0.0004**	**0.0278**	0.3034	0.0769	**<0.0001**

Observations = 65; missing values = 19

also show some level of relationship are use of dictionaries, newspapers, and writing messages – the latter two perhaps because they are more common in general. Also idiomaticity, which is more related to general language proficiency, correlates more strongly with the use of Spanish in literacy practices.

An exploratory Factor Analysis suggested these practices could be grouped (see the Factor Analysis later). Two groupings of practices (formed by simply adding the scores for these) provided interesting data, and both had emerged earlier in the hand analysis. One was private use, consisting of fiction, library and diary writing; and the other was social interaction, consisting of the writing of letters or cards to the family, and the three talk variables. The correlations are shown in Table 6.13.

These groupings clarify and strengthen the relationships between literacy practices and proficiency. The use of Spanish in interactive literacy practices within the family has a strong relationship with the development of grammar and vocabulary, and a significant relationship with scores on the cloze test of scientific register. Personal and private uses of Spanish in literacy, which we noted are quite rare, are nonetheless very important when they do occur. In particular the score on the cloze total is higher than that on either of the individual cloze tests, pointing to a general strength in literate register.

Comparison data from Chile

There were surprisingly few significant correlations between individual literacy practices and the proficiency measures among the Chilean group. However, the general pattern of a relationship between literacy practices

Table 6.12 Correlations of oracy measures with preference for using Spanish in individual literacy practices

		Oral fluency	*Oral accent*	*Oral idiomaticity*	*Oral mixing*	*Oral total*
Encyclopaedia	Corr	0.15	0.11	0.30	0.08	0.19
	p	0.2318	0.3956	**0.0146**	0.5118	0.1206
Dictionary	Corr	0.34	0.28	0.38	0.28	0.39
	p	**0.0047**	**0.0218**	**0.0015**	**0.0222**	**0.0011**
Religious texts	Corr	-0.14	0.20	0.14	0.09	0.08
	p	0.2712	0.1087	0.2698	0.4873	0.5389
Story to a child	Corr	-0.05	0.02	0.17	0.08	0.06
	p	0.6843	0.8504	0.1848	0.5113	0.6097
Newspaper	Corr	0.29	0.38	0.28	0.21	0.35
	p	**0.0167**	**0.0016**	**0.0220**	0.0940	**0.0039**
Magazine	Corr	0.17	0.28	0.40	0.26	0.33
	p	0.1660	**0.0241**	**0.0010**	**0.0382**	**0.0067**
Comic	Corr	-0.02	0.14	0.10	0.07	0.08
	p	0.8504	0.2642	0.4512	0.5548	0.5162
Fiction	Corr	0.16	0.15	0.24	0.20	0.23
	p	0.2004	0.2479	**0.0499**	0.1154	0.0693
Library	Corr	0.03	0.002.84	0.09	0.17	0.01
	p	0.7883	0.9822	0.4783	0.1835	0.9235
Computer	Corr	0.03	0.04	0.12	0.07	0.03
	p	0.8315	0.7583	0.3264	0.5561	0.7890
Write messages	Corr	0.33	0.41	0.40	0.20	0.40
	p	**0.0066**	**0.0006**	**0.0008**	0.1172	**0.0008**
Letters/cards	Corr	0.27	0.43	0.33	0.32	0.41
	p	**0.0265**	**0.0003**	**0.0069**	**0.0095**	**0.0007**
Write diary	Corr	0.16	0.15	0.26	0.12	0.21
	p	0.2034	0.2418	**0.0363**	0.3337	0.0955

Table 6.12 *(continued)*

Politics talk	Corr	0.36	0.38	0.45	0.34	0.46
	p	0.0029	0.0016	0.0002	0.0052	<0.0001
Science talk	Corr	0.31	0.38	0.39	0.25	0.40
	p	0.0126	0.0017	0.0014	0.0454	0.0009
History talk	Corr	0.36	0.38	0.35	0.34	0.43
	p	0.0034	0.0015	0.0041	0.0055	0.0003

Observations = 65; missing values = 19

Table 6.13 Correlations of proficiency measures with use of Spanish in groups of literacy practices

		Basic literacy	*C-test*	*Science cloze*	*History cloze*	*Cloze total*	*Self evaluation*
Social interaction	Corr	-0.06	0.40	0.23	0.10	0.18	0.60
	p	0.5340	<0.0001	0.0219	0.3198	0.0724	<0.0001
Private	Corr	0.04	0.28	0.20	0.18	0.21	0.47
	p	0.7016	0.0057	0.0477	0.789	0.370	<0.0001

Observations = 97; missing values = 9

Table 6.14 Correlations of proficiency measures with all literacy practices: Chile

		Basic literacy	*C-test*	*Science cloze*	*History cloze*	*Cloze total*	*Self evaluation*
All literacy practices	Corr	-0.27	0.40	0.25	0.13	0.25	0.38
	p	0.1967	0.0089	0.0133	0.1994	0.0151	0.0002

Observations = 95; missing values = 1

overall and the proficiency measures emerged clearly (Table 6.14). When we looked at the effects of family background (Table 6.15) we found very

Table 6.15 Correlations of all literacy practices with family background: Chile

		Father's education	*Mother's education*	*Father's occupation*	*Mother's occupation*
All literacy practices	Corr	0.39	0.19	0.26	0.12
	p	**<0.0001**	0.0657	**0.0111**	0.2292

Observations = 95; missing values = 1

strong associations between the father's education and employment and the frequency of literacy practices.

Higher levels in the father's education and employment, which are usually regarded as indicators of social class, seem to be linked to higher usage of literacy practices – in other words the social practice aspect of social class. This may indicate that the effects of the father's background upon register development may to some degree be mediated by literacy practices in this group of Chilean monolinguals.

Conclusion

These findings are particularly significant for the Hispanic community (and perhaps for other minority-language groups). They provide concrete evidence that talking seriously to children in the minority language and encouraging their private reading in that language contribute to the development of both basic grammar and the higher-level registers of the language. Home literacy practices can and do make a difference in these areas of minority language development, not just schooling.

Overall, the message that emerges is that the bilingual's willingness to voluntarily undertake individual literacy practices in the minority language is a crucial factor. The next issue that arises is whether such individual literacy practices are supported by the presence of literacy resources within the home.

Language and Literacy Resources

Measure of language and literacy resources

We also included in our data a request to the caregiver to show us Spanish and English language resources in the home – including the numbers of CDs, tapes, fiction books, reference books. These were simply counted, and the results entered into the computer database, with a maximum entry of 99 to avoid distortions by extreme numbers. The categories of resources are shown in Table 6.16, along with the basic statistics on their numbers.

Table 6.16 Basic statistics concerning language resources

	All Interviewees				Australian-educated			
	Mean	SD	Min	Max	Mean	SD	Min	Max
Spanish videos	13.485	21.957	0	99	11.633	19.616	0	99
English videos	25.495	24.914	0	99	25.139	25.146	0	99
Spanish music	51.566	32.588	1	99	51.051	33.155	1	99
English music	40.980	28.203	3	99	41.013	28.548	3	99
Spanish newspapers	1.889	2.860	0	20	1.696	2.366	0	20
English newspapers	5.162	7.122	0	30	5.253	7.269	0	30
Spanish magazines	4.253	9.698	0	60	3.316	8.498	0	60
English magazines	7.131	14.122	0	99	6.595	14.835	0	99
Spanish religious texts	1.040	1.269	0	8	0.785	0.915	0	4
English religious texts	1.747	2.647	0	25	1.797	2.897	0	25
Spanish comics	3.384	5.890	0	30	3.380	6.173	0	30
English comics	2.828	7.328	0	50	3.089	8.035	0	50
Spanish dictionaries	2.495	1.289	0	6	2.367	1.157	0	5
English dictionaries	3.465	2.782	1	25	3.519	2.991	1	25
Spanish encyclopaedias	0.273	0.491	0	2	0.278	0.0479	0	2
English encyclopaedias	1.131	0.751	0	4	1.114	0.768	0	4
Spanish fiction	16.717	22.380	0	99	16.405	22.201	0	99
English fiction	24.253	26.249	0	99	21.456	24.255	0	99
Spanish non-fiction	8.768	14.401	0	99	7.734	11.133	0	50
English non-fiction	15.051	15.794	0	99	15.671	16.783	0	99
Spanish computer programs	0.374	1.682	0	15	0.190	0.802	0	6
English computer programs	10.475	10.815	0	40	10.443	10.554	0	40
All Spanish literacy resources	104.242	62.635	8	250	98.835	61.321	8	250
All English literacy resources	137.717	75.738	27	370	135.089	78.354	27	370
	n = 99; missing = 7				n = 79; missing = 5			

There was a difference between the entirely Australian-educated interviewees, and those partly educated overseas. As one might predict, on average the Australian-educated had fewer Spanish-language resources in their homes. The profile of resources in the homes of the Australian-educated, based on the means in Table 6.16 is shown in Figure 6.3.

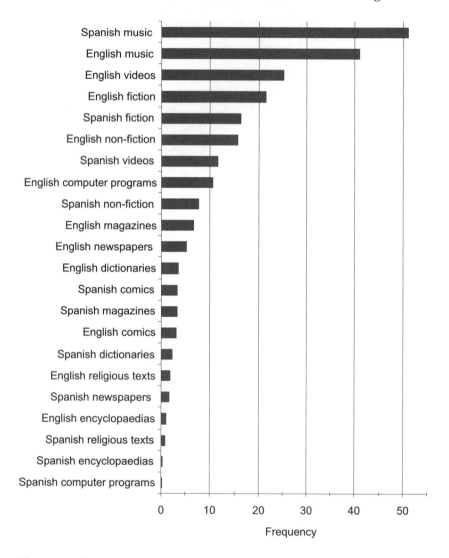

Figure 6.3 Literacy resources in the homes of the Australian-educated

The large volume of Hispanic music points to music as a core identity value for Hispanic Australians, and this is supported by the comments from the open questions. The large amount of English non-fiction probably points to reference books in English, in a context where Spanish equivalents are less available.

Interestingly, some literacy resources showed a relationship with the development of academic register, as is shown in Table 6.17, but not with general Spanish proficiency as measured by the C-test and self-evaluation. Nor was there any relationship either with the oracy measures (not shown).

Perhaps the most striking aspects of this table are that it is not only 'serious' resources, but leisure and entertainment resources in Spanish that affect development of the language. When the sample is limited to the Australian educated the pattern remains similar, but with some slight strengthening of some relationships. When the literacy resources are totalled, the relationships with the proficiency measures become clearer (Table 6.18).

While there is a significant relationship between the amount of English and Spanish resources (Corr = 0.37; p = 0.0003), it is clear from Table 6.18 that a 'literate home' is not sufficient for the development of Spanish

Table 6.17 Correlation of Spanish literacy resources in the home with proficiency measures

Resources		Proficiency measures					
		Basic literacy	*C-test*	*Science cloze*	*History cloze*	*Cloze total*	*Self evaluation*
Videos	p	0.2557	0.1063	**0.0153**	0.3751	0.0737	0.0761
	Corr	-0.12	0.17	0.25	0.09	0.19	0.18
Music	p	0.8852	0.3213	**0.0353**	0.2277	*0.0697*	0.4256
	Corr	0.02	0.10	0.22	0.13	0.19	0.08
Magazines	p	0.9136	*0.0578*	0.1804	0.5302	0.2838	**0.0024**
	Corr	0.01	0.20	0.14	0.07	0.11	0.31
Comics	p	0.4345	0.2061	0.1449	0.2206	0.1375	*0.0508*
	Corr	0.08	0.13	0.15	0.13	0.16	0.20
Encyclopaedia	p	0.5173	0.7403	0.8211	0.3383	0.4985	*0.0569*
	Corr	-0.07	0.03	0.02	0.10	0.07	-0.20

Observations = 93; missing values = 13

Table 6.18 Correlation of all resources in the home with proficiency measures

Resources		Proficiency measures					
		Basic literacy	*C-test*	*Science cloze*	*History cloze*	*Cloze total*	*Self evaluation*
All Spanish	*p*	0.5352	*0.0870*	**0.0040**	*0.0528*	**0.0079**	0.0708
	Corr	-0.07	0.18	0.29	0.20	0.27	0.19
All English	*p*	0.9106	0.5107	0.4862	0.8559	0.7569	*0.5042*
	Corr	-0.01	-0.07	0.07	-0.02	0.03	0.07
All Spanish and English	*p*	0.6773	0.6122	0.1274	0.1504	0.0989	*0.1514*
	Corr	-0.04	0.05	0.16	0.15	0.17	0.15

Observations = 93; missing values = 13

academic register. It is the presence of Spanish resources that is critical. Furthermore, the presence of these resources correlates with scores on the cloze measures of register development more significantly than with other aspects of proficiency. (The pattern for the wholly Australian educated is identical.) Again there is an important message for the Hispanic community (and perhaps other minority language communities) that access to minority language resources in the home is significantly related to the development of the higher levels of the minority language.

There was also a relationship between the presence of particular Spanish literacy resources and the use of Spanish in some of the related literacy practices, as is shown in Table 6.19.

Table 6.19 Correlation of number of Spanish literacy resources with use of Spanish in literacy practices

	All		*Australian educated*	
	Corr	*p*	*Corr*	*p*
Religious texts	0.22	**0.0319**	0.01	0.9086
Magazines	0.40	**<0.0001**	0.43	**<0.0001**
Comics	0.13	0.2061	0.21	*0.0686*
	n = 99; missing values =7		*n* = 79; missing values 5	

Spearman rank correlations, although less conservative than Fisher's R–Z correlations, are particularly sensitive to larger variations in totals, such as those revealed by the raw numbers of literacy resources in the home. Table 6.20 shows the Spearman correlations for all possible combinations of literacy practices with the corresponding literacy resources.

The figures in Table 6.20 demonstrate that, if Spanish literacy resources are available in the home, then Spanish is more likely to be used in the corresponding literacy practice. So if computer programs are accessible in Spanish, Spanish is more likely to be used in computing. Obviously access to literacy resources is a necessary but not sufficient condition for their use.

We also examined our data to see if the recency of literacy practices was related to access in the home to the relevant resources. Of the eight possible relationships, only two were noteworthy, as is shown in Table 6.21.

When Spearman correlations were used, these relationships were greatly strengthened, and computer programs were added.

We were intrigued by the strength of the number of magazines as predictor of Spanish literacy practices, and when we performed correlations on this single variable, they revealed relationships with both the frequency and use of Spanish in other literacy practices. We are at a loss to explain this, other than to say that the presence of magazines in the home is a powerful indicator of literacy practices.

Table 6.20 Spearman correlations: Spanish literacy resources by use of Spanish in the related literacy practices

	ρ	p
Encyclopaedia	0.401	**0.0004**
Dictionaries	0.145	0.2018
Religious texts	0.325	**0.0041**
Newspapers	0.084	0.4579
Magazines	0.308	**0.0065**
Comics	0.335	**0.0031**
Fiction	0.254	**0.0250**
Computer programs	0.649	**<0.0001**

Observations = 101; missing values = 5

Table 6.21 Correlation of number of literacy resources with recency of literacy practices

	ρ	p
Magazines	0.20	*0.0513*
Dictionaries	0.25	**0.0128**

Observations = 99; missing values = 7

Interestingly there is no relationship between literacy resources in English and the frequency of English literacy practices or the use of English in the relevant literacy practices. The English resources also have no impact on the Spanish measures. This probably indicates that, for children who use a minority language in the home, more English literacy practices occur outside the home, presumably largely in school. This suggests that it may be important to support Spanish literacy practices in the home in order to foster the general literacy skills that underlie both English and Spanish literacy practices (the same may also hold for other minority languages).

Unlike in the Chilean sample, there was no correlation between SES and literacy practices. This lack of relationship between SES and literacy practices and language development is open to various interpretations. It may point to the fact that recent migrants often finish up in occupations that do not reflect their SES in their country of origin; it may indicate that higher SES in Australia is attained at the expense of Spanish; or that SES is not a good indicator of home language use and home literacy; or it may indicate weaknesses in our methods of measurement.

Media Use

Chapter 4 describes the availability of various media in Sydney. We are interested here in the actual use of such media among our interviewees.

Open questions

At the beginning of this part of the interview, interviewees were asked the following question.

#1 Q44

These questions are about the media you use in Spanish and English.
Estas preguntas son acerca de los medios de comunicación en español e inglés que utilizas.

Through what media (radio, TV etc) have you mainly encountered Spanish?
¿A través de qué medio de comunicación has tenido más contacto con el español? (radio, TV, etc)

At the end of this part of the interview, they were asked:

#1 Q51

Is there anything else you wish to say about where you have encountered Spanish?

¿Quieres agregar algo más acerca de los contextos en que has sido expuesto al español?

#1 Q52

Is there anything you want to say about these questions?

¿Quieres hacer algún comentario sobre estas preguntas?

It is perhaps worth restating the point made in Chapter 4 concerning the media, that the media in Australia are overwhelmingly in English, and it is in some sense 'marked' or unusual behaviour to access media in other languages. As one of the interviewees put it:

HE ESTADO VIVIENDO EN AUSTRALIA POR LA MAYORIA DE MI VIDA, ENTONCES HE VISTO MAS PROGRAMAS, LETRADOS, Y MUSICA EN INGLES, NO ESPANOL.
I've been living in Australia for most of my life so I have seen most programmes, signs and music in English, not Spanish.

The number of mentions of use of Spanish in specific media were as follows:

- radio: 50 (including *SBS Radio*: 3; *Radio Rio* 2; *Radio Austral* 2)
- television: 43 (including *SBS TV*: 3)
- movies: 8
- videos: 5
- music: 2
- internet: 2
- no use of Spanish media: 14

Some specific comments follow.

Radio

sbs radio ethnica
sbs ethnic radio

On the radio there is sometimes Spanish broadcasts and I loke to sometimes listen to them to test if I am able to understand.

Through 'Radio Rio' in spanish

sometimes we listen to spanish radio (if we find the station)

I listen to AUSTRAL wich is the spanish shanel and my father listens to it every day.

YES I LISTEN TO RADIO ASTRAL

EN AUSTRALIA HE ESCUCHADO ALGUNAS RADIOS DE HABLA

HISPANA
in Australia I have listened to some Spanish language radio stations
I NORMALLY ENCOUNTER SPANISH ON MY GRANDFATHERS
RADIO HE HAS THIS LINK THAT TRANSMITS ALL THE WAY TO
SOUTHAMERCIA.
YO ESCUCHADO LA RADIO NO MAS
I have only listened to the radio
Spanish Radio
my grandmother listenes to a spanish radio when she does the house
work,
RADIO RIO
 mostly on the radio
SBS spanish radio
radio,sometimes on the television but mostly on the radio
SBS spanish radio and sometimes th Chilean news,

Television
veo novelas mejicanas en tv
I watch mexican soap operas on tv
MAINLY TELEVISION
Occasionally i watch the spanish news with my parents .
On channel 1(SBS) there are sometimes Spanish movies, though not
enough.
HE VISTO PROGRAMAS ESPANOLES
I have seen Spanish programmes
on the tv on SBS when we watch some spanish movies
TV MOSTLY
sbs
SOME SPANISH TV NEWS
EN LA TELEVISION[SBS] *On television [SBS]*
 i like to watch alot of spanish soccer games with spanish commentators
TAMBIEN VEO EL NOTICIERO ESPANOL CON MI ABUELITA.
I also watch the Spanish news with my grannie
THE MEDIA WHICH HELPED LEARN MORE SPANISH IS PROBABLY
MOSTLY THE TELEVISION.
TV SHOWS AND SOAP OPERA's
sometimes on the television
sometimes th Chilean news

Videos
Mainly with Spanish videos

VIDEOS QUE MANDAN MIS PRIMOS DE MI PAIS(PERU).
Videos that my cousins send from my country (Peru).

The internet

TAMBIEN EN RADIO PROGRAMAS EN EL INTERNET.
Also in radio programmes on the internet.

YO HE TENIDO CONTACTO MAYORMENTE CON EL ESPANOL
ATRAVEZ DEL USO DE LA INTERNET Y LA MUSICA , LA CUAL
PROVIENE DE LATINO AMERICA.
I have mainly had contact with Spanish through the internet and music coming from Latin America

Music

music

HE OIDO MUSICA LATIN-AMERICA.
I have heard Latin-America music

LA MUSICA , LA CUAL PROVIENE DE LATINO AMERICA.
Music which comes from Latin America

#1 Q 28

listening to music

SI, ME GUSTA LA MUSICA EN ESPANOL MUCHO
Yes I like listening to Spanish music very much

The question at the end elicited various comments of interest, including some comments on street signage.

#1 Q51

cuando voy a la delicatesen veo carteles en español -así como en
panaderías, club de video, farmacia, etc- *when I go to the delicatessen I see
posters in Spanish – also in bakeries, the video club, chemists etc*

WHEN WATCHING FOREIGN FILMS

You don't find many places around this area (i.e. Hurstville, Kogarah,
South Sydney-Cronulla, Miranda) with Spanish signs outside them as you
would find in places like Fairfield and some of the western suburbs,

Closed questions

The format of these questions was discussed with Richard Bourhis and
Rodrigue Landry, who both have considerable experience in designing this
type of question. The careful wording attempted to capture our interviewees' experience of media in their everyday lives. The possibility of the
influence of 'streetscape', here realised as shop signs (the only major
manifestation of bilingual streetscape in New South Wales) was suggested
by Richard Bourhis. The wording referring to exposure 'since early
childhood' made it particularly important that we examine both the whole

sample and also those who had been educated only in Australia. The closed questions began as follows:

Please pick one box which best says your answer.
Escoge el casillero que mejor refleje tu respuesta.

The television programmes that I have been exposed to from early childhood until now were:
Los programas de televisión a que he sido expuesto desde mi niñez hasta ahora han sido:

5   almost always in Spanish / casi siempre en español
4   mostly in Spanish / mayormente en español
3   Spanish and English about equally/tanto español como inglés
2   mostly in English / mayormente en inglés
1   almost always in English / casi siempre en inglés

The same format was used to ask about all the media uses displayed in Table 6.22: the only slightly different question concerned shopsigns, which read as follows:

The signs inside and outside shops that I have been exposed to from early childhood until now were:
Los letreros fuera y dentro de los negocios a que he sido expuesto desde mi niñez hasta ahora han sido

5   almost always Spanish / casi siempre en español
4   mostly Spanish / mayormente en español
3   Spanish and English about equally/tanto español como inglés
2   mostly English / mayormente en inglés
1   almost always English / casi siempre en inglés

The basic statistics concerning media use are in Table 6.22. The figures show that English dominates the media input of our interviewees, with the exception of music, where they appear to listen to slightly more Hispanic-sourced material. It is also clear that the Australian-born have had less exposure to Spanish-language media, as one would expect given the availability of Spanish language material in Australia compared with Spanish-speaking countries.

Figure 6.4 shows more accessibly that the Australian born have had limited exposure to Spanish language media, as one would expect given the availability of Spanish language matter in Australia compared with Spanish speaking countries.

Looking at the individual media, Table 6.23 shows that the entirely Australian-educated group report more access to Spanish music and videos, followed next by radio. This may reflect more broadcast time given to Spanish-language SBS radio in Australia than Spanish-language television, and the existence of local Spanish-language radio stations, but no local Spanish language television. We suspect that some of the 'movies'

Table 6.22 Basic statistics for media use

		All	Entirely Australian educated	Some overseas education
Television	Mean	2.038	1.869	2.750
	SD	0.904	0.803	1.020
Videos	Mean	2.349	2.298	2.600
	SD	0.936	0.954	0.883
Radio	Mean	2.009	1.917	2.400
	SD	0.951	0.908	1.046
Movies	Mean	1.896	1.798	2.350
	SD	0.861	0.773	1.089
Music	Mean	2.679	2.690	2.600
	SD	1.000	1.029	0.940
Shop signs	Mean	1.774	1.607	2.500
	SD	0.865	0.761	0.946
Total	Mean	12.745	12.179	15.200
	SD	4.195	3.912	4.708
		(*n* = 106)	(*n* = 84)	(*n* = 20)

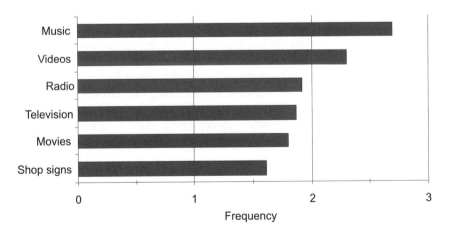

Figure 6.4 Media language: Australian-educated

Table 6.23 Correlations of Spanish media use with oral measures: Australian-educated interviewees

	Fluency		*Accent*		*Idiomaticity*		*Mixing*		*Total*	
	Corr	*p*	*Corr*	*p*	*Corr*	*p*	*Corr*	*p*	*Corr*	*p*
Television	0.17	0.1756	0.21	0.1036	0.37	**0.0025**	0.25	**0.0455**	0.30	**0.0164**
Videos	0.26	**0.0447**	0.14	0.2744	0.39	**0.0017**	0.19	0.1450	0.29	**0.0196**
Radio	0.19	0.1365	0.29	**0.0202**	0.35	**0.0046**	0.33	**0.0078**	0.35	**0.0052**
Movies	0.19	0.1343	0.23	0.0717	0.24	0.0572	0.18	0.1593	0.25	**0.0466**
Music	0.37	**0.0030**	0.22	0.0874	0.39	**0.0015**	0.22	0.0917	0.36	**0.0035**
Signs	0.03	0.8447	0.08	0.5334	0.17	0.1888	0.05	0.7171	0.10	0.4621
Total	0.27	**0.0363**	0.25	**0.0461**	0.42	**0.0007**	0.27	**0.0365**	0.36	**0.003**

Observations = 62; missing values = 22

figures may in fact reflect video usage, despite having designed the questionnaire wording to avoid this problem.

As usual, given our interest in full proficiency language maintenance, we examined the relationship between media use and our proficiency measures (Tables 6.23 and 6.24).

The pattern for the wholly Australian-educated group is very similar to that of the whole sample, even though as we saw earlier, the Spanish-educated group had been exposed less to Spanish media in general. Overall, it is clear that media use is related to oracy, but seems to have no relationship with the development of literate register. This may reflect the language encountered in the popular media, although there is an obvious need for further research in this area into the effect of 'quality' media such as Radio National in Australia that give the impression of using more high-register language. However, in Australia such media attract only 2–5% of the audience, and there is very limited access to 'quality' media in Spanish

Looking at the individual results, television appears to have less effect than one might expect from its dominance as a medium (remembering that the Australian-educated group has had little access to Spanish-language television). Radio and film/videotape (which became significant when the whole sample was used) appear to be more important, perhaps reflecting

Table 6.24 Correlations of Spanish media use with proficiency measures: Australian-educated interviewees

	Basic literacy		C-test		Register cloze total		Self assessment	
	Corr	p	Corr	p	Corr	p	Corr	p
Television	0.15	0.2007	0.04	0.7554	-0.02	0.8518	0.33	**0.0025**
Videos	0.00255	0.9823	0.12	0.2859	0.02	0.8633	0.50	**<0.0001**
Radio	0.03	0.7626	0.30	**0.0067**	-0.06	0.6190	0.38	**0.0005**
Movies	0.09	0.4182	0.20	0.0730	-0.10	0.3675	0.43	**<0.0001**
Music	0.34	**0.0022**	0.16	0.1584	-0.04	0.7310	0.17	0.1284
Signs	0.11	0.3566	-0.09	0.4280	-0.14	0.2217	0.35	**0.0014**
Total	0.16	0.1469	0.17	0.1329	-0.07	0.5410	0.48	**<0.0001**

Observations = 79; missing values = 5

their relatively greater accessibility in the Australian context shown in Figure 6.3.

We mentioned above the possible relationship between media variables and literacy variables, so these were examined through a rotated-principal components analysis. Given the likely effect of previous overseas habits for our 'partly educated overseas' interviewees, we limited the testing to the 'wholly Australian educated' group. The results are shown in Table 6.25.

Factor 1 might be summarised as an orientation to access Spanish material, or 'self immersion' in Spanish. Factor 3 is the 'literate talk' factor that we saw previously in the discussion of literacy practices. Factor 4 is 'writing'. Factor 5 combines videos, fiction, library use and diary writing – this might be an 'imagination' factor. Factor 6 is concerned with radio, newspapers, dictionaries and (oddly) music – this appears to be a 'current affairs' or 'non-fiction' orientation. Factor 7, with its strong positive loading on computers and weaker positive loading on dictionary use, and weak negative loading on radio and movies, may perhaps represent an orientation to the written rather than the spoken word. Factor 8 is difficult to interpret.

These factors were then entered into a correlation with the proficiency measures, with results shown in Table 6.26 (organised so that the factors align with Table 6.25).

There are not many strong correlations, but the pattern is interesting. The self-immersion factor (Factor 1) is related to the history cloze, perhaps

Maintaining a Minority Language

Table 6.25 Rotated-principal component analysis: Media and literacy practices

	Factor 1	Factor 2	Factor 3	Factor 4	Factor 5	Factor 6	Factor 7	Factor 8
Television	**0.698**	0.088	-0.162	-0.185	0.257	-0.055	0.075	0.271
Videos	0.249	0.300	-0.189	-0.115	**0.480**	0.218	-0.037	0.179
Radio	0.389	-0.035	0.185	-0.094	0.280	**0.422**	**-0.414**	-0.180
Movies	**0.620**	0.012	0.203	-0.215	0.222	0.180	-0.309	0.034
Music	**0.561**	0.167	-0.161	-0.303	-0.247	**0.480**	0.085	0.002
Shop signs	**0.739**	-0.003	0.074	0.020	0.121	-0.099	0.069	-0.245
Encyclopaedia	**0.654**	-0.069	0.090	0.030	0.167	-0.072	0.192	-0.103
Dictionary	0.019	-0.012	-0.197	0.250	0.053	**0.746**	0.318	0.088
Religious texts	0.866	-0.065	0.066	0.286	**-0.403**	-0.115	-0.002	0.120
Read story to child	0.176	-0.162	0.289	0.244	0.276	0.014	0.084	**0.527**
Newspaper	-0.137	0.303	**0.440**	0.073	-0.084	**0.714**	-0.138	-0.122
Magazine	**0.725**	-0.066	0.030	0.267	-0.003	0.109	0.031	0.012
Comic	-0.010	0.057	**0.878**	-0.015	0.033	0.036	0.057	0.007
Fiction	0.226	-0.198	-0.232	0.357	**0.540**	0.209	-0.037	0.025
Library	0.286	-0.168	0.012	0.226	0.383	-0.004	0.131	**-0.563**
Computer	0.253	-0.004	0.185	-0.110	0.058	0.131	**0.721**	-0.017
Write messages	-0.121	0.311	0.002	**0.737**	-0.031	0.098	0.058	0.011
Write letters/cards	0.174	**0.447**	0.108	**0.586**	0.012	-0.057	-0.236	-0.046
Write diary	-0.001	0.163	0.176	-0.073	**0.808**	-0.112	0.090	-0.007
Politics talk	-0.070	**0.784**	-0.102	0.084	0.296	-0.003	0.140	0.205
Science talk	0.021	**0.933**	0.039	0.099	-0.027	-0.041	-0.083	-0.101
History talk	0.018	**0.895**	-0.008	0.045	-0.106	0.083	0.026	-0.033

>**0.400 in bold**; factors = 8; observations = 79; missing values = 5; degrees of freedom = 252; Bartlett's Chi Square = 987.127; p = <0.0001; factor extraction method = principal components; extraction rule = method default; transformation method = Orthotran/Varimax

Table 6.26 The relationship of Spanish use factors with proficiency measures

		Factor 1	Factor 2	Factor 3	Factor 4	Factor 5	Factor 6	Factor 7	Factor 8
Basic literacy	Corr	0.10	-0.08	-0.17	-0.06	-0.08	0.14	0.06	-0.03
	p	0.3647	0.5100	0.1436	0.6051	0.4773	0.2036	0.5952	0.7795
C-test	Corr	-0.11	0.17	0.13	0.15	0.11	0.27	-0.13	0.00464
	p	0.3219	0.1386	0.2603	0.1992	0.3188	**0.0156**	0.2561	0.9677
Science cloze	Corr	-0.11	0.21	-0.06	0.10	0.17	-0.05	0.10	0.01
	p	0.3276	0.0689	0.5714	0.3984	0.1384	0.6525	0.3975	0.9347
History cloze	Corr	-0.26	-0.04	-0.11	0.15	0.21	0.10	0.25	0.14
	p	**0.0213**	0.7477	0.3380	0.1739	*0.0620*	0.3880	**0.0282**	0.2216
Cloze total	Corr	-0.21	0.09	-0.10	0.14	0.21	0.03	0.19	0.08
	p	0.0680	0.4295	0.3966	0.2203	*0.0628*	0.8079	0.0906	0.4639
Self assessment	Corr	0.14	0.39	-0.09	0.24	0.21	0.12	-0.02	0.08
	p	0.2064	**0.003**	0.4104	**0.0295**	*0.0685*	0.2948	0.8755	0.4712

showing that immersing oneself in the literature and written language leads to the development of the registers related to the humanities. Likewise the orientation to the written rather than the spoken word, as manifested in Factor 7, plays a role. The imagination and fiction orientation of Factor 5 appears also to be weakly related to the development of humanities register. It is Factor 2, literate talk, that seems most strongly related to the development of scientific register, as we saw in the earlier analyses, as well as confidence in one's proficiency. Factor 6, the non-fiction/current affairs factor, is more related to the development of basic grammatical proficiency as measured by the C-test. These factors and findings are speculative, but the different profiling of the two cloze measures is unexpected and interesting.

Conclusions

Many of our predictions concerning the factors that affect biliteracy were supported by the studies. The strong correlations between months of

Spanish medium education and the C-test and the register cloze test scores underline the importance of educational medium. Furthermore, Cummins view that literacy in the mother tongue supports literacy in the second language is further buttressed by the finding that scores on the English clozes are related to the amount of Spanish-medium education. The valuable role of 'ethnic' community language schools in Australia is affirmed by their contribution to the development of grammar, vocabulary and basic literacy, but it is important to note that they do not replace bilingual education, since the development of register is not affected.

The use of the oral media that we examined seemed to be related, not surprisingly, mainly to oral proficiency.

We found evidence of a relationship between use of Spanish print media and literacy in Spanish, although the amount of use is low, and therefore there is a limited relationship overall. In particular we saw that our interviewees mostly use Spanish literacy only when they have to, preferring English for private literacy uses. When combined with the absence of Spanish-medium education, the prognosis for Spanish literacy in this group is not good. On the more positive side, we found evidence that the presence of Spanish literacy resources in the home fosters their use, and there is a small but measurable overall relationship with the development of academic register

Chapter 7

Attitudes and Beliefs

> *Ever since I know I have no need to feel ashamed of speaking Spanish I have become strong. Now I feel I can speak with the teachers about my children's education and I can tell them I want my children to know Spanish.*
>
> Hispanic mother in the USA, quoted by Ada (1988: 235)

THE ISSUES

Introduction

In keeping with the rest of this book, we are interested in the attitudes and beliefs that support or undermine the maintenance of minority languages. Such attitudes will need to include faith and pride in the minority language and culture (in Hamers & Blanc's 2000 terms, 'valorisation'), and resistance to the hegemonic and homogenising influence of the dominant culture. On the other hand, minorities will also usually need proficiency in the majority language in order to participate in mainstream society, so the dominant language and its culture cannot be rejected outright – bilingualism and biculturalism is desirable. The issue addressed in this chapter is what attitude and belief set is associated with successful language maintenance and bilingualism.

In Australia, politicians who favour the suppression of minority languages and cultures literally drape themselves in the Australian flag, and are so photographed. The association of national identity with majority language monolingualism is an attitude common to many societies around the world. Maintaining a language other than the majority one requires a clear and strong alternative belief structure, in which bilingualism and national identity are not mutually exclusive. Those in the second generation of migrants who lack such a belief structure will often fail to develop their own language beyond semi-speaker level (Dorian, 1981), and may not transmit the minority language to their children.

Attitudes and Beliefs Concerning Language and Maintenance

The quote from Ada (1988) with which this chapter begins illustrates two important propositions. First, people have attitudes to the languages they speak, and second these attitudes can affect language learning and maintenance. As we shall see in this chapter, there is other evidence for both propositions, but they still need proof – in her study Zentella (1997: 141) found that 'No consistent relationship between language proficiency and attitudes towards *el bloque* [the bilingual community] and Spanish was apparent'.

One problem that arises is the classic 'black box' issue. We have no direct access to people's minds, so the only ways that we can attempt to uncover attitudes and beliefs is by examining people's background and experiences (the 'input' to the black box), and people's behaviour (mainly what they say). Putting these together, we can say that attitudes and beliefs are constituted through interaction: they are acquired and constructed in interaction. People bring to any particular interaction their previous experiences, and their mental representations of them. In interaction they may emphasise, suppress or deny aspects of their pre-existing identity and beliefs, as well as negotiating changes to them. This flux compounds the difficulty of identifying attitudes and beliefs.

Like communication, attitudes and beliefs have an ideational/propositional/referential element, and an affective/ interpersonal/ connotative element – roughly speaking, what we think reality is, and how we feel about it. While it is useful to separate these two aspects, in practice they are in such intense interaction that they often merge. Hereafter we will use the term 'attitudes' as shorthand for both beliefs and affective reactions.

There are attitudes about many things, including elements of social identity, such as gender, ethnicity, age, and social class. These all affect language behaviour, and are to some degree constructed and negotiated through language. However, to avoid an unwieldy presentation, we will limit ourselves to those areas of attitudes that are directly relevant to language maintenance. Above all else, these are attitudes to languages, but also attitudes concerning: self identification as a speaker of languages, other speakers of the languages, particular language communities, and the vitality of all these – in other words attitudes concerning the likely future maintenance of these languages by oneself and the language community, and the likely survival of the language community as a distinct entity. Our attempt to limit ourselves to directly-relevant attitudes will have only limited success since attitudes to language interact in particular with attitudes to ethnicity and nationality.

One issue that arises whenever the topic of language attitudes is first introduced is the source of such attitudes. People without a linguistic training often believe that certain languages or language varieties are better than others, and when pinned down they will say that one language or variety is more beautiful or elegant or expressive than another. Trudgill and

Giles (1978) tested this out by recording British dialects, and playing them to English speakers in other countries, some of whom knew the dialects and their social status, while others did not. They found that people who did not know the dialects disagreed widely in their aesthetic judgments, showing that there is little consensus about aesthetic judgments. However, the listeners who did know the social status of the dialects agreed, and their aesthetic judgments mapped directly onto the social status of the dialects – the higher the social status, the 'nicer' the dialect sounded. Put simply, people may believe their judgements are aesthetic, but in reality they are mostly social.

Attitudes to Language

An important pioneering bilingualism study was that performed by Lambert *et al.* (1960). They were examining attitudes towards French and English speakers in Montreal – a highly bilingual city, but one in which there was a clear process of language shift from French to English among French Canadians. Their methodology, which became highly influential and has been replicated in hundreds of subsequent studies, was the 'matched-guise' technique.

In a matched-guise study, recordings are made of a number of bilinguals or bivarietals speaking, first in language/variety A, then in language/variety B. The recordings from the speakers are then mixed up on a tape, putting some distance between the recordings of the same speaker. This usually means that when people listen to a tape they will not recognise that the same speaker has been used more than once. Instead they are misled into believing that the voices are all from different speakers. The listeners hear the voices and usually score the voices on adjective scales (Lickert scales). Typical adjectives would be 'likeable' or 'confident', and when this property is assigned to the speaker, the interviewee might score it on a scale such as:

strongly agree : agree : slightly agree : slightly disagree : disagree : strongly disagree

The advantage of the technique is that it controls for genuine personality differences by using the same speaker for both language/varieties, ensuring that the only real basis for listeners' judgements is the language used. Because there is a deception involved, it is possible to elicit attitudes that the listener holds but might publicly disavow. The findings of such studies reveal two major judgment clusters: *status* (e.g. prestigious, confident, ambitious), and *solidarity* (e.g. friendly, likeable, generous). It is interesting to note that these two variables are realised linguistically in most languages, for instance in pronouns (see Brown & Gilman, 1960;

Morford, 1997), and in register studies under the name of 'appraisal' (Martin, 2000). Another less salient judgement cluster is *dynamism* (active, lively). Similar clusters also emerged in the word connotation studies of Osgood *et al.* (1957).

The study by Lambert *et al.* (1960) revealed stereotypes of English and French speakers held at the time by both Anglophone and Francophone Canadians. Importantly, English speakers were seen as much more prestigious, providing a convincing contribution to the explanation of language shift away from French. (These attitudes have changed in recent times.)

While this elegant and convincing study opened up the study of language attitudes, there were certain things that it could not address (and that continued to cause problems for matched-guise studies). The content of the passages read aloud could not be truly 'neutral' (see Giles & Billings, forthcoming). Moreover, the study did not take into account either the immediate context of language use (for example the acceptability of French in a bar compared with a classroom) or the wider context – at that time in Quebec province French Canadians were a disadvantaged majority. Nevertheless, the disturbing findings of this study were a clarion call that helped to motivate the subsequent strong measure taken to raise the status of French in Quebec (Bourhis, 1984).

There have been many matched-guise studies of other bilingual communities around the world. Studies in Australia have tended to concentrate on accents in English, but Bettoni and Gibbons (1988, 1990) and Hogg *et al.* (1989) revealed negative attitudes towards the Italian varieties actually used in Australia, and positive attitudes to English and to standard Italian (a variety that many Italo-Australians do not speak). The consequence in many cases is a shift to English rather than a shift to standard Italian.

The emergence of these macro clusters of attitudes in so many facets of language and in so many contexts seems to indicate deep categorisations. However, the attention given to these macro clusters may discourage researchers from paying attention to micro and context-based attitudes – but again see Dörnyei (2003). It seems likely that not all beliefs will fall comfortably into these clusters, and that knowledge schemas in particular will not be limited in this way. A limitation to these clusters may be reinforced by limiting research methodology to closed-item questionnaires, which contain the researcher's view of what the beliefs are. Such dominant attitudinal constructs may be important, yet not tell the whole story: they may be necessary but not sufficient as descriptions, and there may be more 'local' elements related to the context in which languages are learned and used.

Over the last two decades, there have been two sustained attacks on the notion of attitudes. It has come under attack from those who believe that attitudes and beliefs are not stable, but are negotiated and constructed through interaction (Potter & Wetherell, 1987, and many others). It is has also come under attack from those who reject a poorly-contextualised and overly-psychological approach in favour of an understanding that is more socially and politically informed (we are thinking in particular of Williams, 1992). We have sympathy with both these views in that they restore balance to explanations that failed to account adequately for both face-to-face inter-action and broader socio-political forces. Nevertheless, we do not believe that these criticisms invalidate the notion that people have beliefs, and that these are present in the minds of participants in interaction. It would be absurd to postulate that people enter interaction as empty slates, awaiting the creation of their belief structure through interaction. Interaction is, rather, a site for the manifestation, negotiation, development and some-times conflict of *existing* belief structures. With regard to the larger picture, it is such beliefs that to a large degree construct, create and change social and political structures. Political battles are to some degree conflicts of ideology or belief (when they are not conflicts of power and advantage).

Attitudes to Bilingualism and Biculturalism

We noted previously that, in many nations, monolingualism in a minority language will not provide access to a full range of services and opportunities. Therefore, in practice, minority-language maintenance normally runs alongside proficiency in the majority language, particularly for second-generation migrants and beyond; so minority-language mainte-nance entails bilingualism. In consequence, attitudes to bilingualism itself can play a role in minority-language maintenance. If people are uncomfort-able with bilingualism, or with the idea of being a bilingual, this may affect the achievement of proficiency in both languages, but more particularly in a vulnerable minority language. Hamers and Blanc (2000: 214) write 'to develop a harmonious bilingual bicultural identity the society must integrate multiculturalism as one of its values'.

Lambert *et al.* (1970), in their study of Franco-American schoolchildren, found that only those who identified strongly with both languages and cultures had above-average achievement in both languages. In Canada, Taylor *et al.* (1973) found that monolinguals identified with other monolin-guals, and bilinguals identified with other bilinguals whether they shared a cultural background or not, suggesting that bilingualism itself can be an independent focus for attitudes. In summary, attitudes that favour bilingualism over monolingualism can support the maintenance of minority languages.

Attitudes to Maintenance/Vitality

In Chapter 4 we saw census research that gives an idea of the strength of language maintenance and shift. However, census approaches in effect ask people what language they *believe* they speak, and what proficiency they *believe* they have, introducing an attitudinal element into even this seemingly objective information. Bourhis (see, for example, Bourhis *et al.*, 1981; Bourhis & Sachdev, 1984) proposed that it is important to see whether people believe their language and its community will survive or not (i.e. their attitudes to ethno-linguistic vitality). He notes that there is a self-fulfilling prophecy involved – a belief in the survival of a language and its community often contributes to their survival, and vice versa i.e. believing in the vitality of a language is a factor in its survival.

Bourhis's methodology involved the development of a Subjective Vitality Questionnaire (SVQ) (see Bourhis *et al.*, 1981), which asked a series of questions about the issues discussed in Chapter 4, such as the likely survival of a language and its separate community of speakers, and the extent of its use in business and the media. There has been a series of studies using this instrument in various countries, including several in Australia. Giles *et al.* (1985) found a convincing partial explanation for the remarkable vitality of Greek in the unrealistic overestimate by Greek youth of the importance and survival of Greek in Australia. Contrasting SVQ studies by Hogg *et al.* (1989) of Italian dialects, and by Gibbons and Ashcroft (1995) of standard Italian, showed poor vitality expectations of the dialects, but strong vitality expectations of standard Italian. Gibbons and Ashcroft's (1995) study also showed that interviewees made a sharp distinction between maintenance of language and maintenance of the community. Nearly all language-maintenance questions favoured English, while community questions favoured Italian. The study also asked interviewees to self-assess their Italian, and on this basis they were evenly divided into groups of higher or lower proficiency. On all the statistically-significant items concerning the vitality of Italian, the higher-proficiency group rated Italian more highly than the lower-proficiency group did, providing support for the 'self-fulfilling prophecy' notion, and the view that those who believe in language maintenance are more likely to achieve it personally.

Identity Beliefs/Attitudes

Cultures vary considerably in the priority that they give to various aspects of identity (Smolicz, 1981 refers to these as 'core values'). For example, Pauwels (1980: 207, reported in Clyne, 1982: 32) found that, among Dutch migrants to Australia, 70% considered it important to maintain family cohesion or *gezelligheid*, while only 5% considered it important to retain the Dutch language. This helps to explain the very high rates of language shift to English among Dutch Australians. By contrast, Taylor *et al.* (1973) found that, for Canadians, language was more important than cultural background.

Giles *et al.* (1976) found that, among Franco-Americans in Maine, those with a high proficiency in French saw French as the only marker of French identity, while those with a low proficiency in French placed their major emphasis on ethnic background (neither group placed much emphasis on geographical origin). This demonstrates the role of language identity in language maintenance, and indicates the need to include it when investigating influences on language maintenance.

In a large-scale study, Rumbaut (1994) found that minority-language adolescents in California who identify themselves more as Americans were more likely to have higher proficiency in English. Those who identified more with their minority nationality were likely to have a higher proficiency in the minority language. The fluent bilinguals (in English and the minority language) were likely to identify as 'hyphenated Americans' (e.g. Cuban-American). The interaction of identity beliefs with language proficiency is demonstrated by this study, as is the type of attitude cluster that may be needed for the maintenance of bilingualism.

Rumbaut's (1994) findings support recent work on language and identity which has revealed a complex, nuanced and variable relationship between them. Various aspects of identity such as class, gender and geographical origin are marked through language; therefore language choice, language use, and language maintenance can all be seen as interacting with other aspects of identity. However, a critical notion in much modern identity theory is that identity *is* language to a large degree (see, for example, Giddens, 1991; Kroskrity, 2000). One way of constructing one's identity as Hispanic is to use Spanish. In other words the phenomenon is not uni-directional – the use of Spanish in interaction can be used to negotiate a Hispanic identity, at the same time that having a Hispanic identity leads to the use of Spanish. In Australia it is common for second-generation Latino-Australians to 'present' as Australian, and to demonstrate a full command of English-speaking Australian cultural practices in English-speaking contexts, and to 'present' as Latino in Latino cultural contexts (even if they are not speaking Spanish). Similar variable identities are found in many other countries. Identity therefore is not a simple unitary phenomenon – people may have/enact multiple identities.

In the context of countries where speaking the dominant national language is essential for full participation in society, the future of languages other than the dominant language lies in maintaining and enacting cultures/languages in addition to the dominant ones. In Australia, minority languages can be supported by constructing multiple identities, and by resisting the monolingual and monocultural hegemony of English which would prevent this. Clément *et al.* (1980) report various studies in which a dominant language poses a perceived threat to ethnic identity.

Taking Language Proficiency Seriously

Another possibly relevant issue is attitudes to language proficiency – what people believe it is, and how they believe it is achieved – i.e. attitudes to language learning. In a well-known though sometimes criticised study, Gardner and Lambert (1972) found two clusters of attitudes that correlated with language learning – instrumental and integrative. Instrumental motivation involves a perception that a particular language is pragmatically useful, particularly in terms of self-advancement. As one interviewee wrote:

> it helps to know a language if you want to get a job.

Integrative motivation is more affective, and has to do with solidarity feelings towards the speakers of the language, to the extent where one wishes to integrate and have contact with them. In minority-language contexts, the integrative motive may be more fruitfully considered in terms of affect (see above): Gibbons and Ashcroft (1995) found an attitudinal cluster that they titled 'pride'.

However, there may be a confusion between beliefs about proficiency, and measurable real command of certain aspects of language, such as grammar, vocabulary, phonemic and phonetic system, and register. Some of the studies described above, perhaps because they emerge from a social-psychological ideology in which belief and action are not distinct, do not include objective measures of the language proficiency, so the interaction of attitudes with proficiency cannot be examined adequately. We have noticed that attitudes are complex and multi-faceted: given the interaction of attitudes and behaviour, it seems likely that different aspects of attitude will be associated with different elements of language proficiency. However, previous studies of language vitality have sometimes limited themselves to *self-assessment* of language proficiency. Self-assessment contains attitudinal elements, particularly self identification as a speaker of a language, as well as confidence (another aspect of attitudes).

Gardner in his many studies (see for instance Gardner, 1979) of second-language acquisition (rather than minority-language maintenance) has consistently used objective proficiency measures, avoiding risk of contamination of proficiency measurement from attitudes. It is possible to extend this approach, examining various attitudes alongside objective measures of different aspects of language proficiency, in order to examine their interactions. This is what we attempted to do.

Summary

We have outlined above a range of attitudes and beliefs that may affect the degree of bilingualism and language maintenance in minority-language communities. We suggest that this range might include attitudes to languages, bilingualism itself, language vitality, identity, and language proficiency. We have also suggested that it is important to have measures of proficiency that are independent of attitudes, so that any relationships revealed between attitudes and proficiency are not a result of contamination.

THE STUDIES

Introduction

Operating within the constraint of avoiding excessive demands on either our interviewees or our limited research budget, we attempted to examine the attitudes of our interviewees by asking both open questions and closed-choice questions. Open questions were asked both before and after the questionnaire section.

Open Questions

The open questions are listed below; they overtly ask about attitudes to the two languages, and towards language vitality. However, the questions are sufficiently vague and general that, as we shall see, they elicited replies concerning all the attitudinal issues discussed above.

Before the questionnaire

How do you feel about Spanish?
What do you think are the chances that the Spanish language will survive in Sydney?

How do you feel about English?

After the questionnaire

Is there anything else you want say about your feelings about Spanish and English?

Is there anything you want to say about these questions?

Questionnaire

Interviewees were asked whether or not they agreed with the 29 items (statements) shown in Table 7.1. Apart from **Q29**, they answered by marking a box on a 5-point scale:

strongly disagree: disagree: mixed feelings: agree: strongly agree.

Question 29 was answered on the following 5-point scale:

almost completely X (insert nationality): mostly X: X and Australian about equally: mostly Australian: almost completely Australian.

Findings from the Open Questions

The five open questions are given above. The interviewees typed in their own responses, so errors in spelling etc. are their own. Responses to the three questions preceding the questionnaires can be divided into positive, negative and uncommitted responses, although uncommitted and negative responses amount to only just over 10% of all responses. For all three questions a great majority of informants (89.7%) gave a positive answer, indicating positive affect both towards their minority language and towards English – a pro-bilingualism stance.

Q1: How do you feel about Spanish?

This question was posed before the questionnaire items, and was worded as broadly as possible to obtain uninfluenced expression of attitudes towards Spanish from the respondents. The responses include attitudes of respondents to their ethnic background and minority language in relation to the dominant language (English), their attitudes towards Spanish as a language of importance (or not) in the world, and their attitudes to learning the language of their parents. The responses can be grouped into the following response types – we have included examples for each type.

Pride

In answer to **Q1** 'How do you feel about Spanish?', the most numerous comments (16) were to do with pride in being a Spanish speaker and/or identity as a Spanish speaker:

Proud! Very proud

I think it is important not to lose touch with your background culture because it is part of who you are as a person

I feel very good that I can speak Spanish (Latino)

The language is beautiful and very useful

I have not experienced a great deal of my Latin American roots, but when I do I feel like involving myself with it

soy muy contenta de ser española *I am very happy to be Spanish*

naci en Colombia entonces entiendo el espanol muy bien y soy muy patriota
I was born in Colombia, so I understand Spanish very well and I am very patriotic

In answer to another question about literacy, one interviewee wrote:

SPANISH IS A GREAT LANGUAGE TO READ AND WRITE, ITS A BEAUTIFUL LANGUAGE AND IAM VERY PROUD OF IT!!

Affect

A number of related comments expressed more general positive affect as follows:

I like to speak Spanish

Yo adoro el español
I adore Spanish

Me gusta español
I like Spanish

Es bueno y es una lengua alegre
it is good and it is a happy language

Yes I like Spanish, I enjoy speaking it

Me gusta
I like it

Yo pienso que el español es una idioma muy Linda para hablar y escuchar
I think that Spanish is a lovely language to speak and listen to

Preference for Spanish over English

Two interviewees liked Spanish enough to prefer it to English.

Me gusta hablarlo y prefiero hablar español antes que ingles con personas que sepan hablarlo
I like it. I like speaking it and I prefer speaking Spanish to English with people that can speak it

I feel that it is a great language and consider myself lucky that I can speak it fluently. I like speaking it more than I like speaking English.

Pro-bilingualism

Thirteen interviewees indicated in their responses attitudes favourable to bilingualism.

Es importante para tener mas que una lengua
It's important to have more than one language

Great because it's very good if you know more than one language and you get to know more people from different countries.

Personalmente a mi me encanta saber una Segunda lengua , y que sea español
Personally I love knowing a second language, and that it is Spanish

... I think it is good to know another languguage.

I feel very proud that I am trilingual

I feel very lucky to know how to speak another language. It's very nice to be able to speak with people who do not speak English, especially relatives.

Pro-maintenance

Another potential support for minority-language maintenance consists of positive attitudes concerning maintenance itself. Eight interviewees expressed opinions about the maintenance of Spanish as a community language.

Yo considero que el español es un idioma muy rico, el cual hay que hacegurarse en mantenerlo ...
I consider Spanish to be a very rich language, which we should ensure is maintained

I think all the children with a Spanish background that can't talk English should have the best facilities to learn how to speak in SpanishIt is a good language to learn, since we should not lose our mother

I think that whether Spanish will survive in Sydney is up to the parents. If a parent arrives in Australia and decides that they want it, it depends on the attitudes of people.

creo que el español es muy importante porque nosotros tenemos que seguir hablando el idioma de nuestros padres y conservar la lengua española
I think that Spanish is very important because we have to continue speaking the language to our parents and maintain the Spanish language

Spanish is my native language

I like to know that I have a second language that I can study deeply and I can pass down to my kids

Contact with Spanish speakers

Seven interviewees indicated that knowing Spanish was important as it enabled them to speak to other Spanish-speakers and to relatives overseas.

I love Spanish I find that I can communicate well with family and friends

It's useful when I talk to friends of my parents. It also enables me to talk to relatives overseas

Es bueno hablarlo, leerlo y escribirlo porque en los diarios de ingles no te enteras de lo que pasa en la comunidad
It is good to speak, read and write it because in the English language newspapers you don't find out what goes on in the community

Es importante para mantener contactos en Argentina
It is important in order to keep contacts in Argentina

Es un idioma util para mi porque la mayoria de la gente que conozco lo habla
It is a useful language for me as the majority of people I know speak it

y tambien lo necesitare cuando visite a mi familia
I will also need it when I visit my family [in Colombia]

Importance of Spanish

Many respondents mentioned the importance of Spanish generally, revealing a belief the 'status' of Spanish, and some of them stated that it would help them in the future, corresponding to Lambert and Gardner's (1972) 'instrumental' attitudes.

It's a good language and a useful one.

I think Spanish is important to learn so that in the future, when I get a job, I have an advantage because I speak two languages

It enables me to understand movies in Spanish that are sometimes spoken in Spanish

I think it's a great language and an advantage for me to know.

Es muy importante
It's very important

Es un idioma que es el segundo despues del ingles
It is the second language after English

I think it is a very important language in today's world

Es una lengua bien importante
it is a very important language

Creo que es muy importante, especialmente porque ... creo que me puede ayudar en el futuro
I think it is very important, especially because ... I believe it can help me in the future

Learning issues

Some interviewees found Spanish easy:

It's a great language and it's easy to learn

I think it is a very beautiful language and easy to grasp and learn . I am very proud of being able to speak it.

It's a very interesting language , I love the language because I can speak it and I think it is a wonderful language.

es facil hablarlo me gusta,
It is easy to speak it, I like it

... no es dificil solo que hay que practicar
it is not hard, you just have to practice

While two interviewees had problems with it:

Es una lengua muy completa, es mas facil que el ingles, a no ser por los acentos y los dieresis
it is a very thorough language, it is easier than English, except for accents and diaeresis

Es un idioma lindo perso dificil a veces
it is a beautiful language but hard at times ... it is a very difficult language to learn

In answer to a question about literacy, some interviewees voiced a desire to improve also:

I DO FIND IT A BIT DIFFICULT BUT I DO TEND TO TRY AND ASK HOW IT IS EITHER SPELT OR SAID

I WOULD LIKE TO SPEAK THE LANGUAGE MORE FLUENTLY AND WRITE IT IN A BETTER WAY

The themes that emerged from the responses were to do both with the languages and with being bilingual. Essentially their attitudes towards being bilingual are favourable – a 'pro-bilingualism' attitude. Views concerning Spanish include its 'usefulness' both for practical purposes and for social contact with other Spanish speakers. However, overwhelmingly the responses had to with the affective, with liking Spanish, with pride in and identification with speaking Spanish – what might be called a 'Spanish pride' attitude. Finally there were attitudes concerning the perceived 'difficulty' of learning Spanish. The fact that these themes emerged without prompting and before the questionnaire items were revealed supports our examination of these themes in the questionnaire items (subsequent analysis also explored the relationship of these attitudes with elements of Spanish proficiency).

Q2: What do you think are the chances that the Spanish language will survive in Sydney?

Answers to this question were divided into positive, negative and uncommitted responses. Of the 106 respondents who completed the survey, 3 did not answer this question.

Uncommitted responses

Fourteen respondents (13.2%) provided answers that were uncommitted. Only three of these respondents gave reasons for their answers. One indicated that the onus was on the community, that some people are embarrassed to speak Spanish in public. Another commented that the survival of Spanish and indeed of other community languages rested in the hands of the government. The third made a demographic argument, stating that the survival of Spanish in Sydney depended on the number of Spanish speakers living in Sydney: and if the number is high, then the language will survive. Some examples of the responses within this category were:

50/50;

medio medio *so so*

no lo se ; un poco
I don't know; a bit

it depends on the actitudes of the people

There are some people who are embarrassed to be talking Spanish who think it is better not to speak it

I don't know

Well, it all depends on what the government will decide

I hope though that the government won't take Spanish or any other language.

Negative responses

There were 6 negative responses (5.7%) to this question. These ranged from zero chances of survival to uncertainty. Reasons provided by respondents were that people do not seem to care whether the language survives or not, and the acute observation that Spanish is not much taught in mainstream education. Examples were:

Ningunas
none

Not so good

No creo que se conserve
I don't believe it will be conserved

They're very low as some people don't really care

Not very big

Not much due to the lack of schools that provide languages.

Positive responses

A total of 87 (82.1%) respondents gave a positive response to this question. The answers ranged from extremely good chances of survival to 'it could survive'. Reasons for their positive responses included demography, politics, education, popularity of Spanish in movies and songs, pride, community activities, uses of the language and language maintenance. Some examples of these responses are:

> extremely good
>
> the chances are good because the amount of people in Sydney are fairly stable
>
> si se va a mantener
> *yes it will survive*
>
> we should have a bit more social events in Spanish as it helps us to talk and socialize with other people in Spanish
>
> As long as there are people from Spanish-speaking countries I feel there will always be an interest in the Spanish language
>
> I think that Spanish will survive in Sydney as it is widely spoken with many Latin American clubs throughout Sydney. It would be nearly impossible to wipe out the language as too many people speak it
>
> a lot
>
> I think it will survive as I know many non-native Latin Americans who love and want to learn the language and many Latin Americans hopefully will keep on teaching their children
>
> I think that the Spanish language will survive in Sydney as it is a respectable language
>
> yo creo que hay muchas posibilidades ya que el idioma es incluido con mucha frecuencia en peliculas inglesas y en diferentes medios de comunicacion
> *I believe that there are high probabilities given that Spanish is frequently included in English language movies and in the mass media*
>
> It has a chance for the culture is widespread.

From the above it can be seen that a considerable majority of informants believed that Spanish would be maintained in Sydney. It should be remembered, however, that this may be in part a result of the sample, which came mainly from families where an effort was being made to retain Spanish.

The forces that were seen to be operating in favour of Spanish were demography, community institutions and activities, the international status of Spanish, positive solidarity attitudes to Spanish, positive status attitudes to Spanish, and media use.

Q3: How do you feel about English?

As with Spanish, the intention was to elicit uninfluenced views concerning English. Of the 106 respondents who completed the questionnaire, 2 failed to answer this question, leaving 104 responses. Answers to this question, like those for question 1, can be grouped into categories. Two responses were negative: 'no' and 'nothing', while four were uncommitted: 'no tengo opinion' (*I have no opinion*); 'not sure'; 'OK'; 'It is OK'.

Affect

Thirty interviewees expressed a liking for English:

ITS A GOOD LANGUAGE

ME GUSTA, ME GUSTA HABLARLO
I like it, I like speaking it

ES BUENO PORQUE YO LO SE MAS QUE ESPANOL
it is good because I know it better than Spanish

I ALSO LOVE THE ENGLISH LANGUAGE AS I WAS BORN IN THIS GREAT COUNTRY.

me ha gustado dessde pequena cuando lo estudiaba en mi pais.
I have liked it since I was a child and studied it in my country.

Its a good language

its cool

i feel good about english

However, two interviewees said that they still prefer Spanish:

ENGLISH IS A GOOD LANGUAGE, BUT NOT AS GOOD AS SPANISH.

I HINK ENGLISH IS A NICE LANGUAGE BUT NOT QUITE AS SPECIAL AND UNIQUE AS THE SPANISH LANGUAGE.

Greater expressive potential of Spanish

One possible reason for preferring Spanish is that three interviewees felt that Spanish is more expressive than English:

no es tan rico como el idioma espanol ni tiene tanto vocabulario..uno se puede expresar mucho mejor en espanol.....
it is not a rich as Spanish and it has not got as much vocabulary. One can express oneself much better in Spanish

REALMENTE NO LO PUEDO COMPARAR CON EL ESPANOL , PARA MI PUNTO DE VISTA DESPUES DE HABER APRENDIDO ESPANOL VEO AL IDIOMA INGLES, FRIO , Y NO MUY EXPRESIVO .
I really cannot compare it with Spanish, from my point of view having studied Spanish I find English cold and not very expressive.

I FEEL THAT IT IS A SIMPLE LANGUAGE AND THINK THAT SPANISH IS A MORE ROMANTIC ESPECIALLY IN SOAPIES (SOAP OPERAS-NOVELAS)

These feelings about a second majority language have much in common with those described in Skutnabb-Kangas (1981: 258–259).

International importance of English

The interviewees seem to be very aware of the international status, importance and utility of English. 25 interviewees comment on this. The examples that follow are roughly sorted into status versus utility, but these categories may not be distinct for most of the interviewees.

es un idioma muy importante, los paises importantes lo hablan
it is a very important language, the important countries speak it

es importante porque casi todo el mundo hablan ingles
it is important because almost the whole world speaks English

me gusta ingles porque es el lenguaje del mundo.
I like english because it is the world language

ENGLISH IS THE UNIVERSAL LANGUAGE AND IS THE MAIN FORM OF COMMUNICATION IN THE WORLD.

EL INGLES ES DE MUCHA IMPORTANCIA YA QUE AHORA ES LA PRIMERA LENGUA.
English is of great importance since it is now the number one language

ES UNA LENGUA QUE SE PUEDE USAR EN TODOS LOS PAISES
It is a language that can be used in all countries

es muy necesario a nivel internacional -gente en Argentina lo sabe; es una de las lenguas más necesarias
it is very necessary at the international level - people in Argentina know it; it is one of the most necessary languages

I'M HAPPY TO KNOW THAT I HAVE A WORLD KNOWN LANGUAGE THAT I KNOW AND WILL HELP MY THROUGHOUT MY LIFE.

English is another important language. Wherever you are in the world, whatever country you are in, they always understand english.

es importante conocer el lenguaje para poder tener oportunidades en el futuro en otro pais, pueda ser hispano hablante.
it is important to know the language to have opportunities in the future in another country, even a Spanish speaking one.

Local importance

Fourteen interviewees mention the need to use English in daily life in Sydney/Australia, including in their schooling.

IT THE MOST COMMON SPOKEN LANGUAGE IN SYDNEY SO IT's VERY IMPORTANT.

pues yo he nacido aqui y es una obligacion para hablarlo. porque yo voy a una escuela inglesa y hablan ingles.
well I was born here and it is an obligation to speak it because I go to an English speaking school.

es el idioma con el que trabajo
it is the language I work with

ENGLISH IS IMPORTANAT IN MY SOCIETY BECAUSE I NEED TO USE IT ON A DAY TO DAY BASIS.

i think that english is great because if i did not know how to speak english i wouldn't know much in this country and i would fall behind in my education.

I like speaking in english because i can communicate with people from here like friends, teachers , etc....

CREO QUE ES NECESARIO PARA COMUNIC ARME CON LA MAYORIA DE GENTE EN AUSTRQLI

I think it is necessary for communicating with the majority of people in Australia

ENGLISH IS VERY IMPORTANT TO MY SOCIAL LIFE. I USE ENGLISH ALMOST EVERYWHERE I GO.

el ingles es imporante por lo que vivimos en un pais de habla inglesa.

English is important because we live in an English speaking country.

Pro-bilingualism

A pro-bilingualism orientation again emerged in comments from six interviewees:

AMI ME GUTA MUCHO EL INGLES PORQUE ES BUENO SABER DOS O MAS IDIOMAS.

I like English very much because it is good to know two or more languages

SOCORRO!!! NO ES UNA BROMA ESPERO PODER SENTIR LO MISMO QUE CIENTO SOBRE EL ESPANOL,PIENSO QUE EL TENER LA CHANCE DE PODER SABER COMUNICARCE MAS DE UNA LENGUA ES COMO UN REGALO MARAVILLOSO QUE HABRE PUERTAS ASIA OTRO MUNDO (CULTURAS,COSTUMBRES,TRADICIONES)

Heavens!!! It is no joke I hope, to be able to feel exactly the same as for Spanish, I think to have the chance to be able to communicate in more than one language is a marvellous gift that opens doors to another world (cultures, customs, traditions)

NOW I KNOW TWO LANGUAGES

Unfortunately in our closed-item questionnaire we did not include any items on beliefs about bilingualism itself – this was unpredicted.

Learning issues

Learning issues also emerged among our interviewees. Seventeen of them claimed to find the language easy to learn.

ES FACIL DE APRENDER
It is easy to learn

ES UN IDIOMA FACIL
It is an easy language

es una lengua facil y la puedo hablar facilamente
It is an easy language and I can speak it easily

i think it's a good language which is easy to learn

ES UN IDIOMA SENCILIO
It is a simple language
FAIRLY BASIC AND FAIRLY EASY TO GRASP.

However, some take the more sophisticated view that a language you learn in early childhood always seems easier:

That it is an easy language to understand, practically if you have lived all your life in Australia.

si lo aprendés de chico es fácil
if you learn it from very young it is easy

cuando llegue a este pais era muy joven o sea que no me fue dificil aprenderlo
when I arrived in this country I was very young so it was not difficult for me to learn it

I think that english is probably the easiest language in the world. I don't know whether it is because I have lived here since I was very young, but i find it a lot easier thatn other lnguages even Spanish.

Some interviewees (mainly those who came to Australia later in child-hood) find the language hard.

es un idioma dificil para aprender
it is a hard language to learn

es más dificil de habla que el español
it is harder to speak than Spanish

i'm glad i was born with it i believe it's one of the hardest languages to learn.

For foreigners, english is a hard language to learn. As I find it easy.

Resistance to the hegemony of English

Two interviewees expressed resistance to the hegemony of English, one in regard to the world, the other in regard to Australia.

I don't think that people in other countries should have to learn it

I FEEL PROUD ASWELL.EVEN IN MEXICO TEACHER's TEACH ENGLISH THERE AND THERE HAS BEEN NO ATTEMPT TO STOP TEACHING IT LIKE THIS GOVERNMENT WANTS TO TAKE AWAY OUR OWN LAUNGE THAT WE HAVE BEEN GROWN UP WITH AND STRUGGLED TO LEARN PROPABLY.

Q4: Is there anything else you want to say about your feelings about Spanish and English?

Asked after the closed questions, this was intended to gather additional reactions that may have been stimulated by filling in the closed-item questionnaire. Twenty-one respondents did not answer this question, and 67 indicated that they had nothing else to add. This left only 19 respondents who wished to add comments. Of these, 8 expressed pride in their *bilingualism*, in knowing both languages because of the importance of both Spanish and English. Two respondents made a comment concerning the richness of the Spanish language, Spanish culture and Spanish history – the *Spanish pride* attitude that had emerged in response to **Q1** previously. Similarly, one respondent explicitly expressed a preference for Spanish over English, and another indicated that feelings can be better expressed in Spanish (i.e. *expressive potential*: see also Skutnabb-Kangas, 1981, for a discussion of the difficulty of expressing feelings in a second language). Two responses indicated that Spanish should continue to be taught in schools for future generations – the *maintenance* theme from **Q1**. One expressed a need to see more information on what is taking place in Spanish-speaking countries. In general, our questions had little impact on the views of interviewees, but where they did the probing of feelings and the reflection involved in the questionnaire process appears to have elicited feelings of support for Spanish and bilingualism.

Q5: Is there anything you want to say about these questions?

This was a reflective question, designed to provide information concerning the reactions of respondents to our instruments, both to control for any problems, and to enable us to improve our research. Twenty-four respondents did not answer this question, and 76 stated that they had nothing else to say. Three of the remaining respondents commented that the questions were good and/or interesting. Two wrote that the questions had made them realise how important Spanish was to them, while another said that s/he felt more Colombian than Uruguayan given that s/he had spent more time in that country. It can be seen from this that only six interviewees actually responded to this question, which at least indicates the absence of problems. Indeed the small number that did reply seem to have found the process rewarding.

Conclusions from the open questions

The topics that emerged from these questions were mainly those described in the introduction. Some interesting themes that we did not predict, however, were notions of difficulty and ease of learning, differences in expressive potential and, perhaps most interesting of all, resistance to the hegemony of English.

The Questionnaire

Individual items

Table 7.1 contains the original questions, which were answered, as we noted earlier, on 5-point scales. The items drew on the SVQ, but were supplemented from matched-guise studies and comments from Sydney Hispanic teenagers and discussion among the bilingual researchers of attitudes that they felt were typical of the Hispanic community in Sydney. They addressed attitudes to English and Spanish in a range of domains (international, Sydney, the community, in public, and the self); they addressed instrumental, affective, status, identity and maintenance attitudes; and they looked at both productive and receptive uses of Spanish.

With regard to the processing of responses, where necessary the responses are reverse-scored, so that a more positive attitude to Spanish is always coded higher. This table shows the correlations between the individual questions and the Spanish assessments. (For conventions used in tables, see p. *x*, at the beginning of the book.)

Once more, to avoid the effects of education in Spanish-speaking country on Spanish proficiency, we mostly limited the statistical processing to the 84 interviewees who were entirely educated in Australia. As one of our early interviewers did not tape record her interviews, the data on oral proficiency have missing values (15 cases were affected).

We begin by examining the relationship between the oracy measures and the individual attitude items. We were agreeably surprised to see how many of these correlations were significant.

Although it is clear that the oracy measures have a shared element, there are also some interesting differences between them. Fluency seems to be associated mainly with a strong affective pro-Spanish orientation (items 3, 5, 14, 17, 18 and 25). A good accent seems to be associated with a rejection of the hegemony of English (items 8, 10 and 27), and a resentment that Spanish is not respected in Sydney (item 16). Idiomaticity (which is associated with more general language proficiency) is related to a valuing of Spanish for international use (items 1 and 7; and 21 when all interviewees are included). There is also a pro-maintenance orientation (items 15 and 26), and a core Spanish pride (items 5, 14 and 25). Mixing seems to be associated primarily with a recognition of a need to learn more Spanish (items 5, 15, 20, 23 and 26).

We ran the same correlations on the whole sample), and results were similar, with the exception of item 27. Only among the Australian-educated is the need to reject the hegemony of English associated with higher Spanish proficiency.

It is important to note that the different aspects of proficiency relate to

Table 7.1 Correlations: Individual questions by Spanish oracy measures (Australian-educated only)

	Fluency		Accent		Idiomaticity		Mixing		Total	
	Corr	p	Corr	p	Corr	p	Corr	p	Corr	p
1 Spanish will not be very useful internationally in the future	0.38	**0.0017**	0.10	0.4247	0.35	**0.0044**	0.18	0.1489	0.32	**0.0107**
2 English will not be very useful internationally in the future	0.26	**0.0395**	0.10	0.4542	0.07	0.5706	0.10	0.4501	0.16	0.1975
3 Spanish is a beautiful language	0.27	**0.0314**	0.04	0.7433	0.12	0.3612	0.00419	0.9741	0.14	0.2799
4 English is a beautiful language	0.04	0.7297	0.04	0.7387	0.01	0.9167	0.06	0.6357	0.05	0.7017
5 I really like being around people when they are speaking Spanish	0.31	**0.0125**	0.20	0.1182	0.38	**0.0019**	0.35	**0.0045**	0.38	**0.0019**
6 I really like being around people when they are speaking English	-0.06	0.6398	-0.06	0.6351	-0.10	0.4457	-0.00472	0.9708	-0.07	0.5983
7 Spanish is important for international business	0.17	0.1842	0.16	0.2230	0.27	**0.0291**	0.18	0.1606	0.24	0.0619
8 English is important for international business	0.23	0.0687	0.26	**0.0407**	0.27	**0.0305**	0.24	0.0575	0.30	**0.0153**
9 Spanish is not highly regarded internationally	0.07	0.6034	0.01	0.9625	0.06	0.6215	-0.01	0.9127	0.04	0.7637
10 English is not highly regarded internationally	0.28	**0.0243**	0.27	**0.0304**	0.27	**0.0350**	0.11	0.3734	0.28	**0.0236**
11 You only need Spanish in the modern world	-0.11	0.3988	0.04	0.7560	-0.08	0.5137	0.09	0.4742	-0.02	0.8627
12 You only need English in the modern world	-0.20	0.1146	-0.17	0.1711	-0.23	0.0686	0.04	0.7363	-0.17	0.1797
13 In Sydney most people want Spanish to be kept alive	0.06	0.6543	0.01	0.9183	0.06	0.6504	0.08	0.5305	0.06	0.6144
14 I feel good when I speak Spanish	0.41	**0.0008**	0.36	**0.0037**	0.46	**0.0001**	0.28	**0.0241**	0.46	**0.0001**

Table 7.1 (*continued*)

15	For cultural reasons, families from Spanish speaking countries should keep up their Spanish	0.34	0.0061	0.33	0.0079	0.41	0.0009	0.41	0.0007	0.45	0.0002
16	Spanish is not highly regarded in Sydney	-0.10	0.4358	-0.31	0.0123	-0.22	0.0822	-0.20	0.1094	-0.25	0.0498
17	I do not like people from my parents' country(s)	0.26	0.0411	0.16	0.2248	0.06	0.6343	0.02	0.8950	0.15	0.2328
18	Spanish speakers should be proud of their language	0.28	0.0281	0.18	0.1512	0.24	0.0570	0.24	0.0610	0.29	0.0221
19	In Sydney most people like hearing Spanish spoken	0.16	0.2165	0.04	0.7666	0.02	0.8748	0.05	0.7160	0.08	0.5151
20	I want to learn more Spanish	0.17	0.1789	0.22	0.0856	0.17	0.1874	0.25	0.0453	0.25	0.0526
21	It is important to retain Spanish for international use	0.18	0.1619	0.05	0.7075	0.20	0.1245	0.18	0.1537	0.19	0.1430
22	Spanish is a language without a great culture	0.14	0.2902	0.08	0.5574	0.09	0.4986	0.04	0.7857	0.10	0.4232
23	If you speak Spanish you can get a better job	0.13	0.3026	0.08	0.5532	0.16	0.2086	0.29	0.0203	0.20	0.1130
24	In Sydney, Spanish is well represented in the media (e.g. newspapers, TV, radio)	-0.10	0.4314	-0.06	0.6553	-0.07	0.6064	-0.14	0.2633	-0.11	0.3787
25	I am happy to speak Spanish in public	0.32	0.0096	0.09	0.4686	0.27	0.0354	0.20	0.1191	0.27	0.0300
26	Children from Spanish speaking homes should be made to learn Spanish	0.23	0.0703	0.35	0.0049	0.36	0.0040	0.31	0.0143	0.37	0.0024
27	In Australia you only need English	0.24	0.0539	0.30	0.0181	0.34	0.0062	0.25	0.0447	0.34	0.0058
28	The Spanish language is not an important part of my identity	0.18	0.1674	0.07	0.5919	0.07	0.5934	0.02	0.8855	0.10	0.4173
29	What is your identity?	0.23	0.0761	0.22	0.0785	0.35	0.0042	0.31	0.0125	0.34	0.0065

Observations = 63; missing values = 21

Table 7.2 Correlations: Individual questions by Spanish proficiency measures – Australian-educated

	Basic literacy		C-test		History cloze		Science cloze		Span cloze total		Self-prof	
	Corr	p	Corr	p	Corr	p	Corr	p	Corr	p	Corr	p
1 Spanish will not be very useful internationally in the future	0.10	0.3881	0.03	0.8195	0.11	0.3571	0.03	0.7935	0.08	0.5090	0.32	**0.0043**
2 English will not be very useful internationally in the future	-0.05	0.6375	0.29	**0.0090**	0.13	0.2682	0.12	0.3037	0.14	0.2377	0.19	0.0948
3 Spanish is a beautiful language	0.10	0.3708	0.26	**0.0244**	0.17	0.1409	0.08	0.5056	0.14	0.2345	0.14	0.2236
4 English is a beautiful language	-0.01	0.9218	0.24	**0.0388**	-0.02	0.8331	0.06	0.6259	0.02	0.8859	0.07	0.5278
5 I really like being around people when they are speaking Spanish	0.28	**0.0137**	0.29	**0.0092**	0.15	0.1898	0.15	0.1933	0.17	0.1488	0.36	**0.0013**
6 I really like being around people when they are speaking English	0.13	0.2447	0.11	0.3638	$3.13E^{5}$	0.9998	0.17	0.1395	0.09	0.4290	0.07	0.5658
7 Spanish is important for international business	0.07	0.5688	0.07	0.5373	0.28	**0.0150**	0.12	0.2895	0.22	0.0526	0.26	**0.0202**
8 English is important for international business	-0.04	0.7057	0.19	0.0894	0.31	**0.0067**	0.32	**0.0048**	0.34	**0.0021**	0.17	0.1368
9 Spanish is not highly regarded internationally	0.09	0.4559	-0.09	0.4175	0.04	0.7127	-0.05	0.6700	-0.00252	0.9827	0.03	0.7728
10 English is not highly regarded internationally	0.22	**0.0504**	0.39	**0.0004**	0.02	0.8333	0.16	0.1733	0.10	0.3958	0.18	0.1267
11 You only need Spanish in the modern world	-0.21	0.0662	-0.10	0.3880	$-3.65E^{-3}$	0.9750	-0.01	0.9520	-0.01	0.9600	-0.03	0.7657
12 You only need English in the modern world	-0.07	0.5525	-0.08	0.4725	-0.10	0.4117	0.06	0.6148	-0.02	0.8483	-0.30	**0.0089**
13 In Sydney most people want Spanish to be kept alive	0.23	**0.0427**	$2.29E^{3}$	0.9843	0.12	0.2806	-0.04	0.7532	0.05	0.6620	0.15	0.1970
14 I feel good when I speak Spanish	0.20	0.0797	0.22	0.0526	0.24	**0.0376**	0.16	0.1709	0.22	0.0555	0.35	**0.0017**

Table 7.2 (*continued*)

#	Item												
15	For cultural reasons, families from Spanish speaking countries should keep up their Spanish	0.13	0.2695	0.30	**0.0083**	0.25	**0.0293**	0.20	0.0769	0.25	**0.0284**	0.29	**0.0090**
16	Spanish is not highly regarded in Sydney	0.16	0.1634	-0.11	0.3604	0.04	0.7537	0.06	0.6024	0.05	0.6470	-0.04	0.7532
17	I do not like people from my parents' country(s)	0.15	0.1957	0.21	0.0725	0.12	0.3074	0.07	0.5505	0.10	0.3691	0.05	0.6398
18	Spanish speakers should be proud of their language	0.19	0.1026	0.09	0.4406	0.08	0.5167	0.11	0.3499	0.10	0.3842	0.02	0.8381
19	In Sydney most people like hearing Spanish spoken	0.23	**0.0403**	0.03	0.7772	0.23	**0.0444**	0.16	0.1553	0.22	0.0569	0.14	0.2349
20	I want to learn more Spanish	0.30	**0.0073**	0.11	0.3259	0.07	0.5368	0.04	0.7007	0.06	0.5782	0.19	0.0977
21	It is important to retain Spanish for international use	0.19	0.0980	0.01	0.9117	0.43	**<0.0001**	0.36	0.0014	0.44	<0.0001	0.14	0.2325
22	Spanish is a language without a great culture	0.21	0.0633	0.14	0.2114	0.16	0.1590	0.07	0.5716	0.13	0.2719	0.22	0.0552
23	If you speak Spanish you can get a better job	0.13	0.2559	-0.01	0.9291	0.20	0.0821	0.17	0.1442	0.20	0.0763	0.10	0.3741
24	In Sydney, Spanish is well represented in the media (e.g. newspapers, TV, radio)	0.07	0.5315	-0.20	0.0753	0.17	0.1301	0.12	0.2830	0.17	0.1514	-0.07	0.5638
25	I am happy to speak Spanish in public	0.20	0.0859	0.15	0.1800	0.15	0.1827	0.13	0.2768	0.15	0.1802	0.34	**0.0026**
26	Children from Spanish speaking homes should be made to learn Spanish	-0.01	0.9341	0.21	0.0703	$2.81\mathrm{E}^{-3}$	0.9807	$3.52\mathrm{E}^{-3}$	0.9759	$3.48\mathrm{E}^{-3}$	0.9761	0.32	**0.0040**
27	In Australia you only need English	0.10	0.4049	0.06	0.5804	-0.06	0.6130	-0.15	0.1928	-0.11	0.3241	0.25	**0.0292**
28	The Spanish language is not an important part of my identity	0.11	0.3459	0.09	0.4162	0.10	0.4097	0.20	0.0830	0.16	0.1621	0.20	0.0856
29	What is your identity?	0.07	0.5402	0.10	0.3842	0.03	0.7903	0.10	0.3856	0.07	0.5372	0.39	**0.0004**

Observations = 77; missing values = 7

different attitude sets. As far as we know this is a new finding. Looking at the aspects of proficiency in turn, *basic literacy* is associated with a valorisation of the use of Spanish in Sydney (items 5, 13 and 19). Mastery of this basic skill is also associated with a desire to learn more Spanish (item 20). The development of *grammar and vocabulary* as measured by the C-test is associated with a love of Spanish (items 3, 5 and 15), Spanish maintenance (item 15), and most interestingly, a rejection of the international hegemony of English (items 2, 10 and perhaps 4). *High register* in Spanish, as measured by the clozes, is associated most strongly with item 21, which contains the notion of maintaining Spanish for international use, and this is supported by the maintenance item 15, and the international-use items 7 and 8. An internationalist and global orientation appears to be related to the development of this aspect of Spanish. There is also an element of Spanish pride (items 14 and 19). *Self-assessment* has an attitudinal element, so there is some contamination in this result. It is interesting to note, however, that interviewees who assess their own Spanish higher (thereby showing confidence in their Spanish), also reveal confidence to use Spanish (items 14 and 25), a valuing of Spanish for international use (items 1, 7, and 12), strong pro-maintenance views (items 15 and 26), and a Hispanic rather than Australian identity (item 29).

We can conclude from this that there is value in looking at different aspects of proficiency, and, perhaps most importantly, the development of core proficiency in Spanish is associated with pride in Spanish and a rejection of the international hegemony of English. Those in Australia who master the higher registers tend to be oriented to international uses of the language. This is rational, since the use of Spanish in Australia is mostly limited to domestic and community domains, and higher registers would be deployed mainly in overseas contacts.

There are echoes here of the results from the oracy measures, with a recurrence of Spanish pride and a rejection of the hegemony of English. There is also a strong relationship with the findings from the open questions, since questions about pride in speaking Spanish, and Hispanic identity have a strong relationship with these self-reported proficiency measures.

Turning now to the English measures, only one of the English cloze tests showed significant associations with the attitude measures. This is shown in Table 7.3.

The view revealed here is one of acceptance of the hegemony of English, and a rejection of the role of Spanish both internationally (items 1 and 9) and locally (item 24), and a consequent rejection of being forced to learn

Table 7.3 Correlations: Individual questions by English cloze test

		English cloze: water	
		Corr	*p*
1	Spanish will not be very useful internationally in the future	-0.23	**0.0370**
2	English will not be very useful internationally in the future	-0.04	0.7083
3	Spanish is a beautiful language	0.09	0.4438
4	English is a beautiful language	-0.05	0.6362
5	I really like being around people when they are speaking Spanish	-0.11	0.3500
6	I really like being around people when they are speaking English	-0.04	0.7123
7	Spanish is important for international business	-0.17	0.1421
8	English is important for international business	-4.04E-3	0.9717
9	Spanish is not highly regarded internationally	-0.24	**0.0317**
10	English is not highly regarded internationally	0.10	0.3568
11	You only need Spanish in the modern world	0.01	0.9295
12	You only need English in the modern world	0.11	0.3487
13	In Sydney most people want Spanish to be kept alive	-0.20	0.0721
14	I feel good when I speak Spanish	-0.22	*0.0534*
15	For cultural reasons, families from Spanish-speaking countries should keep up their Spanish	-0.06	0.5706
16	Spanish is not highly regarded in Sydney	-0.20	0.0715
17	I do not like people from my parents' country(s)	0.03	0.7703
18	Spanish speakers should be proud of their language	-0.10	0.3689
19	In Sydney most people like hearing Spanish spoken	-0.17	0.1212
20	I want to learn more Spanish	-0.20	0.0816
21	It is important to retain Spanish for international use	-0.19	0.0846
22	Spanish is a language without a great culture	0.04	0.7494
23	If you speak Spanish you can get a better job	-0.12	0.2827
24	In Sydney, Spanish is well represented in the media (e.g. newspapers, TV, radio)	-0.40	0.0002
25	I am happy to speak Spanish in public	-0.15	0.1929

Table 7.3 *(continued)*

26	Children from Spanish speaking homes should be made to learn Spanish	-0.25	0.0274
27	In Australia you only need English	-0.11	0.3478
28	The Spanish language is not an important part of my identity	0.04	0.7144
29	What is your identity?	-0.22	0.0522

Observations = 80; missing values = 4

Spanish (item 26). This could be seen as the reverse of the some of the attitudes that support Spanish, but the evidence for this is limited.

Groupings of attitudes

One interesting issue that arises from these figures is whether attitudes to English are negatively related to attitudes to Spanish, and whether negative attitudes to English favour the maintenance of Spanish. To examine this question, all items in support of Spanish were added, and all items in support of English were added, then a Fisher's R–Z correlation was performed with the proficiency measures. The results are in Table 7.4.

Perhaps the most important thing to notice is that support for English is positively scored against all the Spanish tests, significantly so in two cases. This seems to show that support for *bilingualism* (the 'pro-bilingualism'

Table 7.4 Correlations: Overall support by proficiency measures

	English support		Spanish support	
	Corr	*p*	*Corr*	*p*
Spanish basic literacy	0.05	0.6820	0.30	**0.0068**
Spanish C-test	0.34	**0.0023**	0.17	0.1418
Spanish history cloze	0.16	0.1773	0.28	**0.0148**
Spanish science cloze	0.23	**0.0477**	0.19	0.0970
Spanish cloze total	0.21	0.0670	0.26	**0.0229**
Spanish self-proficiency rating	0.09	0.4545	0.35	**0.0017**
English cloze, water	0.04	0.7008	-0.27	**0.0161**

Observations = 77; missing values = 7

attitude found in the responses to the open questions), not just support for Spanish is favourably related to the maintenance of Spanish. Furthermore, the tests that were most strongly related were those which tested the more difficult and advanced aspects of Spanish – the science cloze and the C-test. Cummins (1984) in his model of 'Common Underlying Proficiency' proposes that it is precisely these higher aspects of language that are common across the languages of bilinguals. There was also a non-significant positive relationship between support for English and support for Spanish, indicating that there was not a simple 'either–or' notion in the minds of our interviewees. The other finding of importance is that support for Spanish overall has a strong relationship with proficiency in Spanish as measured by the tests. However, the last result indicates that English proficiency may have some relationship to the negative view of Spanish that we observed in the results for the individual questions.

The open questions reveal clusters of attitudes, namely 'pro-bilingualism', the importance of 'maintenance' of Spanish, the 'international usefulness' of Spanish, the 'solidarity', liking Spanish, 'Spanish pride', and 'resistance to the hegemony of English'. These groupings were supported by what we observed in the pattern of responses on the individual questions, as well as by an exploratory factor analysis of the questionnaire items. Another cluster that emerged in the closed questions was the notion of 'Sydney vitality', and we felt it important to separate out the specific measures of 'identity'. To clarify the picture, individual items were grouped and added together as follows:

- Spanish pride: 5, 14, 15, 18, 25
- Spanish affect: 3, 17, 22
- Spanish international usefulness: 1, 7, 21
- Spanish maintenance: 15, 21, 26
- Sydney vitality: 13, 16, 19, 24
- Resistance to the international hegemony of English: 2, 4, 8, 10
- Identity: 28, 29

These groups of items were then correlated with the Spanish and English proficiency measures, as shown in Table 7.5.

These groupings were also correlated with the English clozes, but were not significant apart from Sydney vitality and international use, where the correlation showed that this variable correlated negatively with scores on the English 'water' cloze (Table 7.6).

The intriguing possibility mentioned earlier, that clusters of attitudes are related to different aspects of proficiency, are supported by these findings. Basic literacy (spelling and accents) is associated with 'feeling good' about

Table 7.5 Correlations: Groups of questions by proficiency measures – written and oral Spanish

	Pridel confidence		Affect		Maintenance		Sydney vitality		Spanish international value		Spanish identity		Resist English international hegemony	
	Corr	p	Corr	p	Corr	p	Corr	p	Corr	p	Corr	p	Corr	p
(a) Written Spanish														
Basic literacy	0.26	**0.0247**	0.26	**0.0239**	0.11	0.3310	0.25	**0.0307**	0.15	0.1800	0.11	0.3559	0.06	0.6203
C-test	0.23	**0.0478**	0.32	**0.0048**	0.22	0.0572	-0.09	0.4129	0.05	0.6727	0.12	0.3092	0.47	**<0.0001**
History cloze	0.18	0.1086	0.24	**0.0318**	0.25	**0.0264**	0.20	0.0882	0.35	**0.0016**	0.07	0.5268	0.15	0.1861
Science cloze	0.16	0.1638	0.11	0.3290	0.21	0.0692	0.11	0.3640	0.22	0.0580	0.18	0.1257	0.25	**0.0278**
Cloze total	0.19	0.0969	0.20	0.0828	0.25	**0.0250**	0.17	0.1467	0.32	**0.0050**	0.14	0.2378	0.22	0.0532
Self assessment	0.32	**0.0041**	0.24	**0.0370**	0.32	**0.0042**	0.07	0.5714	0.32	**0.0042**	0.36	**0.0011**	0.24	**0.0315**
(b) Oral Spanish														
Fluency	0.39	**0.0013**	0.34	**0.0058**	0.30	**0.0162**	0.00176	0.9891	0.32	**0.0107**	0.26	**0.0405**	0.32	**0.0115**
Accent	0.25	**0.0482**	0.14	0.2755	0.31	**0.0133**	-0.11	0.3719	0.13	0.2956	0.19	0.1388	0.26	**0.0401**
Idiomaticity	0.40	**0.0009**	0.14	0.2610	0.39	**0.0013**	-0.07	0.5671	0.36	**0.0037**	0.27	**0.0299**	0.24	0.0586
Mixing	0.32	**0.0114**	0.03	0.8009	0.37	**0.0029**	-0.08	0.5492	0.24	0.0605	0.21	0.0927	0.19	0.1312
Oral total	0.42	**0.0006**	0.21	0.1056	0.41	**0.0006**	-0.08	0.5515	0.32	**0.0096**	0.29	**0.0231**	0.31	**0.0139**

Observations = 77; missing values = 7

Table 7.6 Correlations: Questions by proficiency measures – English

	Sydney vitality orientation		Spanish international value	
	Corr	*p*	*Corr*	*p*
English cloze, water	-0.34	0.0018	-0.26	0.0190

Observations = 80; missing values = 4

Spanish, with both taking pride in it and liking the language and its speakers. It is also the only aspect of proficiency associated with a Sydney vitality orientation. Grammar and vocabulary, the 'core' aspects of general language proficiency, are related very strongly to a resistance to the hegemony of English, and to a lesser degree to feeling good about Spanish.

In so far as higher register is concerned, it seems that it is necessary to wish to retain the language for international use (where such register is needed); this also involved the need to resist English hegemony. Self-assessment, which as we have seen involves an element of confidence as well as awareness of one's grammatical proficiency and pronunciation, is predictably associated with Spanish pride and identity, a maintenance orientation, and a valorisation of Spanish for international use.

Looking at the oracy measures, in general pride and confidence, and a maintenance orientation are strongly linked to all aspects of oral proficiency, while affect is associated only with fluency (marking the distinctiveness of the two attitude clusters). It is mainly fluency and idiomaticity, like the higher levels of written proficiency, that are associated with international utility of Spanish and to lesser degree with resistance to the hegemony of English. Spanish identity plays a less important role.

English proficiency is negatively associated with Sydney vitality, and a valorisation of Spanish for international use, but so few of the figures involving English are significant that this finding should be treated with caution.

Discussion of the Questionnaire Findings

The first thing to notice is that it is quite clear that beliefs do affect minority-language maintenance. Many of the correlations are strong and convincing. Furthermore, unpredicted beliefs, strong beliefs in favour of bilingualism and minority language maintenance, and the related determination to resist the hegemony of the dominant language are as important in our community as more familiar affect, pride, status and instrumental beliefs. Vitality beliefs concerning the Sydney community seem to be relatively unimportant in this sample

The findings of this research are encouraging, since we found a widespread and solid pride in being a Spanish speaker among our Sydney respondents. As we noted in the introduction, this is a fundamental prerequisite if the Spanish community is to resist the overwhelming hegemony of English in Australia (and elsewhere). Indeed the statistical strength of the 'anti-hegemony' attitude provides strong support for the notion that, for a minority language to survive, its speakers need to resist the (sometimes overwhelming) pressure to assimilate to the majority community and adopt the majority language, along with feeling happy with their mother tongue. A logical consequence of this is the pro-bilingualism attitudes that we found, since anyone being educated in an Australian school must speak English, so the only real issue is whether or not to become monolingual in English. For a Spanish speaker to both succeed in Australian society and maintain Spanish, a pro-bilingualism orientation is needed.

More advanced aspects of proficiency, particularly literate register, are associated with the view that the minority language should be maintained for international use. In the context of Sydney this makes sense, since a conversational ability is adequate for most local purposes. Most matters demanding high register, such as education, public affairs, and contacts with institutions are dealt with in English. It is in contacts with Spanish-speaking countries and Spanish speakers overseas that this aspect of Spanish proficiency becomes an asset. Those interviewees who perceive this and who wish to interact in Spanish internationally may tend to work on it: in other words, the development of the literate high register of Spanish may be supported by this pragmatic realisation. The weaker link to resistance to English hegemony (particularly for international use) forms part of this value set.

These groupings resemble the classic findings of Gardner and Lambert (1972) concerning 'integrative' and 'instrumental' reasons for becoming bilingual (corresponding roughly to our 'affective' and 'usefulness' categories). However, Gardner and Lambert did not discover a relationship between these attitude clusters and different *aspects* of language proficiency. Our findings may go some way towards explaining their sometimes contradictory results and, we believe, make a particular contribution to this area.

For this community, a Hispanic identity does not appear to be as significant as some recent literature would lead us to predict. Earlier, we mentioned the manner in which Latino culture and identity for the younger generation in Australia is supported by English-language publications, providing a possible explanation for this finding.

The largest number of relationships was between self-assessed proficiency and the questions. What this probably shows is that self-assessment contains an attitude as well as a proficiency element – it is a measure of confidence as well as of command of language resources. This is important, because much research done in the area of language and social psychology routinely uses such measures, and refers to them as proficiency measures, which is inexact and potentially misleading.

Looking at oracy, we mentioned previously that a poor accent and extensive mixing have on occasions been linked with incipient language loss (Dorian, 1981; Bettoni, 1981). Fluency and idiomaticity indicate higher proficiency. What emerges clearly is the strong association of pride and confidence in the minority language with the development of an oral proficiency in it. However, as with the written language, the development of higher aspects such as fluency and idiomaticity are favoured by an orientation to international use, and to a lesser degree by a resistance to the hegemony of English.

However, there is only limited support for the complementary view that English proficiency is supported by negative views of Spanish. The two significant findings may point to higher English proficiency among those who have a pessimistic view of Spanish vitality in Sydney, or a lack of appreciation of the international usefulness of Spanish, perhaps believing instead that English is sufficient for such purposes.

Conclusions

Methodology

We see once more the value of using both objective and qualitative methods. The qualitative measures give a rich profile of the attitudes of our interviewees, including some unexpected and illuminating insights. A nuanced and delicate approach is needed to attitudes and beliefs, and this methodology leaves space for the unpredicted to appear. The objective measures allow us to further define the attitude clusters, and also to perform statistical correlations with the proficiency measures. These provide objective evidence of the relationship between attitudes and proficiency, and the particular relationships between certain attitude clusters and certain aspects of proficiency, something that would be extremely difficult to achieve with qualitative assessment alone.

Findings

With the wisdom of retrospection it is clear that in many major countries of migration there is a strongly dominant language, and resistance to the hegemony of this language is necessary for the maintenance of minority languages. Pride in the minority language and culture is also a potent variable. Furthermore, since the dominant language is essential for an adequate life in such societies, it is important that beliefs support, not just the survival of the minority language, but bilingualism in both the dominant and the minority language. In effect, much of the ideology and argument emerging from minority-language political groups is shown here to form part of the belief structure that works to support minority language maintenance in the individual and community.

Chapter 8

Conclusions

Methodology

In general terms our findings on methodology are no surprise. With open questions, it is clearly important and interesting to allow interviewees space to state their views in comparative privacy, and with minimal controls over content. We were both emotionally touched and intellectually stimulated by the comments of our interviewees. They showed remarkable depth of insight into their own situation, and more generally into what it is like to be bilingual. They provided angles and elements that we had not considered, and this book would be greatly impoverished by their absence. This provides support for the gathering of qualitative data.

The closed questionnaires that we used were based on the best that we could find, and we would in particular like to thank Josiane Hamers for access to her QIRUL battery, Rodrigue Landry for copies of various instruments, Gordon Wells for input to the literacy section, and Richard Bourhis, Jim Cummins and John Edwards for comments and suggestions. To these sources we added elements from previous studies, and questions and suggestions that arose from our team and from the interviewees in our pilot studies. Tried and tested instruments were used in the attitude study. The instruments used to examine contact and literacy practices were mostly new, and consequently included some items that made little contribution to the overall picture. Nevertheless, these instruments now in turn constitute a resource for future researchers, especially as it is possible to gauge the usefulness of individual questions on the basis of the data provided in the book. As we noted earlier, this type of quantitative data has certain specific advantages. It can be more comparable across communities (always remembering that the reading given to questions is locally situated and culturally based). It is more easily used in statistical processing, to provide evidence of linkages and patterns within the data – in particular in our data, the factors could be correlated with the proficiency measures to provide evidence of linkages.

Our original research design also included an observational element, in which, for example, the specific literacy practices of bilingual families would have been observed. The type of analysis of code mixing and code choice found in Gibbons (1987) and Zentella (1997) would have enabled a more detailed understanding of how language contact was concretely manifested. We also intended to do our studies in families both where Spanish was being maintained, and in families where it was not, in order to understand more about the dynamic processes of maintenance and shift, along the lines of the study in Kulick (1992). Zentella (1997) gives an enlightening portrayal of a Spanish bilingual community, based on such data. Sadly, the Australian Research Council consistently refused funding for this study. We still believe that ethnographic research would have provided additional information and triangulation, since there is considerable evidence of the desirability of this approach when researching bilingualism.

Finally, and providing a bridge into the next section, we used a range of proficiency measures, not just self-assessment.

Taking Proficiency Seriously

The main concern of many parents and community representatives who spoke to us was for the Spanish proficiency of the teenagers. They wanted clear understandings of how much Spanish the interviewees knew, and where any gaps or deficiencies lay, so that these could be directly addressed. The community's preoccupation with minority-language maintenance is to a large degree a concern about language proficiency. Self-assessments of proficiency alone are clearly inadequate measures to meet these needs. Our proficiency measures are imperfect, but they provided far more information about a central issue in the language maintenance – what is maintained and what is lost. In addition, using yardstick data from a mostly monolingual comparison group in a source country of emigration as well as the country of immigration means that people do not make unrealistic judgements about the proficiency of bilinguals. Indeed nearly half of our interviewees were performing near the monolingual standards of Chile.

Another serious proficiency issue was that of register. The difference between conversational language and academic or 'high' register has been a given of bilingual studies for decades, yet there have been few studies where it has been operationalised and measured. Part of the problem is that the register studies performed on languages other than English are small in number, and some of the most important ones performed by Biber (1988) are difficult to apply to the measurement of proficiency. We hope that the comparatively simple technique for analysing such differences and developing measures based on them, described in Chapters 2 and 3, is of use to other researchers.

Looking now at some of the more interesting findings emerging from this emphasis on proficiency, Chapter 5 shows how the use of Spanish with the mother and older siblings benefits the development of academic register, while good relationships with younger siblings and cousins seem to be linked mostly to the development of basic literacy (spelling and punctuation). If we remember who is likely to help whom with homework and literacy, this makes eminent sense, but only in retrospect.

Chapter 6 gives evidence that education through the medium of Spanish contributes particularly to the development of grammatical and register proficiencies. By contrast, instruction at ethnic Saturday school had its major effects on basic literacy, oracy, and to a lesser degree grammar, reinforcing perceptions of the differences in the outcomes of language instruction compared with content instruction. It also emerged that the presence of Spanish literacy resources in the home influenced register development rather than other aspects of proficiency (something that might not have emerged in the absence of register-sensitive testing).

In the area of language attitudes, differentiation among the proficiency measures produced particularly interesting findings. The relationships between various clusters of attitudes and various aspects of proficiency illuminated areas that were previously obscure. Mastery of basic literacy is associated with both the desire to improve one's Spanish, and local uses. Grammar and vocabulary, by contrast, are associated with an emotional commitment to Spanish, and resistance to the hegemony of English. Higher register is associated with a valuing of Spanish for international use. In retrospect, these linkages make sense, but it is unlikely that they could have been predicted.

Factors in Maintenance

Early on, we introduced Landry and Allard's (1991) engaging metaphor of 'weights in a scale'. This metaphor proved particularly apt, because the work displayed here revealed no one variable or factor that could alone explain language maintenance and shift. Repeatedly we saw correlations ranging between 0.2 and 0.5, showing that a particular variable contributed to an explanation, but did not alone explain maintenance. On the other hand, there was little in the models that did not make some contribution, however small. There will be other variables that we did not examine, although the answers to the open questions testify that many important elements were included. We did not have sufficient confidence in our measures of the various factors to compare the results. If one factor seemed to be more influential, it may have been only that our measure of it was more effective, especially when comparing the results from tried and tested instruments with mostly new ones.

The societal

Looking now at the various factors, the role of status, both economic and political, is clearly important in the case of English and Spanish in Australia. The information from government reports revealed the economic disadvantage associated with a lack of English proficiency. This cogent argument in favour of English proficiency has long been recognised in Australia, although government funding has not always kept pace with perceptions. Similar arguments can be made for other countries where there is no single widely-spoken minority language. Concerning political status, the reality is that there is overwhelming majority support for English as the national language in Australia. There is ample historical evidence of people in many places feeling the emotional need for a symbolic national language as well as a rational need for a practical means of communication. (This is not an appropriate place to dwell on the consequent potential for exploitation of these feeling by the power hungry, and the risks of abuse.) The political and economic arguments strongly support English in Australia, and show why the public status of minority languages is one of subordinate coexistence with English, and why the 'private language plan' of minority families is usually one of emphasis on English, with the minority language as a desirable addition. It also shows why the only viable approach to long-term minority-language maintenance is one of bilingualism alongside English.

This pattern flows through into almost all the other societal areas, with English dominance and Spanish minor support across institutions, such as education, the law, health services and the bureaucracy. It also explains why in demographic contexts such as intermarriage, minority languages lose out when they compete with English. Sheer numbers also clearly play a role in Australia. In the other societal arena, the media, English once again dominates, although there is a surprising volume of Spanish media.

The educational medium is probably the most important single institutional variable in minority-language maintenance, even though bilingual education is no panacea, and needs to be well implemented and contextually appropriate. In Sydney, the almost-exclusive use of English places a large weight on the scales for English, and offers no support for Spanish. In particular, it militates against the acquisition of educational registers of Spanish. Our findings also show that current ethnic Saturday schooling, while it promotes general proficiency, does not seem to be imparting academic register, perhaps because a few hours outside school hours cannot compensate for full-time schooling.

The societal variable 'social class' seems in general to play a limited role. However, there is evidence that a more sophisticated modelling of social class in terms of social practices, particularly literacy practices, can reveal stronger associations.

Interpersonal contact

The tripartite division into strong network ties (with intimates), weak network ties, and distance network ties, proved its worth. Strong network ties support the development of basic language proficiency, including speaking, vocabulary and grammar. The support for higher registers is weaker. Weak network ties proved to be just that – weak in their support for language development and maintenance. We did not fully investigate distance ties, but the open questions suggested some influence, since the need to communicate with (often Spanish monolingual) family members overseas is a spur to higher proficiency.

Media use and literacy practices

The literacy practices of the interviewees played a limited role in their proficiency in Spanish, probably because they engage in little Spanish literacy. Where the literacy practices could work, they did. The findings for media use were similar. The most important medium for contact with Spanish is music, which has a limited linguistic content. Music, particularly for Latinos, seems to play a strong role in identity.

Attitudes

The range and variation in attitude types found in the literature and in the data were unexpected. Attitudes and beliefs concerning language, vitality, bilingualism, identity, language proficiency, language learning and the hegemony of English all seem to play a part. As in earlier studies, pride and affect were powerful forces, as were vitality beliefs. There were some influential attitudes that are less reported, such as the understanding of the international usefulness of Spanish (associated particularly with develop- ment of higher register). More unusual was the uncovering of the impor- tance of resistance to the hegemony of English in minority language maintenance. The relationships between the attitude clusters and profi- ciency were particularly strong and convincing.

Practical Maintenance Measures

There is a rich literature on practical measures to retain or revive languages, much of it associated with Fishman (e.g. Fishman, 1991, 2000). We will not repeat this directly here, but rather will comment on what has emerged from the studies reported in earlier chapters.

Societal

Chapter 4 shows the impact of the societal variables. In so far as institutions are concerned, in a true minority context it is unlikely that all government institutions will become effectively bilingual, although it should be noted that this is not impossible. In Singapore it is possible to communicate with government agencies in all four official languages, and much written material is available in multilingual form. Even in Australia, some health and public-welfare material is available multilingually. At present this is regarded as a transition phase for new migrants, and it is unlikely, for both practical and political reasons, that the second generation will be invited to communicate with the government in languages other than English.

The main arena in which progress could be made in Australia is that of education. There is some indication of a policy of resistance to bilingual education in the New South Wales Education Department. This is not the case in Victoria, so this is an area where political pressure might be applied. For the reasons given in this book, bilingual education is a heavy weight in the scale, particularly concerning the acquisition of higher registers of a minority language. Attendance at community language classes also plays a role in language proficiency.

The community can take action by applying pressure through their representatives for the development of some form of bilingual education, and for further development of community language programmes. Parents might like to consider a year or two of schooling for their children in their country of origin.

As we have seen, the media are a positive area for minority languages, particularly Spanish. Communities will decide what they are prepared to support in terms of the quantity and quality of minority-language publications. There is still the potential for concrete political action to obtain permission for more widespread broadcasting in languages other than English, opening the airwaves to community funded and developed broadcasting.

Contact

There is evidence in Chapter 5 and 6 that the quantity and quality of Spanish language interaction within the family is an important influence on Spanish-language maintenance. Perhaps most significant is the finding that talking to children and young adults about history, politics, science and other serious topics plays a major role in the development of higher forms of proficiency. This new finding is one that parents and other intimates might find useful – concretely, by making an effort to discuss serious issues with young people in minority languages. It is often counter productive, however, to attempt to force teenagers to do what does not appeal to them.

Distance contact seems salient in the interviewees' perceptions of when Spanish is particularly necessary, so encouragement to maintain overseas contact, particularly with loved ones, is another area where family might place a small weight in the scales. Weak contact, in cafés, churches, etc., is not particularly influential, in part because Spanish is rare in these contexts. However, French Canadians in New Brunswick are increasingly adopting a policy of insisting on using French in shops, government offices, and other places where bilingualism might be expected. Some bravery by minority Australians may be needed to reclaim such contexts as possibilities for minority-language use, overcoming an Australian norm that, in public, minorities use mainly English.

Media and literacy

One finding of particular importance is that the raw volume of publications and other material in Spanish in the home fosters literacy practices in Spanish. The concrete advice for families is clear – increase the amount of these materials in the home. Leave minority-language books, newspapers and magazines around the home. Install minority language computer programs, and share in cooking with minority-language cook-books. Play the minority-language music that young people may find engaging (for Latino youth this is more likely to be salsa than folk songs).

Foster engagement with literacy materials, perhaps by showing their interest and relevance, since both the quality and quantity of literacy practices are associated with higher levels of language proficiency. Literacy practices can be joint, so talking through a Spanish-language magazine article or television documentary, or working together to construct a letter or poster, may all help to inculcate literacy practices, literacy skills and literate language. There is also evidence from other studies of the importance for literacy development of reading bedtime stories to young children.

Attitudes

All cultures have their own particular riches, and this is notably the case for Hispanic cultures. Raising teenagers' awareness of this, to develop pride and identity as a Hispanic-Australian, is an important factor in the maintenance of Spanish.

Developing some resistance to the hegemony of English, while not alienating children from the surrounding Anglo culture, is a difficult and delicate matter. It may help to discuss such notions as ecological richness in culture, respect for all languages and cultures, and the avoidance of a dull monolingual, monocultural world, while at the same time shunning negativity about the dominant culture.

Positive attitudes to bilingualism itself are influential. Concrete action might include talking to young people about the benefits of being bilingual, and the evident lack of advantages in being monolingual.

Conclusion

There are three findings that we wish to highlight. The first is that it is possible to maintain a high level of proficiency in a minority language in the second generation – we found that a proportion of our interviewees had proficiency levels comparable with those of their monolingual peers in Chile. This high-level proficiency is not easily achieved; rather it demands commitment and work from both the second generation, and those that surround them. The family, in particular, plays a major role when, as in Australia, there is a lack of institutional support, and sometimes there are unsupportive attitudes in the majority community.

Second, the common emphasis on command of the everyday conversational aspects of language may affect the development of high or literate aspects of language. We do not believe that this is usually what communities want, but it has come about as a result of impoverished understandings of language in the wider community and among many linguists. Broader understanding supports broader proficiency.

Third, we wish to reiterate the range and complexity of the factors that affect bilingual proficiency. We have probably not dealt with all of them, but even in this study we find ample evidence of a broad range of elements that play their role in the maintenance of minority languages.

References

Abbasi-Shavasi, M.J. (1998) The fertility of immigrant women in Australia. *People and Place* 6 (3), 30–38.

Abdoolcader, L. (1989) *Sydney Voices: A Survey of Languages Other Than English in Catholic Schools*. Sydney: Catholic Education Office.

Ada, A. (1988) The Pajaro Valley experience: Working with Spanish-speaking parents to develop children's reading and writing skills in the home through the use of children's literature. In T. Skutnabb-Kangas and J. Cummins (eds) *Minority Education: From Shame to Struggle*. Clevedon: Multilingual Matters.

Alderson, J.C., Clapham, C. and Wall, D. (1995) *Language Test Construction and Evaluation*. Cambridge: Cambridge University Press.

Allard, R. and Landry, R. (eds) (1994) 'Ethnolinguistic Vitality', *International Journal of the Sociology of Language*, special edition, 105/6.

Ammerlaan, A. (1995) You get a bit wobbly: Exploring bilingual lexical retrieval in the context of first language attrition. Unpublished PhD thesis, Nijmegen University.

AusStats (1999) *Australian Social Trends 1999: Population Composition: Languages Spoken in Australia*. Canberra, ACT: Australian Government Publishing Service.

Australian Bureau of Statistics, Queensland (1994) *The Social Characteristics of Immigrants in Australia*. Canberra, ACT: Bureau of Immigration and Population Research and the Australian Government Publishing Service.

Bachman, L.F. (1990) *Fundamental Considerations in Language Testing*. Oxford: Oxford University Press.

Bachman, L. and Palmer, A. (1996) *Language Testing in Practice*. Oxford: Oxford University Press.

Baetens Beardsmore, H. (1995) The European School experience in multilingual education. In T. Skutnabb-Kangas (ed.) *Multilingualism for All* (pp. 21–68). Lisse: Swets & Zeitlinger.

Baker, C. (2001) *Foundations of Bilingual Education and Bilingualism* (3rd edn). Clevedon: Multilingual Matters.

Baynham, M. (1995) *Literacy Practices: Investigating Literacy in Social Contexts*. London: Longman.

Bettoni, C. (1981) *Italian in North Queensland: Changes in the Speech of First and Second Generation Bilinguals*. Townsville, QLD: Dept of Modern Languages, James Cook University of North Queensland.

Bettoni, C. (1985) Italian language attrition: A Sydney case study. In M. Clyne (ed.) *Australia, Meeting Place of Languages*. Canberra, ACT: Pacific Linguistics, Australian National University.

Bettoni, C. and Gibbons, J. (1988) Linguistic purism and language shift: A guise-voice study of the Italian community in Sydney. *International Journal of the Sociology of Language* 72, 15–35.

234

Bettoni, C. and Gibbons, J. (1990) L'influenza della generazione e della classe sociale sugli atteggiamenti linguistici degli italiani in Australia. *Rivista Italiana di Dialettologia* 14, 113–137.

Biber, D. (1988) *Variation across Speech and Writing.* Cambridge: Cambridge University Press.

Biber, D. (1995) *Dimensions of Register Variation: A Cross-linguistic Comparison.* Cambridge: Cambridge University Press.

Bourdieu, P. and Passeron, J.C. (1990) *Reproduction in Education, Society and Culture.* London: Sage.

Bourhis, R.Y. (ed.) (1984) *Conflict and Language Planning in Quebec.* Clevedon: Multilingual Matters.

Bourhis, R., Giles, H. and Rosenthal, D. (1981) Notes on the construction of a 'Subjective Vitality Questionnaire' for ethnolinguistic groups. *Journal of Multilingual and Multicultural Development* 2 (2), 145–155.

Bourhis, R. and Sachdev, I. (1984) Vitality perceptions and language attitudes Some Canadian data. *Journal of Language and Social Psychology* 3 (2), 97–125.

Brice Heath, S. (1983) *Ways with Words: Language, Life, and Work in Communities and Classrooms.* Cambridge: Cambridge University Press.

Brown, R. and Gilman, A. (1960) The pronouns of power and solidarity. In T. Sebeok (ed.) *Style in Language.* New York, NY: John Wiley.

Campbell, S.J. (1994) Aspects of a model of translation competence: Translation competence into a second language. PhD thesis, University of Sydney.

Canale, M. and Swain, M. (1980) Theoretical bases of communicative approaches to second language teaching and testing. *Applied Linguistics* 1 (1), 1–47.

Chafe, W. (1985) Linguistic differences produced by differences between speaking and writing. In D.L. Olson, W. Torrance and A. Hildgard (eds) *Literacy, Language and Learning* (pp. 105–123). Cambridge: Cambridge University Press.

Chafe, W. and Tannen, D. (1987) The relation between written and spoken language. *Annual Review of Anthropology* 16, 383–409.

Christie, F. (1990) The changing face of literacy. In F. Christie (ed.) *Literacy for a Changing World* (pp. 1–25). Hawthorn, VIC: Australian Council for Educational Research.

Clahsen, H., Meisel, J.M. and Pienemann, M. (1983) *Deutsch als Zweitsprache Der Sprachwerb ausländischer Arbeiter.* Tübingen: Gunter Narr.

Clément, R., Gardner, R. and Smythe, P. (1980) Social and individual factors in second language acquisition. *Canadian Journal of Behavioural Science* 12 (4), 293–302.

Clyne, M. (1982) *Multilingual Australia: Resources – Needs – Policies.* Melbourne, VIC: River Seine.

Clyne, M. (1991) *Community Languages: The Australian Experience.* Cambridge: Cambridge University Press.

Clyne, M. and Kipp, S. (1997a) Linguistic diversity in Australia. *People and Place* 5 (3), 6–11.

Clyne, M. and Kipp, S. (1997b) Language maintenance and language shift: Community languages in Australia, 1996. *People and Place* 5 (4), 19–27.

Coulmas, F. (1984) (ed.) *Linguistic Minorities and Literacy.* Berlin: Mouton.

Crystal, D. and Davy, D. (1969) *Investigating English Style.* London: Longman.

Cummins, J. (1979) Linguistic interdependence and the educational development of bilingual children. *Review of Educational Research* (49) 222–251.

Cummins, J. (1984) *Bilingualism and Special Education: Issues in Assessment and Pedagogy.* Clevedon: Multilingual Matters.

Cummins, J. (1996) *Negotiating Identities: Education for Empowerment in a Diverse Society.* Ontario, CA: California Association for Bilingual Education.

Cummins, J. (2000) *Language, Power, and Pedagogy: Bilingual Children in the Crossfire.* Clevedon: Multilingual Matters.

Cummins, J., Lopes, J. and Ramos, J. (1987) The development of bilingual proficiency in the transition from home to school: A longitudinal study of Portuguese-speaking children. In B. Harley, P. Allen, J. Cummins and M. Swain (eds) *The Development of Bilingual Proficiency: Final Report* (Vol. 3): *Social Context and Age.* Toronto: Modern Language Centre, OISE.

Cummins, J. and Nakajima, K. (1987) Age of arrival, length of residence, and interdependence of literacy skills among Japanese immigrant students. In B. Harley, P. Allen, J. Cummins and M. Swain (eds) *The Development of Bilingual Proficiency: Final Report* (Vol. 3): *Social Context and Age* (pp. 183–202). Toronto: Modern Language Centre, OISE.

Cziko, G.A. (1992) The evaluation of bilingual education: From necessity to probability to possibility. *Educational Researcher* 21 (2), 10–15.

Danet, B. and Bogoch, B. (1994) Orality, literacy and performativity in Anglo-Saxon wills. In J. Gibbons (ed.) *Language and the Law* (pp. 100–135). London: Longman.

DIMA (2001) *English Proficiency 1996 Census* (Statistical Report 30). Statistics Section, Department of Immigration and Multicultural Affairs.

Dorian, N. (1981) *Language Death: The Life Cycle of a Scottish Gaelic Dialect.* Philadelphia, PA: University of Philadelphia Press.

Dörnyei, Z. (2003) *Attitudes, Orientations, and Motivations in Language Learning.* Oxford: Basil Blackwell.

Edelsky, C. (1982) Writing in a bilingual program: The relation of L1 and L2 texts. *TESOL Quarterly* 16, 211–221.

Edwards, J. (1994) *Multilingualism.* London: Routledge.

Ferguson, C. (1981) *Language in the USA.* Cambridge: Cambridge University Press.

Fishman, J. (1991) *Reversing Language Shift.* Clevedon: Multilingual Matters.

Fishman, J. A. (2000) Why is it so hard to save a threatened language? In J.A. Fishman (ed.) *Can Threatened Languages be Saved?* Clevedon: Multilingual Matters.

Fishman, J., Cooper, R.L. and Ma, R. (1971) *Bilingualism in the Barrio.* The Hague: Mouton.

Francis, N. (2000) The shared conceptual system and language processing in bilingual children: Findings from literacy assessment in Spanish and Nahuatl. *Applied Linguistics* 21 (2), 170–204.

Frasure-Smith, N., Lambert, W. and Taylor, D.M. (1975) Choosing the language of instruction for one's children: A Quebec study. *Journal of Cross-Cultural Psychology* 6, 131–155.

Gal, S. (1979) *Language Shift: Social Determinants of Linguistic Change in Bilingual Austria.* New York: Academic Press.

Gardner, R.C. (1979). Social psychological aspects of second language acquisition. In H. Giles and R. St Clair (eds) *Language and Social Psychology* (pp. 193–220). Oxford: Basil Blackwell.

Gardner, R.C. and Lambert, W.E. (1972) *Attitudes and Motivation in Second Language Learning.* Rowley, MA: Newbury House.

Gass, S. and Selinker, L. (eds) (1983) *Language Transfer in Language Learning.* Rowley, MA: Newbury House.

Genesee, F. (1987) *Learning Through Two Languages: Studies of Immersion and Bilingual Education.* Cambridge, MA: Newbury House.

Gibbons, J. (1987) *Code-Mixing and Code Choice: A Hong Kong Case Study.* Clevedon: Multilingual Matters.

Gibbons, J. (1994a) Depth or breadth: Some issues in LOTE teaching. *Australian Review of Applied Linguistics* 17 (1), 1–22.

Gibbons, J. (ed.) (1994b) *Language and the Law.* London: Longman.

Gibbons, J. (1997) Australian bilingual education. In J. Cummins and D. Corson (eds) *Encyclopedia of Language and Education* (Vol. 5): *Bilingual Education* (pp. 209–215). Dordrecht: Kluwer.

Gibbons, J. (2003). *Forensic Linguistics: An Introduction to Language in the Justice System.* Oxford: Blackwell.

Gibbons, J. and Ashcroft, L. (1995) Multiculturalism and language shift: A subjective vitality questionnaire study of Sydney Italians. *Journal of Multilingual and Multicultural Development* 16 (4), 281–299.

Gibbons, J., White, W. and Gibbons, P. (1994) Combating educational disadvantage among Lebanese Australian children. In T. Skutnabb-Kangas and R. Phillipson (eds) *Linguistic Human Rights Overcoming Linguistic Discrimination* (pp. 253–262). New York: Mouton de Gruyter.

Giddens, A. (1991) Modernity and self-identity: Tribulations of the self. In A. Giddens (ed.) *Modernity and Self-Identity.* Oxford: Basil Blackwell.

Giles, H. and Billings, A. (forthcoming) Assessing language attitudes: Speaker evaluation studies. In A. Davies and C. Elder (eds) *Handbook of Applied Linguistics.* Oxford: Basil Blackwell.

Giles, H., Bourhis, R. and Taylor, D. (1977) Towards a theory of language in ethnic group relations. In H. Giles (ed.) *Language, Ethnicity and Intergroup Relations.* London: Academic Press.

Giles, H., Rosenthal, D. and Young, L. (1985) Perceived ethnolinguistic vitality: The Anglo- and Greek-Australian setting. *Journal of Multilingual and Multicultural Development* 6 (3–4), 253–269.

Giles, H., Taylor, D., Lambert, W. and Albert, G. (1976) Dimensions of ethnic identity: An example from Northern Maine. *The Journal of Social Psychology* (100), 11–19.

Gooch, A. (1967) *Diminutive, Augmentative and Pejorative Suffixes in Modern Spanish (A Guide to their Use and Meaning).* Oxford: Pergamon.

Granovetter, M. (1982) The strength of weak ties: A network theory revisited. In P.V. Marsden and N. Lin (eds) *Social Structure and Network Analysis* (pp. 105–130). Beverley Hills, CA: Sage.

Haley, A. (1976) *Roots.* Garden City, NY: Doubleday.

Halliday, M.A.K. (1975) *Learning How to Mean.* London: Arnold.

Halliday, M.A.K. (1978) *Language as Social Semiotic: The Social Interpretation of Language and Meaning.* London, Arnold.

Halliday, M.A.K. (1985) *Spoken and Written Language.* Geelong, VIC: Deakin University Press.

Halliday, M.A.K. (1988) On the language of physical science. In M. Ghadessy (ed.) *Registers of Written English: Situational Factors and Linguistic Features* (pp. 162–178) London: Pintner.

Halliday, M.A.K. and Hasan, R. (1985) *Language, Context and Text: Aspects of Language in a Social-Semiotic Perspective*. Geelong, VIC: Deakin University Press.

Halliday, M.A.K. and Martin, J.R. (1993) *Writing Science: Literacy and Discursive Power*. London: Falmer.

Hamers, J.F. (1994) L'interaction entre les réseaux sociaux, la valorisation du langage et les croyances dans le développement biculturel. In J. Blomart and B. Krewer (eds) *Perspectives de l'Interculturel*. Paris: L'Harmattan.

Hamers, J.F. and Blanc, M.H.A. (1989) *Bilinguality and Bilingualism* (1st edn) Cambridge: Cambridge University Press.

Hamers, J.F. and Blanc, M.H.A. (2000) *Bilinguality and Bilingualism* (2nd edn) Cambridge: Cambridge University Press.

Harley, B., Allen, P., Cummins, J. and Swain, M. (eds) (1990) *The Development of Second Language Proficiency*. Cambridge: Cambridge University Press.

Haugen, E. (1972) *The Ecology of Language*. Stanford, CA: Stanford University Press.

Hogg, M., d'Agata, P. and Abrams, D. (1989) Ethnolinguistic betrayal and speaker evaluations among Italian Australians. *Genetic, Social and General Psychology Monographs* 115, 153–181.

Hornberger, N. (1997) Literacy, language maintenance and linguistic human rights: Three telling cases. *International Journal of the Sociology of Language* 127, 87–103.

Hudson, T. (1993) Nothing does not equal zero. Problems with applying developmental sequence findings to assessment and pedagogy. *Studies in Second Language Acquisition* 15 (4).

Johnson, R.K. and Swain, M. (eds) (1997) *Immersion Education: International Perspectives*. Cambridge: Cambridge University Press.

Jones, S. and Tetroe, J. (1984) Composing in a second language. In A. Matsuhashi (ed.) *Writing in Real Time: Modelling Production Processes*. New York: Longman.

Klein, W. and Dittmar, N. (1979) *Developing Grammars: The Acquisition of German Syntax by Foreign Workers*. Berlin: Springer.

Klein-Braley, C. and Raatz, U. (1984) A survey of research on the c-test. *Language Testing* 1, 134–146.

Kloss, H. (1966) German-American language maintenance efforts. In J. Fishman (ed.) *Language Loyalty in the United States* (pp. 206–252). The Hague: Mouton.

Kroskrity, P.V. (2000) Identity. *Journal of Linguistic Anthropology* 9 (1), 111–114.

Kulick, D. (1992) *Language Shift and Cultural Reproduction: Socialization, Self, and Syncretism in a Papua New Guinean Village*. Cambridge: Cambridge University Press.

Labov, W. (1969) The logic of nonstandard English. *Georgetown Monographs on Language and Linguistics* 22, 1–31.

Lambert, W.E. (1977) Effects of bilingualism on the individual. In P.A. Hornby (ed.) *Bilingualism: Psychological, Social and Educational Implications*. New York, NY: Academic Press.

Lambert, W.E., Hodgson, R., Gardner, R. and Fillenbaum, S. (1960) Evaluational reactions to spoken language. *Journal of Abnormal and Social Psychology* 60 (1), 44–51.

Lambert, W.E., Just, M. and Segalowitz, N. (1970) Some cognitive consequences of following the curricula of Grades One and Two in a foreign language. *Georgetown Monographs on Language and Linguistics* 23, 229–279.

Landry, R. and Allard, R. (1991) Can schools promote additive bilingualism in minority language children? In L. Malave and G. Duquette (eds) *Language, Culture and Cognition*. Clevedon: Multilingual Matters.

LePage, R. and Tabouret-Keller, A. (1985) *Acts of Identity*. Cambridge: Cambridge University Press.

Li, W. (1994) *Three Generations, Two Languages, One Family: Language Choice and Language Shift in a Chinese Community in Britain*. Clevedon: Multilingual Matters.

Li, W., Milroy, L. and Ching, P.S. (1992) A two-step sociolinguistic analysis of code-switching and language choice: An example of a bilingual Chinese community in Britain. *International Journal of Applied Linguistics 2* (1), 63–86.

Lindholm-Leary, K. (2001) *Dual Language Education*. Clevedon: Multilingual Matters.

Martin, J.R. (1990) Literacy in science: Learning to handle text as technology. In F. Christie (ed.) *Literacy for a Changing World*. Hawthorn, VIC: Australian Council for Educational Research.

Martin, J.R. (2000) Beyond exchange: Appraisal systems in English. In S. Hunston and G. Thompson (eds) *Evaluation in Text: Authorial Stance and the Construction of Discourse* (pp. 142–175). Oxford: Oxford University Press.

Martin-Jones, M. and Romaine, S. (1986) Semilingualism: A half-baked theory of communicative competence. *Applied Linguistics 7*, 26–38.

Milardo, R.M. (1988) Families and social networks: An overview of theory and methodology. In R.M. Milardo (ed.) *Families and Social Networks* (pp. 13–47). Newbury Park, CA: Sage.

Milroy, L. (1980) *Language and Social Networks*. Oxford: Basil Blackwell.

Milroy, L. and Li, W. (1995) A social network approach to code-switching: The example of a bilingual community in Britain. In L. Milroy and P. Muysken (eds) *One Speaker, Two Languages: Cross-Disciplinary Perspectives on Code-Switching* (pp. 136–157). Cambridge: Cambridge University Press.

Morford, J. (1997) Social indexicality in French pronominal address. *Journal of Linguistic Anthropology 7* (1), 3–37.

Ng, S.H. and He, A. (forthcoming). Code-switching in tri-generational family conversations among Chinese immigrants in New Zealand. *International Journal of Language and Social Psychology*.

Ong, W.J. (1982) *Orality and Literacy: The Technologizing of the World*. London, Methuen.

Opie, I. and P. Opie (1959) *The Lore and Language of Schoolchildren*. Oxford: Oxford University Press.

Osgood, C.E., Suci, G.J. and Tannenbaum, P.H. (1957) *The Measurement of Meaning*. Urbana, IL: University of Illinois Press.

Pauwels, A.F. (1980) The effects of mixed marriages on language shift in the Dutch community in Australia. Unpublished MA thesis, Monash University.

Potter, J. and Wetherell, M. (1987) *Discourse and Social Psychology: Beyond Attitudes and Behaviour*. London: Sage Publications.

Rumbaut, R.G. (1994) The crucible within: Ethnic identity, self-esteem and segmented assimilation among children of immigrants. *International Migration Review 28*, 748–794.

Schumann, J. (1978) The acculturation model for second language acquisition. In R. Gingras (ed.) *Second Language Acquisition and Foreign Language Teaching*. Arlington, VA: Center for Applied Linguistics.

Senate Standing Committee on Foreign Affairs, Defence and Trade (1992) *Australia and Latin America*. Canberra, ACT: Senate Printing Unit, Parliament House.

Shokrpour, N. and Gibbons, J. (1998) Register complexity and the inadequacy of readability formulae as a measure of difficulty. *Indian Journal of Applied Linguistics* 24 (2), 19–36.

Skutnabb-Kangas, T. (1981) *Bilingualism or Not: The Education of Minorities*. Clevedon: Multilingual Matters.

Silva-Corvalán, C. (1991) Spanish language attrition in a contact situation with English. In H. Seliger and R. Vargo (eds) *First Language Attrition* (pp. 151–171). Cambridge: Cambridge University Press.

Slade, D. and Gibbons, J. (1987) Testing bilingual proficiency in Australia: Issues, methods, findings. *Evaluation and Research in Education* 1 (2), 95–106.

Smolicz, J.J. (1981) Core values and cultural identity. *Ethnic and Racial Studies* 4 (1), 75–90.

Swain, M. and Lapkin, S. (1982) *Evaluating Bilingual Education: A Canadian Case Study*. Clevedon: Multilingual Matters.

Taylor, D.M., Bassili, J.N. and Aboud, F. E. (1973) Dimensions of ethnic identity: An example from Quebec. *The Journal of Social Psychology* (89), 185–192.

Trudgill, P. and Giles, H. (1978) Sociolinguistic and linguistic value judgements: Correctness, adequacy and aesthetics. In F. Coppiertiers and D. Goyvaerts (eds) *The Function of Language and Literature Studies*. Ghent: Storia Scientia.

Turell, M.T. (ed.) (2000) *Multilingualism in Spain*. Clevedon: Multilingual Matters.

Tuominen, A. (1999) Who decides the home language? A look at multilingual families. *International Journal of the Sociology of Language* (140), 59–76.

UNESCO (1953) *The Use of Vernacular Languages in Education*. Paris: UNESCO.

Valverde, E., Hale, S. and Ramirez, E. (1994) *Unlocking Australia's Language Potential* (Vol. 9): *Spanish*. Canberra: The National Language and Literacy Institute of Australia.

Verhoeven, L. (1991a) Acquisition of biliteracy. In J.H. Hulstijn and J.F. Matters (eds) *Reading in Two Languages*. Amsterdam: AILA.

Verhoeven, L. (1991b) Predicting minority children's bilingual proficiency: Child, family and institutional factors. *Language Learning* (41), 205–233.

Wenger, E. (1998) *Communities of Practice: Learning Meaning and Identity*. Cambridge: Cambridge University Press.

Williams, G. (1992) *Sociolinguistics: A Sociological Critique*. London: Routledge.

Wong-Fillmore, L. (1985) When does teacher talk work as input? In S. Gass and C. Madden (eds) *Input in Second Language Acquisition* (pp. 17–50). Rowley, MA: Newbury House.

Wong-Fillmore, L. (1991) Second-language learning in children: A model of language learning in social context. In E. Bialystok (ed.) *Language Processing in Bilingual Children* (pp. 49–69). Cambridge: Cambridge University Press.

Yagmur, K., de Bot, K. and Korzilius, H. (1999) Language attrition, language shift and ethnolinguistic vitality of Turkish in Australia. *Journal of Multilingual and Multicultural Development* 20 (1), 51–69.

Zentella, A.C. (1997) *Growing up Bilingual: Puerto Rican Children in New York*. Oxford: Blackwell.